ISLAMOPHOBIA IN CYBERSPACE

For Hiba, Amel, Sobia and Tasvir

Islamophobia in Cyberspace

Hate Crimes Go Viral

Edited by

IMRAN AWAN
Birmingham City University, UK

ASHGATE

Published by
Ashgate Publishing
2 Park Square
Milton Park
Abingdon
Oxon OX14 4RN
England

Ashgate Publishing
711 Third Avenue
New York, NY 10017
USA

Ashgate is an imprint of the Taylor & Francis Group, an informa business

www.ashgate.com

British Library Cataloguing in Publication Data
A catalogue record for this book is available from the British Library.

The Library of Congress has cataloged the printed edition as follows:
Islamophobia in cyberspace : hate crimes go viral / [edited] by Imran Awan.
    pages cm
    Includes bibliographical references and index.
    ISBN 978-1-4724-5809-4 (hardback) – ISBN 978-1-4724-5810-0 (ebook) – ISBN 978-1-4724-5811-7 (epub) 1. Hate crimes. 2. Computer crimes. 3. Islamophobia. I. Awan, Imran.
    HV6773.5.I83 2016
    364.15'6088297–dc23

2015022702

ISBN: 9781472458094 (hbk)
ISBN: 9781472458100 (ebk – PDF)
ISBN: 9781472458117 (ebk – ePUB)

Printed in the United Kingdom by Henry Ling Limited,
at the Dorset Press, Dorchester, DT1 1HD

Contents

List of Figures

List of Tables

Notes on Contributors

Imran Awan is Deputy Director of the Centre for Applied Criminology and Senior Lecturer in Criminology at Birmingham City University. He has published widely in national and international journals in the area of anti-Muslim hate crime, human rights and Islamophobia. Imran has previously been invited by the Equality and Human Rights Commission to take part in a review of anti-Muslim hate crime and civil liberty issues. He is currently involved in a research project that examines the impact of online anti-Muslim hate crime and has published a number of peer-reviewed journal articles in the field of Islamophobia on the Internet. He is an ambassador for the Make Justice Work Campaign and a Fellow of the Higher Education Academy. He is co-editor, with Brain Blakemore, of the critically acclaimed *Policing Cyber Hate, Cyber Threats and Cyber Terrorism* (Ashgate 2012) and, also with Brian Blakemore, of the book on far-right extremism *Extremism, Counter-terrorism and Policing* (Ashgate 2013). As well as appearing regularly in the media, Imran has submitted both written and oral evidence to the All-Party Parliamentary Group on Islamophobia. Imran is also an adviser and a steering group member of the Government-funded third party reporting service for victims of Islamophobia, Tell MAMA (Measuring Anti-Muslim Attacks). He also is an independent member of the Cross Government Working Group for Anti-Muslim Hate, based in the Department for Communities and Local Government. Imran is the Founder and Director of the Ethnic Minority Research Network in Criminology.

Brian Blakemore is an associate head in the School of Health Sport and Professional Practice. Brian has previous experience on a wide range of academic awards and academic management positions including divisional head of Police Sciences during his 30 years within the University of South Wales. Brian teaches on a range of modules including Science for Law Enforcement, Crime Investigation, and Researching Contemporary Issues. He has published on cognitive processes in investigation, higher education for police officers and professionalising the police force, the human rights aspects and investigative effectiveness of the national DNA database, and has co-edited texts with Professor Colin Rogers (*Crime Analysis and Evaluation*, *Problem Orientated Partnerships* and *Community Safety* all published in 2009 by Willan) and with Imran Awan (*Policing Cyber Hate, Cyber Threat and Cyber Terrorism* [2012] and *Extremism Counter-terrorism and Policing* [2013] both published by Ashgate).

Jeane Gerard, PhD, is a research associate at Coventry University in the Faculty Research Centre in Psychology, Behaviour and Achievement. Her research focuses on different types of homicide (e.g., sex-related homicide, juvenile homicide, and school shootings). Her research interests include investigative and forensic psychology, offender profiling, as well as violent and interpersonal aggression

Ewan Kirk is currently the Senior Personal Tutor on the LLB Programme at Birmingham City University. Ewan currently teaches EU Law and Intellectual Property Law at undergraduate and postgraduate level. His areas of research interest include intellectual property law and Internet law. Ewan was also a JASB Representative for revalidations. His has previously been an external examiner at the University of Glamorgan.

Andre Oboler is CEO of the Online Hate Prevention Institute. He has worked at the leading edge of international efforts to combat online hate in social media since 2008, and has been active in the broader field of combating internet based hate since 2004. Internationally recognised as a leading expert in the field of online hate, Dr Oboler has presented testimony to the Italian Parliament and has appeared on national television in Australia, Italy and Israel. He is co-chair of the Online Antisemitism Working Group of the Global Forum to Combat Antisemitism and has served as an expert to the Inter-Parliamentary Coalition to Combat Antisemitism. He is a Distinguished Visitor for the IEEE Computer Society. Dr Oboler holds a PhD in Computer Science from Lancaster University (UK) and a Juris Doctor from Monash University (Australia). He has also completed a Post-Doctoral Fellowship at Bar-Ilan University (Israel). He is a Senior Member of the IEEE and a member of the IEEE Computer Society and the IEEE Society for the Social Implications of Technology.

Jane Prince is Principal Lecturer in Psychology at the University of South Wales. Her research and teaching interests focus round the study of threatened identities and the ways in which identity challenges are managed, with a particular focus on the experiences of migrants (both voluntary and involuntary) and on on-line experiences of identity threats. She has worked in universities in the UK, the Netherlands and France.

Mohammed Rahman is a Visiting Lecturer in Criminology at Birmingham City University. His PhD level research investigates the relationship between 'violence' and 'crime' in the West Midlands, England. Recently, Mohammed has contributed towards several peer-reviewed academic articles, investigating 'murder in the media'. His previous academic qualifications include an MA Criminology and a BSc (Hons) Forensic Computing.

Kate C. Whitfield holds an MSc in Investigative Psychology and a PhD in Forensic Psychology, both from the University of Liverpool. She is currently a lecturer in Investigative and Forensic Psychology, and contributes to teaching on both undergraduate and postgraduate courses. Dr Whitfield's research interests include online victimisation, child protection, hate crime, critical and major incident management, and forensic organisational issues.

Introduction

> The last few weeks, where he has been specifically targeting me and a few others making reference to my personal life and family, has had a negative impact spiralling from anger to depression and I then resorted to trying to connect with other victims online as to what he will do next. I then had episodes of despair as I was pushed from pillar to post, with the police not taking my concerns seriously. He (the perpetrator), had chosen a few targets and accused them of being paedophiles, also using photographs of victim's relatives and creating fake accounts. When he cloned my own account and sent messages to my followers it made me angry and further depressed. (Tell MAMA 2015)

This is an interview with a victim of targeted online anti-Muslim abuse. This victim's personal account of online abuse is important for a number of reasons. Firstly, it provides us with an insight into the online abuse victims suffer, secondly, it demonstrates that online abuse can have real and direct impact upon an individual's health and wellbeing because of their perceived difference and finally it shows how the convergence of hate crime and technology can lead to cyber hate. In 2013, I was invited to present evidence, as part of my submission regarding online anti-Muslim hate, at the House of Commons (Awan 2013). I attempted to show how hate groups on the internet were using this space to intimidate, cause fear and make direct threats against Muslim communities – particularly after the murder of Drummer Lee Rigby in Woolwich in 2013. Following this, the issue of Islamophobia on social media, was also raised by the Home Affairs Select Committee in 2015, before the Attorney General Jeremy Wright, who stated that companies such as Twitter and Facebook needed to act upon the hate speech espoused online on their platforms (Morris 2015).

According to Tell MAMA (Measuring Anti-Muslim Attacks) recent data analysis they found 548 verified incidents (of 729) reported to them concerning anti-Muslim abuse. The majority of incidents took place online (402 out of 548). Almost, a fifth of service users reported repeat offline incidents of anti-Muslim hate with Muslim women suffering more offline incidents than men. Typically, the victim was wearing traditional Islamic clothing at the time of the incident and the perpetrators were overwhelmingly white male (Littler and Feldman 2015). A breakdown of the statistics shows these tend to be mainly from male perpetrators and are marginally more likely to be directed at women.

Digital Hate-speak

It has become easy to indulge in racist hate crimes online and many people take advantage of the anonymity to do so. These messages are then taken up by virtual communities who are quick to amplify their actions by creating webpages, blogs and forums of hate. Online anti-Muslim hate therefore intensifies, as has been shown after the Rotherham abuse scandal in the UK (2010), the beheading of journalists James Foley, Steven Sotloff and the humanitarian workers David Haines and Alan Henning by Islamic State in 2014, the Woolwich attacks in 2013 and the terrorist attacks in Paris in 2015. Indeed, after the attacks in Paris, the hashtag #KillAllMuslims was one of the words trending in the UK on Twitter (see Figure I.1 below of tweets collected).

Abuse is Not a Human Right

Clearly, hate on the internet can have both a direct and indirect effect on the victims and communities being targeted. It can be used to harass and intimidate victims and it can also be used for opportunistic crime. Few of us will forget the moment when Salma Yaqoob appeared on BBC Question Time and tweeted the following comments to her followers: 'Apart from this threat to cut my throat by #EDL supporter (!) overwhelmed by warm response to what I said on #bbcqt' (see Figure I.2 below).

The internet is a powerful tool by which people can be influenced to act in a certain way and manner. This is particularly strong when considering hate speech that aims to threaten and incite violence. This also links into the convergence of emotional distress caused by hate online, the nature of intimidation and harassment and the prejudice that seeks to defame groups through speech intending to injure and intimidate. Some sites which have been relatively successful here include BareNakedIslam[1] and IslamExposed[2] which has a daily forum and chatroom about issues to do with Muslims and Islam. The strong anti-Muslim tone begins with initial discussion about a particular issue – such as banning halal meat – before turning into abuse using provocative language.

Most of this anti-Muslim hate speech hides behind a fake banner of English patriotism, but is instead used to demonise and dehumanise Muslim communities. It goes without saying that the internet is just a digital realisation of the world itself – all shades of opinion are represented, including those Muslims whose

---

1   See http://www.barenakedislam.com/2012/09/30/yes-we-hate-islam-yes-we-will-mock-your-paedophile-prophet-mohammed-as-much-as-we-want-no-we-dont-care-what-you-think-or-how-offended-you-are-we-are-americans-and-we-are-free-to-say-what-we-w/..

2   See http://www.islamexposed.com/.

Trending

🔥 **#JeSuisCharlie**
811.1K Tweets about this trend

🔥 **#KillAllMuslims**

🔥 **#TheFallOnNetflix**
13.4K Tweets about this trend

ore trends

sailboat22
@sailboat22

Islam is a vicious cult.
no place in any civilize
Deport and kill them be
you!

11:20 PM · 07 Jan 15

 Daviðe Gandølfi
@EchtGandolf

I'm so sorry for those French
journalists, fucking Muslims I always
hated and always will hate them
#KillAllMuslims

 The Angry Patriot
@BigBobbyTCOT

KILL ALL MUSLIMS! WE HAVE
TOLERATED THEM LONG ENOUGH!
#ParisShooting #TCOT #P2 #MRA
12:32 AM · 08 Jan 15

 The Angry Patriot
@BigBobbyTCOT

KILL ALL MUSLIMS! WE HAVE
TOLERATED THEM LONG ENOUGH!
#ParisShooting #TCOT #P2 #MRA

12:32 AM · 08 Jan 15

 Daviðe Gandølfi   ⊕☰
@EchtGandolf

I'm so sorry for those French
journalists, fucking Muslims I always
hated and always will hate them
#KillAllMuslims

11:41 PM · 07 Jan 15

 Steven Renner
@EpikMani

@maishams You're right.
#KillAllMuslims is the only viable
response to this war on Western
Culture.

1:00 AM · 08 Jan 15

**Figure I.1   Selection of tweets after Paris attacks and the hashtag
#KillAllMuslims**

Figure I.2 Threats made against Salma Yaqoob on social media

hatred of the West prompts them to preach jihad and contempt for 'dirty kuffar'. Clearly, freedom of speech is a fundamental right that everyone should enjoy, but when that converges with incitement, harassment, threats of violence and cyber-bullying then we as a society must act before it's too late. There is an urgent need to provide advice for those who are suffering online abuse. It is also important to keep monitoring sites where this sort of thing regularly crops up; this can help inform not only policy but also help us get a better understanding of the relationships forming online. This would require a detailed examination of the various websites, blogs and social networking sites by monitoring the various URLs of those sites regarded as having links to anti-Muslim hate.

It is also important that we begin a process of consultation with victims of online anti-Muslim abuse – and reformed offenders – who could work together highlighting the issues they think are important when examining online Islamophobia. The internet offers an easy and accessible way of reporting online abuse, but an often difficult relationship between the police and Muslim communities in some areas means much more could be done. This could have a positive impact on the overall reporting of online abuse. The improved rate of prosecutions which might culminate as a result could also help identify the issues around online anti-Muslim abuse.

Cyber hate can take many forms from online material which can lead to actual offline abuse and violence, secondly cyber violence, thirdly cyber stalking and finally online harassment with the use of visual images, videos and text which are intended to cause harm. This book examines the case for current guidelines dealing with online Islamophobia and concludes that we require a new emphasis that recognises online Islamophobia and the impact it can have on vulnerable communities. The book is unique as it focuses on new technology in the form of social media and explores the challenges the police and other agencies face when confronting hate crime in cyberspace. It also provides a critique of how people are targeted by online offenders and helps us understand online Islamophobia in a much more detailed and comprehensive way.

The growth of the internet has meant there is an urgent need to examine how the online world has been used to commit hate crimes. In particular, the level of anonymity the internet offers means it will be continuously used as a way of committing crime. It also poses major challenges for the security services and the police. Privacy and isolation on the internet allows such offenders to display a willingness to target a specific group for targeted abuse or what is commonly referred to as trolling.

This is the first comprehensive critique of online Islamophobia. It brings together a diverse range of multidisciplinary ideas to explore the extent of online Islamophobia and at how online offenders are targeting communities. It also provides a critical analysis and understanding to how victims are perceived and feel about it. It also explores what measures the police can take to tackle issues of cyber hate and online Islamophobia. The USP of this text is that it is a 'one stop shop' for all aspects of online Islamophobia and similar related issues. The book will look at a wide range of issues that deal with Islamophobia on the internet. This includes providing a definition for the term, the psychology of online offenders, online hate groups promoting Islamophobia such as the EDL and Britain First, and the use of social media sites to perpetuate online anti-Muslim abuse.

The book includes a study of the behaviour and motivations of individuals viewed as online offenders. The policing, legal frameworks and legislation regarding online Islamophobia and its limitations in an international setting will also be analysed. The public perception and media portrayal of Muslims is also examined, alongside helping us understand the nature of Islamophobia in cyberspace. There has been very little literature in this area and this will be the first book looking at Islamophobia in the virtual world and therefore makes an important contribution to understating of this form of hate crime. The book is multi-faceted as it covers the origins of online hate crime and helps give us a better understanding of government policy and the methods towards tackling online Islamophobia. It gives a practitioner and academic based rationale alongside specific approaches and case studies looking at social media sites such as Twitter and Facebook to discuss how online Islamophobia is formed.

References

Awan, I. 2013. *Written Evidence Submitted to the All-Party Parliamentary Group on Islamophobia* (December), House of Commons, [Online]. Available at: http://tellmamauk.org/wp-content/uploads/2013/09/appg.pdf [accessed: 7 January 2015].

BBC News. 2014. 'Muslim hate crime rises 65% in London', [Online]. Available at: http://www.bbc.co.uk/news/uk-england-london-29424165 [accessed: 8 January 2015].

Littler, M. and Feldman, M. 2015. *Tell MAMA Reporting 2014/2015: Annual Monitoring, Cumulative Extremism, and Policy Implications*, Teesside: Teesside University Press.

Morris, N. 2015. 'Attorney General steps into social media racism row', *The Independent*, [Online]. Available at: http://www.independent.co.uk/news/uk/politics/attorney-general-steps-into-social-media-racism-row-9961364.html [accessed: 27 January 2015].

Tell MAMA, 2014. 'Anti-Muslim Hate Crime', [Online]. Available at: http://tellmamauk.org/tag/lee-rigby/ [accessed: 8 January 2015].

Tell MAMA. 2015. 'A victims' personal perspective on the impacts of online hate', [Online]. Available at: http://tellmamauk.org/a-victims-personal-perspective-on-the-impacts-of-online-hate/ [accessed: 8 January 2015].

Chapter 1

Cyber-Islamophobia and Internet Hate Crime

Imran Awan

The term 'hate crime' has come under increasing scrutiny and sharp focus after cases such as Stephen Lawrence, who was murdered in a racist attack in Britain in 1993, to the long history of racially-motivated hate crimes and violence committed against minorities in Europe and the United States, which culminated in new hate crime legislation and policies. Whilst there is no universal definition of a hate crime, in the United Kingdom, it is acknowledged that hate crime is not simply motivated by hate, but can be categorised as crimes that are targeted at a person because of hostility or prejudice towards that person's disability, race or ethnicity, religion or belief, or sexual orientation/transgender identity. Indeed, hate crime has received increasing media attention following major incidents such as the September 11, 2001 attacks in the United States, the July 2005 bombings in London and the Woolwich attack in the UK in 2013, which led to a spate of reprisal attacks against Muslim communities. Whilst hate crimes can affect a wide range of people who are frequently persecuted and targeted, this chapter will focus on the concepts and terminology around hate crime and examines how the convergence of hate crime on the internet has also led to a new spate of online Islamophobic responses, which have become more prevalent post Woolwich and the Paris shootings of 2015.

Background and Context

Hate crime is not limited to just physical attacks, but includes a wide range of potential crimes from offensive graffiti, damage to property, abusive and threatening messages, harassment, intimidation and verbal abuse (Perry 2001). Anti-Muslim hate crime falls under the category of religious hate crime, which is where it is perceived, by the victim or any other person, to be motivated by a hostility or prejudice based upon a person's religion or perceived religion (Keats 2014). In particular, post Woolwich and the death of drummer Lee Rigby in the UK, evidence shows that there has been an increase and rise in online

Islamophobia and this chapter will provide some background and context into the reasons and causes for the proliferation of this online hate.

As noted previously, online hate can come in many different forms and shapes, from racial harassment, religiously motivated abuse including anti-Semitic abuse, and directed abuse more generally which targets someone because of their disability, gender, culture, race and beliefs (Gerstenfeld 2013). Cyberspace therefore becomes a virtual minefield where offenders or 'trolls or trolling' specifically target people through online pre-meditated abuse and specific targeting of a victim, which a perpetrator has identified (Perry and Olsson 2009). The internet troll, who is named after the character from a children's story, specifically aims to target and harass an individual(s) because of their perceived difference (see Chapter 5 for further discussion). In effect, the internet troll aims to use cyberspace as a means to create a hostile space, where online hate can permeate (Keats 2014).

For example, the ex-football player, Stan Collymore has been repeatedly targeted by internet trolls and suffered a widespread amount of online racist abuse as a result. Collymore used Twitter to tell his 739,000 followers (at the time of writing) about the systematic online abuse which he was suffering. He stated that:

> In the last 24 hours I've been threatened with murder several times, demeaned on my race, and many of these accounts are still active. Why? ... I accuse Twitter directly of not doing enough to combat racist/homophobic/sexist hate messages, all of which are illegal in the UK. (BBC News 2014)

It does appear that the use of social media in particular, has profound consequences when misused and allows perpetrators a safe space to create a hostile virtual environment by using threatening messages. For example, the UK Member of Parliament, Stella Creasy and the feminist campaigner and freelance journalist Caroline Criado-Perez, were subjected to abusive threats which included rape via Twitter. Some of the comments posted online included: 'Everyone jump on the rape train, @CCriadoPerez is the conductor'. And: 'Hey sweetheart, give me a call when you're ready to be put in your place' (cited online in *The Huffington Post* 2013). Since those cases, Twitter has tried to alleviate people's fears by creating a button that would help report abuse and flag up tweets considered to be in breach of their code of conduct (Waldram 2013). But is that enough?

Clearly, online abuse is therefore not restricted to online Islamophobia, however this chapter aims to shed light on this 'new' digital form of racism, which following the Woolwich attacks has become the prime focus for the police and other agencies having to investigate online hate crime. Moreover, this is reinforced by statistics from the police and organisations, such as Tell

MAMA (Measuring Anti-Muslim Attacks) who are based in the UK and who have reported a significant increase in the amount of people reporting online anti-Muslim abuse to them (Tell MAMA 2013). Feldman et al. (2013: 21) found that: 'The majority of the incidents of Muslim hate crime reported to Tell MAMA are online incidents and 300 (69%) of these online cases reported a link to the far right.'

These facts are not isolated, as the Association of Chief Police Officers (ACPO), also revealed a similar trend that had seen them receive over 136 complaints of online anti-Muslim abuse reported through its 'True Vision website' which deals with hate crimes, since the death of Lee Rigby (ACPO 2013). True Vision is the police's main cyber tool in tackling online hate and is used as a means of helping the police create a safer online environment.

The website states that it will examine illegal content that threatens or harasses a person or group of persons because of hostility towards their race, religion, sexual orientation, disability or transgender status (see Chapter 7, for more detail). It adds, however that: 'Most hateful or violent website content is not illegal' and gives victims of online hate three options in dealing with the incident. These include reporting the material to the police, or reporting the material to a hosting company or contacting the website administrator to remove the material (True Vision 2013).

Clearly, threatening and abusive comments, whether it be by visual images, fake online profiles, Facebook messages, YouTube videos and tweets such as the above, can have a detrimental direct effect on the victims who are targeted as well as their families (Waddington 2010). What the above cases demonstrate is that online behaviour can be normalised by offenders which allows a perpetrator to use in many cases anonymity, manipulation and social control to target their victims (Douglas et al. 2005). However, whilst this form of cyber hate often remains invisible, sometimes due to offenders deleting tweets, comments or posts and also because the perpetrator can hide their identity, the threat remains very real for the victims it targets (Hall 2013).

Indeed, trying to ascertain all the potential threats and risks posed online does pose a major challenge for the security services, the police and the government (see Chapter 7). Cyber hate within the policing context therefore requires due diligence and an investigation that determines potential online offenders, offensive online messages and those they believe can be prosecuted alongside the Crown Prosecution Service (CPS) rules. Communications via social media sites, like Twitter, can also be a criminal offence. The new CPS guidelines published in 2013 state that there must be either a credible threat of violence or communications which specifically target an individual or group of people, communications which amount to a breach of a court order and communications which may be considered grossly offensive, indecent, obscene or false (CPS Guidelines 2013).

In many of these cases people can be charged for comments made via social networking sites under 'racially motivated' or 'religiously motivated' crimes through the Crime and Disorder Act 1998, the Malicious Communications Act 1988, the Communications Act 2003 and the Public Order Act 1986 (Coliandris 2012). Overall, policing cyberspace and people's activity via social media sites remains difficult and the recent Leveson Inquiry (2012) in the UK which was set up by the British government to investigate the culture, practices and ethics of the Press also acknowledges that it is problematic to regulate.

Following the Woolwich attack, a number of arrests were made where people had posted comments on Twitter and Facebook which were deemed to incite racial hatred or violence. In one case, a person was convicted under the Malicious Communications Act 1988 after an offensive message was posted on Facebook (Urquhart 2013). Cyber hate regulation therefore requires the police and other agencies to act quickly and more effectively in relation to online Islamophobic abuse. At the moment cyberspace does resemble a virtual minefield of hate and therefore policing it requires a shift in thinking from authorities which gets them thinking and acting not in an abstract black and white way, but in a more innovative and nuanced way that helps the police prosecute people for cyber hate as well as educating people of the dangers of online abuse (Chan 2007). I will now begin to explore some of the complexities around the term 'hate crime'.

Complexities Surrounding the Term Hate Crime

There is no universal definition of a hate crime, although we have a myriad of interpretations and examples of terms that have been used to define what might constitute a hate crime. In the United Kingdom, a hate crime is any criminal offence which is perceived, by the victim or any other person, to be motivated by a hostility or prejudice based on a person's race or perceived race because of their disability, race or ethnicity, religion or belief, sexual orientation, or transgender identity. Craig (2002: 86) states that this equates to any illegal act which intentionally selects a victim because of those prejudices against the victim.

This type of crime can also be committed against a person or property and the victim does not have to be a member of the group at which the hostility is targeted. Indeed, the notion that an offender must be motivated by hate for there to be a hate crime is problematic. Chakraborti and Garland (2009:4) make the case that: 'in reality crimes do not need to be motivated by hatred at all', and Hall (2013: 9) states that 'hate crime isn't really about hate, but about criminal behaviour motivated by prejudice, of which hate is just one small and extreme part', which does raise important questions about re-thinking what hate crime actually means. For example, how should we define it? Why is it happening?

And how do we prevent it from happening in the future? Perry (2001: 10) argues that hate crime is about offenders pursuing a level of control and power and states that a hate crime must involve:

> acts of violence and intimidation, usually directed towards already stigmatized and marginalized groups. As such it is a mechanism of power and oppression, intended to reaffirm the precarious hierarchies that characterize a given social order. It attempts to re-create simultaneously the threatened (real or imagined) hegemony of the perpetrator's group and the appropriate subordinate identity of the victim's group. It is a means of marking both the Self and the Other in such a way as to re-establish their 'proper' relative positions, as given and reproduced by broader ideologies and patterns of social and political inequality.

Interestingly, Chakraborti and Garland (2009: 6) note how Perry's definition extends to all 'members and groups' who are victimised and marginalised and as such they argue Perry's definition provides a more fluid and comprehensive interpretation of the meaning of hate crime. They state that: 'Crucially, it recognizes that hate crime is not a static problem but one that is historically and culturally contingent, the experience of which needs to be seen as a dynamic process, involving context, structure and agency.'

In respect to the motivation element surrounding the term, Hall (2013: 3) makes the case that:

> In this sense then it is society's interest in the motivation that lies behind the commission of the crime that is new. That motivation is, of course, an offender's hatred of, or more accurately, prejudice against, a particular identifiable group or member of a particular identifiable group, usually already marginalized within society, whom the offender intentionally selects on the basis of that prejudice.

Thus for Hall (2013: 16) it is clear that hate crime is a social construct and is susceptible to a process of crime which can relate to the new socio-legal problems of how we deconstruct hate crime. Similarly, Gerstenfeld (2013: 9) argues that hate crime has no borders and therefore we cannot simply measure it through domestic problems but that instead it requires an international approach that involves working with wider partners such as the United Nations, the European Union and the Organisation for Security and Cooperation in Europe (OSCE) to share ideas, experience and good practice that can help tackle the problem of hate crime.

Furthermore, this involves dialogue and discussion about how cyberspace is policed since hate crime on the internet has become a more widespread problem since the rapid growth of the internet (Iganski 2008). Indeed, the convergence of hate crime and Islamophobia on the internet has provided a new platform by which a number of anti-hate websites and groups have appeared online in order to perpetuate a level of cyber hate not seen previously (these are discussed in further detail in Chapter 4). Sheffield (1995: 438) argues therefore that hate crime is: 'violence motivated by social and political factors and is bolstered by belief systems which (attempt to) legitimize such violence'.

In 2007, the Police Service, Crown Prosecution Service (CPS), Prison Service (which is now the National Offender Management Service) and other similar agencies that make up the criminal justice system agreed that hate crime should only consist of five separate strands and that this could be monitored centrally. As noted previously, those monitored strands are: race, religion/faith, sexual orientation, disability and gender-identity. Interestingly, UK policy also deems crimes committed against a person because of hostility towards someone's age, gender and/or appearance could also constitute a hate crime, despite not being part of the five monitored strands. Hall (2013: 5) argues that: 'These definitions are notable because they allow for anyone to be a victim of hate crime, and for any offence or incident to be recorded and investigated by the police as a hate crime'. The UK policy and legal interpretation of hate crime has also divided the term into different areas from hate motivation, hate incidents and hate crimes. The operational definition in England and Wales states that hate motivation is where: 'Hate crimes and incidents are taken to mean any crime or incident where the perpetrator's hostility or prejudice against an identifiable group of people is a factor in determining who is victimized' (College of Policing 2014: 3). The definition included here is broader in the sense that the victim does not have to be a member of a group.

A hate incident on the other hand is described as: 'Any non-crime incident which is perceived by the victim or any other person, to be motivated by a hostility or prejudice based on a person's race or perceived race, religion or perceived religion, sexual orientation or perceived sexual orientation, disability or perceived disability, or transgender or perceived to be transgender' (College of Policing 2014: 3). In this context, the victims could be classified as any racial group or ethnic background which includes countries within the United Kingdom and 'Gypsy and Traveller groups' and any other religious group including those who have no faith. Hate incidents are important because they are defined as particular crimes that can often escalate into further crimes or tension in a community. For example, comments made by an evangelical Protestant preacher named Pastor James McConnell who described Islam as a 'heathen' doctrine and argued Muslims 'could not be trusted' were investigated by police as a potential hate incident, because of the nature of the comments which were construed as potentially aiding an act that could lead to an escalation of violence and community tensions (BBC News 2014).

Cyber hate therefore is a nexus of those communications and concepts where a perpetrator utilises electronic technology and the convergence of space, movement and behaviour in a 'safe' virtual environment to 'control' and target 'opponents' considered to be a threat (Awan and Blakemore 2012). This type of control allows the perpetrator to act in a dominant way against groups they deem to be subordinate, often as is the case with Muslims, attacking their faith and ethnicity (Perry 2001). It also allows offenders to use the online world and other social networking platforms to target individuals they deem to be 'different' from them in an ideological, political and religious sense.

As noted above, cyber hate is a complex phenomenon and is used to promote a particular ideology that promotes racial hatred, religious intolerance and also allows 'lone wolfs' and 'hate groups' to exert cyber power and social control in a systematic and targeted manner that has no respect for a victim's rights (Perry 2001). This therefore can result in them trying to use online methods as a means of self-protectionism and false patriotism for groups like the far-right which fuel anti-Muslim hate and abuse (Cole and Cole 2009).

In the online world, this can often be played out by abusive, threatening and co-ordinated tweets, or through the use of sites like Twitter (see Chapter 2) to send messages of hate which include the use of visual images to target particular individuals (Whine 2003). Clearly, it should be noted that cyberspace can also be an extremely valuable tool in helping detect and tackle online cybercrime and increasingly is being used by the police to help engage with the communities. Blakemore (2013) for example, argues that the use of social networking sites by the police can have an important impact on people's level of 'fear of cybercrime' and also can help assist them report such incidents to the police. However, it is the phenomenon of online Islamophobia, and trying to categorise how to deal with this issue that has caused most problems.

In March 2012, the UK Government published its plan to tackle hate crime entitled: 'Challenge it, Report it, Stop it'. The document contained there three core objectives which included preventing hate crime happening in the first instance. These included: 1) increasing awareness of reporting hate crime; 2) access to support mechanisms for victims; and 3) improving the operational response towards hate crime. Statistics have also revealed that hate crime remains on the increase in the UK with the Home Office, Ministry of Justice and the Office for National Statistics in December 2013 publishing an overview of hate crime in England and Wales. The data covers police-recorded hate crime, which revealed that between 2012 to 2013 43, 927 hate crimes were recorded by the police, of which the breakdown was as follows:

- 35,885 (85%) were race hate crimes;
- 1,573 (4%) were religion hate crimes;
- 4,267 (10%) were sexual-orientation hate crimes;
- 1,841 (4%) were disability hate crimes;
- 361 (1%) were transgender hate crimes.

Findings also from the combined Crime Survey for England and Wales for 2011 to 2012 and for 2012 to 2013 estimated that there were 278,000 incidents of hate crime on average each year. Around 40% of these incidents came to the attention of the police. However what these statistics do not show is the amount of hate crime that remains under-reported (Home Office 2013). Despite this, we have seen examples in particular around tackling racial hatred and religiously aggravated offences that have led to successful prosecution. For example, two Middlesbrough football club fans were convicted of a religiously aggravated public order offence whilst also participating in offensive chanting in 2014 after tearing up a copy of the Quran and throwing pieces of it into the air during a football match (Muslim News 2014). Below, the chapter examines in more detail the issues around internet hate crime.

Internet Hate Crime

Social media platforms have a huge global reach and audience, with YouTube boasting more than 1 billion users each month. The number of people watching YouTube each day has also increased by 40% since March 2014 (YouTube Statistics 2015). Similarly, Twitter has on average 350,000 tweets being sent per minute and 500 million tweets per day (Twitter 2014), whilst Facebook remains the largest social media network with 500 million active users and 55 million people sending updates (Fiegerman 2014). This growth and expansion of the internet has created many positive opportunities for people to communicate and engage in a manner not seen previously (Social Media Today 2010). However, it has also acted as a double-edged sword by creating a virtual vacuum and platform for people using hate as a means to appeal to a wider audience often under the cloak of anonymity that allows them to supersede and bypass any sort of editorial control or regulation. It should also be noted here however that whilst there is a large amount of online material that could cause offence, this does not equate to it necessarily being illegal in the UK.

The internet therefore provides new opportunities for associated crimes to be committed. Messages can be spread at great speed, people can remain anonymous and the nature of cyberspace remains unregulated. In particular for hate groups wanting to recruit people for their cause this can also give them a platform to spread unsolicited material which can go unnoticed. This allows them to capture new audiences and use the internet as a propaganda tool for those purposes (discussed in more detail in chapter four). Indeed, these communicative messages can spread and cause a lot of discontent (McNamee et al. 2010) and these hate based groups are quick to create websites that create more hate through blogs and forums of hate and Islamophobia. Keats and Norton (2011) for example found social media sites were being used to facilitate this form of online hate.

Hall (2013: 204) states that: 'The increase in the use of the Internet as a vehicle for hate is therefore seemingly undeniable, be it organized hate groups or those expressing prejudice and hostility in a more casual manner.'

Hate on the internet can also have direct and indirect experiences for victims and communities being targeted. In one sense, it can be used to harass and intimidate victims and on the other hand it can also be for opportunistic crimes. The internet therefore is a powerful tool by which people can be influenced to act in a certain way and manner. What is left in terms of direct impact is important because it impacts upon local communities and the understanding of how this could constitute acts of violence offline. This is particularly strong when considering hate speech online that aims to threaten and incite violence. Hate speech in this context is any form of language used to depict someone in a negative fashion with regard to their race, ethnicity, gender, religion, sexual orientation or physical and mental disability which promotes hate and incites violence (Yar 2013). This also links into the convergence of emotional distress caused by hate online, the nature of intimidation and harassment online, and the prejudice that seeks to defame groups through speech intending to injure and intimidate (see Chapter 10 for further discussion). Some of those sites include the Bare Naked Islam site which has a daily forum and chatroom about issues to do with Muslims and Islam.

In one of its more provocative posts in September 2012 it stated that 'Yes, we hate Islam'. There were 850 comments accompanied by the piece which included statements such as 'Muslims are not human', 'One day we will get you scum out' and 'Muslim men are pigs ... I am all for annihilation of all Muslims'.[1] ACPO (2013) notes how hate material can cause damage to community cohesion. ACPO (2013) states that: 'We understand that hate material can damage community cohesion and create fear, so the police want to work alongside communities and the internet industry to reduce the harm caused by hate on the Internet.'

Another problem with internet hate crime is the issue of how to police it (discussed in more detail in Chapter 6). This can be problematic when individuals are using hate material from outside the UK and as such it becomes very difficult to prosecute anyone, because they are outside the jurisdiction of UK courts. Indeed, a lot of the material online can also cause a lot of fear and it is imperative that the police and other agencies work together to tackle hate crime on the internet. Hate crimes on the internet have also been used as a means to create storage and communicative messages that go beyond the physical to the virtual dimension. For Perry (2003: 19) this means the spectrum of hate crime

---

1 See http://www.barenakedislam.com/2012/09/30/yes-we-hate-islam-yes-we-will-mock-your-paedophile-prophet-mohammed-as-much-as-we-want-no-we-dont-care-what-you-think-or-how-offended-you-are-we-are-americans-and-we-are-free-to-say-what-we-w/.

does cross the invisible line and as such Coliandris (2012: 82) argues hate crimes 'are capable of "sending a message" to particular communities'.

The internet therefore has become a safe haven for many of these groups and individuals, who are using it effectively to target, marginalise and demonise a group or community. A lot of this has been dedicated to far-right groups and lone wolf actors who have engaged in what has been defined as cybersquatting and Google bombing. These are anti-hate webpages and online sources which are used to create content that creates a measure of intolerance and targets specific individuals or groups. For example, this has been used by far-right groups and those such as Britain First, the Anti-Defamation League and the English Defence League who have used the internet to create a public presence and been successful in using the internet as a platform to disseminate further hate and intolerance. Moreover, Feldman et al. (2013) found that from the 74% of online hate incidents reported to Tell MAMA, the majority of online incidents also included threats made about offline action. They also found that most of the online hate was committed by males and 70% of online incidents had a link to the far-right, specifically to the English Defence League (EDL) and the British National Party (BNP). The EDL is a far right organisation based in the UK, which has at its core the aim to tackle 'militant Islam' and the BNP is a far-right political party in Britain.

As noted above, in England and Wales it can be an offence to stir up and incite hatred through illegal hate content on the grounds of race, religion and sexual orientation. Indeed, there are also other offences such as using the content of a website which can is illegal when it threatens or harasses a person or a group of people. Furthermore, if it can be proved that such material was posted because of hostility based on race, religion, sexual orientation, disability or transgender status then it is also a hate crime offence. In practice this is not confined to words or pictures but could include videos, chatrooms and even music.

Cyber-Islamophobia in a Digital Age

The Runnymede Trust defined Islamophobia as 'unfounded hostility towards Muslims, and therefore fear or dislike of all or most Muslims'. The seminal Runnymede Trust report (1997) also identified eight components that they define as being Islamophobia. They include where people view:

1. Islam as a faith that is unresponsive to change;
2. the values of Islam to be incompatible with other cultures and faiths;
3. Islam as a religion that is barbaric and sexist;
4. Islam as a religion that is both violent and aggressive;
5. Islam as a political ideology;

6. Islam and criticisms made about the faith are unwarranted;
7. discriminatory practices are used to justify exclusion of Muslim communities; and
8. Anti-Muslim crime as normal.

Interestingly, very little discussion is made of online Islamophobia. They argue that Islamophobic views are shaped by a 'closed set' of narrow views on Islam and Muslims, which has helped contribute to the 'othering' of Muslim communities through discriminative practices and affects (Awan 2012). The Forum against Islamophobia and Racism (FAIR) (2013) argue that Islamophobia constitutes fear and hostility against Muslim communities. However, like the above interpretations, they confine Islamophobia to physical attacks such as abuse and targeted violence against Muslim communities, mosques, cemeteries and discrimination in places of education (Allen 2001). Islamophobia therefore is seen as 'dangerous' because of the 'expansion' of Muslim communities. Whilst these definitions remain limited in scope with regards to the online dimension of Islamophobia, they do however give us a starting point for further discussion and discourse in this area. The author of this chapter however argues that we need a separate definition of online Islamophobia which is recognisable both at a policy level and an academic level.

For example, a definition which includes: 'Anti-Muslim prejudice that targets a victim in order to provoke, cause hostility and promote intolerance by means of harassment, stalking, abuse, incitement, threatening behaviour, bullying and intimidation of the person or persons, via all platforms of social media, chatrooms, blogs and forums' could be used as a means to help assist the police. Tell MAMA also provides a working definition of anti-Muslim prejudice, which includes prejudice or hatred of Muslims, which may be expressed as hatred or outward hostility towards Muslims.

Academics such as Taras (2012: 4) make the point that Islamophobia has become a term that is misunderstood and indeed lacking in clarity. Taras states that Islamophobia entails 'the spread of hostile public attitudes towards Muslims, in this case across Europe. The spread of Islamophobia is based on a conviction that Europe is in peril because of Islamisation'. This sense of securitisation and fear for Taras is about how visual representations of Islam have become synonymous with people who fear the pervading sense of history. For example, the depiction of mosques, headscarves and minarets helps contribute towards the 'othering' of such communities. Taras (2012: 4) notes that: 'Islamophobia thus entails a cultural racism that sets Muslims apart. As a result, the Islamic migrant is constructed as someone burdened by alien attributes and as a carrier of antagonistic, threatening values'.

It should be noted here that Islamophobia did not come into existence post 9/11 or indeed post-Woolwich. Muslims as a group have suffered from marginalisation and faced high risk of being victims of racially motivated crimes prior to this, including after the 'Cold War' (Chakraborti and Garland 2009: 44). However these incidents do tend to show a sharp increase in attacks against Muslims post 9/11 and events such as the 7/7 attacks in 2005 in London. For example, McGhee (2005) found an increase in racist attacks reported to the police because of the way Muslims looked. Similarly, Muslims have faced a backlash whether it was in Europe (Modood 2003) or the United States (Perry 2003) with a widespread range of anti-Muslim attacks being reported.

The Woolwich attacks also triggered a backlash against Muslims across the world mainly because Islam was being used to justify the terror attacks. Whilst Islamophobia has been viewed as a new term it has long roots back from the time of the Christian Crusades to the Prophet Muhammad (Allen 2010). Taras (2012: 119) notes how 'Islamophobia is a backlash to the expanded presence of Muslim communities in Europe'. Indeed, a recent BBC Radio 1 Newsbeat poll found that one in four young people in Britain distrust Muslims. Additionally, 16% said they did not trust Hindus or Sikhs, 15% said they did not trust Jewish people, 13% for Buddhists and 12% said they did not trust Christians. Indeed, 44% said they believe Muslims did not share the same values, whilst 28% said the UK would be a better place with fewer Muslims there (Kotecha 2013).

Clearly, prejudice towards Muslim communities post events such as 9/11, 7/7 and more recently Woolwich are intensified. This marginalisation of Muslim communities appears to be rooted in the narrative that Islam is a barbaric faith and that Islam and the West are, in actual fact, involved in a clash of civilisations. This belief often creates the space whereby Muslims are targeted and also vilified for what they believe in, both offline and online. This demonisation is captured in studies with Muslim communities conducted by Awan (2012) and Allen et al. (2014) which looked at online Islamophobia and the demonisation of Muslim women. Their studies found that Muslims were being targeted both online and offline which had culminated in Muslims feeling isolated and alienated.

Conclusion

Since the emergence of key events such as 9/11, 7/7 and now Woolwich, there has been an increase in hate crimes committed against Muslim communities. Whilst many of these incidents have led to offline violence, there is also a sense that such incidents are now common place online. Such attacks online mean that the police, social media companies and government must do more to tackle online anti-Muslim hate crime. One way is to help build trust and confidence, so that victims of online hate crime can come forward and report such incidents. This is important because victims of online hate crime can feel isolated and alienated. For example, the UK based charity ChildLine, recently found an increase in the number of children contacting them with concerns about online bullying. They saw 4,507 cases of cyber bullying in 2012/13, which was up from 2, 410 from the previous year in 2011/12 (Sellgren 2014).

The use of social media and the internet provide safe online spaces which have created a vacuum for perpetrators to target vulnerable people by using anti-Semitic abuse, racist abuse, homophobic abuse, gender-based abuse, anti-disability abuse and Islamophobic abuse. As a result online anti-Muslim hate crime has also been increasing and there is an urgent need to examine the implications this has for community cohesion and society as a whole.

Further Reading

Grabosky, P., Wright, P. and Smith, R. 1998. *Crime in the Digital Age: Controlling Telecommunications and Cyberspace Illegalities*, New Brunswick, NJ: Transaction.
Jewkes, Y. and Yar, M. 2010. *Handbook of Internet Crime*, Cullompton: Willan.
Mansell, R. and Collins, B. 2005. *Trust and Crime in Information Societies*, Cheltenham: Edward Elgar.

References

Allen, C. 2001. *Islamophobia in the Media since September 11th, Forum against Islamophobia and Racism*, [Online]. Available at: http://www.fairuk.org/docs/islamophobia-in-the-media-since-911-christopherallen.pdf [accessed: 26 April 2013].
Allen, C. 2010. *Islamophobia*, Farnham: Ashgate.
Association of Chief Police Officers. 2013. *True Vision Records*, [Online]. Available at: http://www.report-it.org.uk/true_vision_records_a_significant_weekly_reduct [accessed: 2 September 2013].
Awan, I. 2012. 'The impact of policing British Muslims: A qualitative exploration', *Journal of Policing, Intelligence and Counter-Terrorism*, 7 (1): 22–35.
Awan, I. and Blakemore, B. 2012. *Policing Cyber Hate, Cyber Threats and Cyber Terrorism*, Farnham: Ashgate.
BBC News. 2014a. 'Ex-football Collymore accuses Twitter over abusive messages', [Online]. Available at: http://www.bbc.co.uk/news/uk-25838114 [accessed: 10 December 2014].
BBC News 2014b. 'Pastor James McConnell Islamic remarks investigated by Police', [Online]. Available at: http://www.bbc.co.uk/news/uk-northern-ireland-27501839 [accessed: 10 December 2014].
Blakemore, B. 2013. 'Extremist Groups and Organisations', in *Extremism, Counter-Terrorism and Policing*, edited by I. Awan and B. Blakemore, Farnham: Ashgate, 87–102.

Chakraborti, N and Garland, J. 2009. *Hate Crime: Impact, Causes and Responses*, London: Sage.

Chan, J.B.L. 2007. 'Police and New Technologies', in *Handbook of Policing*, edited by T. Newburn, Cullompton: Willan Publishing, 655–79.

Cole, J. and Cole, B. 2009. *Martyrdom: Radicalisation and Terrorist Violence Among British Muslims*, London: Pennant Books.

Coliandris, G. 2012. 'Hate in a Cyber Age', in *Policing Cyber Hate, Cyber Threats and Cyber Terrorism*, edited by I. Awan and B. Blakemore, Farnham: Ashgate, 75–95.

College of Policing, 2014. *Hate Crime Operational Guidance*, [Online]. Available at: http://www.report-it.org.uk/files/hate_crime_operational_guidance.pdf [accessed: 12 December 2014].

Craig, K. 2002. Examining Hate-motivated Aggression: A Review of the Social Psychological Literature on Hate Crime as a Distinct Form of Aggression, *Aggression and Violent Behaviour*, 7 (1): 85–101.

Crown Prosecution Service. 2013. *Guidelines on Prosecuting Cases Involving Communications sent via Social Media*, [Online]. Available at: http://www.cps.gov.uk/legal/a_to_c/communications_sent_via_social_media/ [accessed: 10 December 2014].

Douglas, K., McGarty, C., Bliuc, A. and Lala, G. 2005. 'Understanding Cyberhate: Social Competition and Social Creativity in Online White Supremacist Groups', *Social Science Computer Review*, 23 (1): 68–76.

Feldman, M., Littler, M., Dack, J. and Copsey, N. 2013. *Anti-Muslim Hate Crime and the Far Right*, Teeside University, [Online]. Available at: http://tellmamauk.org/wp-content/uploads/2013/07/antimuslim2.pdf [accessed: 4 September 2013].

Fiegerman, S. 2014. *Facebook Messenger now has 500 million monthly active users,* [Online]. Available at: http://mashable.com/2014/11/10/facebook-messenger-500-million/ [accessed: 22 December 2014].

Forum against Islamophobia and Racism, 2013, [Online]. Available at: http://www.fairuk.org/introduction.htm [accessed: 10 July 2014].

Gerstenfeld, P.B. 2013. *Hate Crimes: Causes, Controls and Controversies.* 3rd edition, Thousand Oaks, CA: Sage.

Hall, N. 2013. *Hate Crime.* 2nd edition, London: Routledge.

HM Government. 2012. *Challenge it, Stop it, Report it: The Government's Plan to Tackle Hate Crime*, [Online]. Available at: https://www.gov.uk/government/uploads/system/uploads/attachment_data/file/97849/action-plan.pdf [accessed: 29 June 2014].

Home Office. 2013. *An Overview of Hate Crime in England and Wales*, [Online]. Available at: https://www.gov.uk/government/uploads/system/uploads/attachment_data/file/266358/hate-crime-2013.pdf [accessed: 10 December 2014].

The Huffington Post. 2013. *Twitter Rape Abuse of Caroline Criado-Perez Leads to Boycott Threat*, [Online]. Available at: http://www.huffingtonpost.co.uk/2013/07/27/twitter-rape-abuse_n_3663904.html [accessed: 1 September 2014].

Iganski, P. 2008. '*Hate Crime' and the City*, Bristol: The Policy Press.

Keats, C. and Norton, H. 2011. 'Intermediaries and Hate Speech: Fostering Digital Citizenship for Our Information Age'. *Boston University Law Review*, 91: 1435.

Keats, D. 2014. *Hate Crimes in Cyberspace*, Cambridge, MA: Harvard University Press.

Kotecha, S. 2013. 'Quarter of young British people 'do not trust Muslims', *BBC Newsbeat*, [Online]. Available at: http://www.bbc.co.uk/newsbeat/24204742 [accessed: 10 December 2014].

Leveson Inquiry. 2012. *Culture, Practice and Ethics of the Press*, [Online]. Available at: http://www.levesoninquiry.org.uk/about/the-report/ [accessed: 11 February 2014].

McGhee, D. 2005. *Intolerant Britain? Hate, Citizenship and Difference*, Milton Keynes: Open University Press.

McNamee, L.G., Peterson, B.L. and Pena, J. 2010. 'A Call to Educate, Participate, Invoke and Indict: Understanding Communication of Online Hate Groups', *Communication Monographs*, 77 (2): 257–80.

Modood, T. 2003. 'Muslims and European Multiculturalism', in *The Politics of Migration: Managing Opportunity, Conflict and Chance*, edited by S. Spencer, Oxford: Blackwell Publishing, 100–115.

Muslim News. 2014. 'Middlesborough fan convicted of ripping Qur'an pages', *Muslim News*, [Online]. Available at: http://www.muslimnews.co.uk/ newspaper/islamophobia/middlesborough-fan-convicted-ripping-quran-pages/ [accessed: 10 December 2014].

Perry, B. 2001. *In the Name of Hate: Understanding Hate Crimes*, London: Routledge

Perry, B. 2003. 'Where do we go from here? Researching Hate Crime', *Internet Journal of Criminology*, [Online]. Available at: http://www.internetjournalofcriminology. com/where%20do%20we%20go%20from%20here.%20researching%20 hate%20crime.pdf [accessed: 10 December 2014].

Perry, B. and Olsson, P. 2009. *Cyberhate: The Globalisation of Hate: Information & Communications Technology Law*, [Online]. 18 (2): 185–99. Available at: http://www.informaworld.com/smpp/content-content=a912569634-db=all~jumptype=rss [accessed: 10 December 2014].

Sellgren, K. 2014. 'Cyberbullying 'on rise' – ChildLine', [Online]. *BBC News*, Available at: http://www.bbc.co.uk/news/education-25639839 [accessed: 10 December 2014].

Sheffield, C. 1995. 'Hate Violence', in *Race, Class and Gender in the United States*, edited by R. Rothenberg, New York: St Martin's Press, 431–41.

Social Media Today. 2010. *Statistics on Social Media*, [Online]. Available at: http:// www.socialmediatoday.com/tompick/176932/best-social-media-stats-and-market-research-2010-so-far [accessed: 10 December 2014].

Taras, R. 2012. *Xenophobia and Islamophobia in Europe*, Edinburgh University Press.

Tell MAMA, 2013. *Anti-Muslim Hate Crime*, [Online]. http://tellmamauk.org/ [accessed: 2 September, 2014].

The Runnymede Trust. 1997. *Islamophobia A Challenge for Us All*, [Online]. Available at: http://www.runnymedetrust.org/uploads/publications/pdfs/islamophobia.pdf [accessed: 29 April 2014].

True Vision, 2013. *Internet Hate Crime*, [Online]. Available at: http://www.report-it.org.uk/reporting_internet_hate_crime [accessed: 2 September 2014].

Twitter, 2014. Usage Statistics [Online]. Available at: http://www.internetlivestats.com/twitter-statistics/ [accessed: 8 January 2015].

Urquhart, C. 2013. 'Attacks on Muslims soar in wake of Woolwich murder', *The Guardian*, [Online]. Available at: http://www.theguardian.com/uk/2013/may/25/woolwich-murder-attacks-on-muslims [accessed: 2 September 2014].

Waddington, P.A.J. 2010. 'An Examination of Hate Crime', *Police Review*, 23 April, 118 (6077): 14–15.

Waldrum, H. 2013. 'Twitter rolls out "report abuse" button for individual tweets: will you use it?' *The Guardian*, [Online] Available at: http://www.theguardian.com/technology/blog/2013/aug/30/twitter-report-abusebutton [accessed: 5 September 2014].

Whine, M. 2003. 'Far right extremists on the Internet', in *Cyber Crime: Law Enforcement, Security and Surveillance in the Information Age*, edited by D. Thomas, D. and B. Loader, London: Routledge, 234–50.

Yar, M. 2013. *Cybercrime and Society*, London: Sage.

YouTube Statistics, 2015. Viewership [Online] Available https://www.youtube.com/yt/press/en-GB/statistics.html [accessed 8 October 2015].

Chapter 2
Virtual Islamophobia: The Eight Faces of Anti-Muslim Trolls on Twitter

Imran Awan

The Woolwich attack in May 2013 in the UK has led to a spate of hate crimes committed against Muslim communities. These incidents include Muslim women being targeted for wearing the headscarf and mosques being vandalised. For example, the Al-Rahma community centre in Muswell Hill in North London was burnt down soon after the Woolwich incident (BBC News 2013a). Other examples of hate incidents included graffiti being scrawled against mosque walls and petrol bombs being left outside mosques (Saul 2013). All these incidents have led to a heightened atmosphere for British Muslims, fearful of reprisal attacks against them because of the Woolwich incident. However, whilst street level Islamophobia, remains an important area of investigation, a more equally disturbing picture is emerging with the rise in online anti-Muslim abuse (Tell MAMA 2013).

This chapter explores a case study conducted by the author of this chapter, which examined 500 separate tweets, to try and find out how Muslims are being viewed and targeted by perpetrators of online abuse who are using social media sites such as Twitter to espouse anti-Muslim prejudice. The study used three hashtags, namely; #Woolwich, #Muslims and #Islam, to note and look at patterns emerging regarding online Islamophobia via the Twitter search engine. The chapter provides a typology of offender characteristics, made up of people who are committing the online abuse and argues that online Islamophobia must be given the same level of attention as street-level Islamophobia.

In May 2013, Michael Adebowale and Michael Adebolajo murdered British soldier Lee Rigby in Woolwich, south-east London. Adebowale and Adebolajo were both convicted of the murder of Lee Rigby in December 2013. At the time, the incident provoked strong public anger and outrage by politicians, policy makers and the media. British Prime Minister David Cameron argued that the Woolwich attack would not 'divide us' but instead make us 'stronger' in the fight against global and home-grown terrorism. However, the tragic events of that day also led to a series of attacks against Muslims, mosques and Islamic institutions which amounted to a sharp increase in Islamophobic related incidents. Indeed, a number of police forces saw a dramatic surge in the number of reported hate crimes against Muslims, with the Metropolitan police recording 500 Islamophobic crimes since Woolwich (*The Guardian* 2013).

Whilst a number of these incidents took place offline (i.e. with the use of direct physical force) there were also people who used social media sites to either vent their anger or to make actual death threats against Muslim communities (BBC News 2013c). Clearly, major incidents such as the Woolwich attack can provoke public outrage, anger, and can lead to stereotyping of all Muslim communities as being violent extremists (Larsson 2007). Indeed, the internet and social media sites such as Twitter,[1] have become a popular arena for online hate, partly due to their accessibility and the anonymity they offer for offenders who use it to intimidate, harass and bully others (Christopherson 2007). Moreover, following the Woolwich attack, we also witnessed how Twitter was used by offenders who were promoting this type of online Islamophobic hate, which was loaded with tactics of harassment and threats of reprisal attacks (BBC News 2013c). Below is a selection of some of the tweets that appeared post the Woolwich attack.

Clearly, online abuse is not restricted to online Islamophobia as noted in chapter one. Indeed, this is reinforced by statistics from the police and organisations such as Tell MAMA (Measuring Anti-Muslim Attacks) who reported a significant increase in the amount of people reporting online anti-Muslim abuse to them (Tell MAMA 2013). Feldman et al. (2013: 21) found that: 'The majority of the incidents of Muslim hate crime reported to Tell MAMA are online incidents and 300 (69%) of these online cases reported a link to the far right.'

This study analysed and examined 500 separate tweets, to try and find out how Muslims were being viewed and the way in which perpetrators of online abuse were targeting them through social media sites such as Twitter. All of the tweets were analysed between January 2013 and April 2014, and are available and accessible in the open public domain. The overwhelming number of tweets were written and posted by people who were living in the UK, although there were some tweets from users who were based in Australia and the United States. From the data collected, the majority of tweets were posted by males (72%) in comparison to females who accounted for 28%. The study used three hashtags, namely; #Woolwich, #Muslim and #Islam, to note and look at patterns emerging regarding online Islamophobia on Twitter. The reason those

---

1 Twitter is a social media platform that allows people to stay up to date with the news of friends, family and co-workers in a way that makes them easily accessible and stay connected through the exchange of quick and frequent messages.

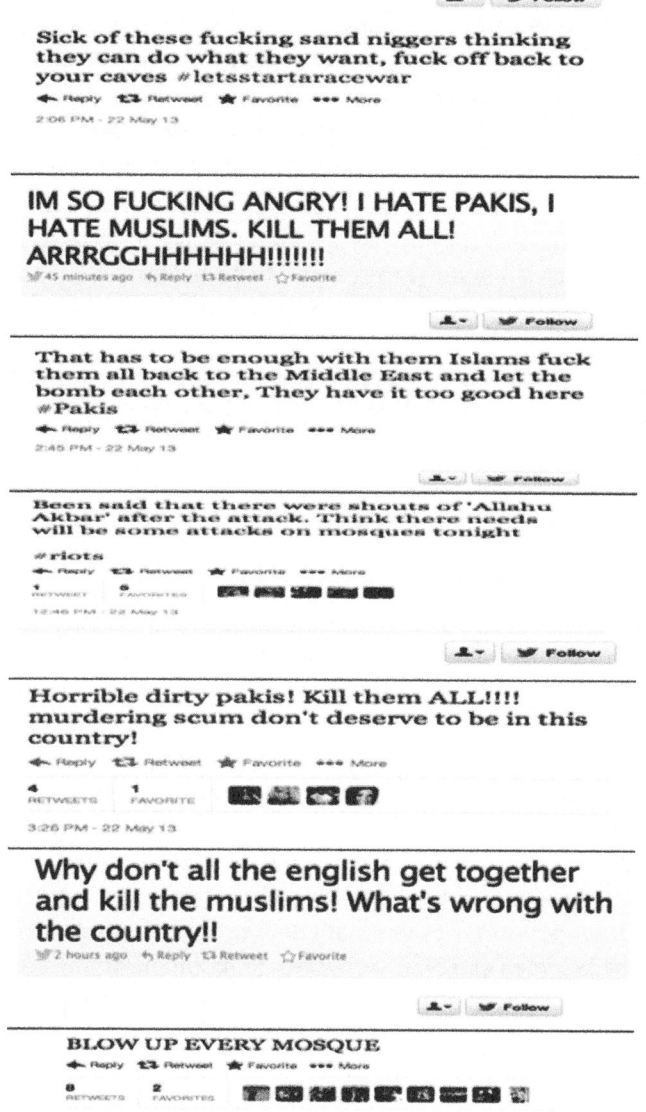

Figure 2.1 Selection of tweets following the Woolwich attack

Note: These can also be accessed via http://publicshaming.tumblr.com/search/woolwich.

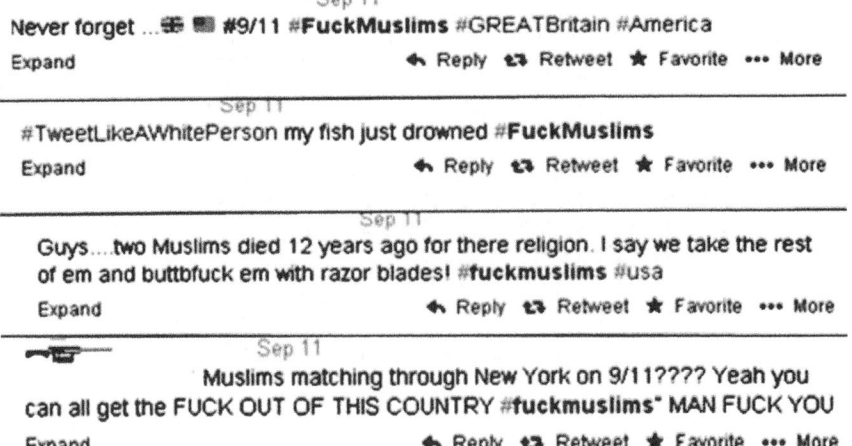

Figure 2.2   A selection of trending tweets on 11 September 2013

hashtags[2] were used was because they had appeared on the Twitter search engine as words that had been recently 'Trending' in the United Kingdom. Trending words on Twitter is when the most mentioned words are posted on Twitter and are considered to be important or 'hot' topics that people are discussing. For example, on 11 September 2013, the hashtag #FuckMuslims was trending (see Figure 2.2 for examples of the tweets that were trending that day). Following this, the chapter provides a typology of offender characteristics. This chapter therefore makes an important contribution to helping us understand the role of Islamophobia on social media sites such as Twitter.

Online Islamophobia remains under-researched. Indeed, a recent report conducted by Feldman et al. (2013: 10) regarding online anti-Muslim prejudice highlighted how: 'The online domain remains under-researched' and 'much less attention has been paid to online hate crime, which can be the precursor to more physically threatening offline incidents'. As noted above, the debate about Islamophobia is often centred on street-level incidents, including the pulling of headscarves and attacks against mosques (Allen 2010). However, increasingly a number of cases reported to organisations such as Tell MAMA include online anti-Muslim abuse which is directed against Muslim communities, including high profile Muslim figures such as Baroness Warsi (the former Minister of Faith and Communities) and Jemima Khan (ex-wife of the Pakistani cricketer

2   A hashtag is used as a symbol and reference to a particular topic that is closely linked towards a subject matter.

turned politician, Imran Khan) both of whom were subjected to online threats which were reported to the police by Tell MAMA (Sinha 2013).

Furthermore, a number of high profile Muslim public figures have also expressed their frustration at the lack of support available for Muslims suffering online abuse and discussed the direct impact it has had upon them. Mehdi Hasan, the former political editor of the Huffington Post, recalls the impact of the online anti-Muslim hate comments made against him. He states that:

> To say that I find the relentlessly hostile coverage of Islam, coupled with the personal abuse that I receive online, depressing is an understatement. There have been times – for instance, when I found my wife curled up on our couch, in tears, after having discovered some of the more monstrous and threatening comments on my New Statesman blog – when I've wondered whether I's all worth it. (cited online in *The Guardian*, Mehdi Hasan 2012)

These comments are not isolated and other Muslims in the public eye such as Inayat Bunglawala, Huma Qureshi and Nadiya Takolia have all described the online abuse they have suffered. Below is an example of the type of online abuse they have directly suffered in an article published in *The Guardian* in 2012:

> the true face of pakiland is the cleansing of Hindu and Sikh minorities since 1948, and the ongoing deceptions practiced by Pakistanis, not some fluff piece about an honest man. Exception to the rule. There is a lamppost and noose waiting for every jihadi that comes back to Britain and their scum enablers and sympathizers .... (cited online in *The Guardian*: Inayat Bunglawala, 2012)

Clearly, the above 'hate' comments made online can have a negative impact on the victims who are targeted and can be very upsetting and unsettling for them and their families (Bunglawala 2012). Evidence from Feldman et al.'s (2013) study also suggests that post Woolwich, the internet and social networking sites have been used by far-right groups such as the EDL, to promote online cyber hate attacks against Muslim communities. This type of prejudice follows a 'drip drip' effect, which has intensified post Woolwich (Feldman et al. 2013).

Another problem when dealing with online abuse seems to be the laissez-faire attitude from some of the social media sites such as Twitter who simply ask the victim either to block someone or close their account. In response to the criticisms by Stan Collymore, Twitter stated that: 'We cannot stop people from saying offensive, hurtful things on the internet or on Twitter. But we take action when content is reported to us that breaks our rules or is illegal' (BBC News 2014). Cyberspace can become a safe environment for some offenders but equally internal and external mechanisms are required to support victims of online hate (Sayyid and Vakil 2010). The above examples of online abuse also show that a number of the cyber hate incidents that have occurred online have done so via social networking sites, such as Twitter. These incidents can be categorised as being forms of 'cyber harassment', 'cyber bullying', 'cyber abuse', 'cyber incitement/threats' and 'cyber hate' (Wall 2001). Many of the comments posted online through social networking sites like Twitter have extremist and incendiary undertones. Moreover, they are not confined to social networking sites and include sites dedicated to blogging, online chat rooms and other virtual platforms that promote online cyber hate and online Islamophobia (Allen 2014).

Many of these prejudicial statements are often used by perpetrators to target a particular group or person. This is often personified by racist jokes and stereotypical 'banter' (Weaver 2013). If these incidents go unchecked physical attacks can also take place and could culminate from extreme online prejudice and discrimination which are intertwined (Allport 1954). Indeed, this type of negativity can also lead to an escalation of online abuse and the normalisation of such behaviour.

For example, a number of sites such as the http://anti--islam.blogspot.co.uk/ and http://www.jihadwatch.org/, all aim to tackle what they call the 'anti-civilisation of Islam'. Whilst many of these blogs and websites use the cloak of freedom of expression to perpetuate an anti-Muslim rhetoric, it does inevitably attract users who are quick to post comments on pieces that have a deeply embedded anti-Muslim narrative (JihadWatch 2013). This chapter argues that online anti-Muslim hate therefore requires a multi-faceted and international approach from different agencies, including the police, social networking sites and a government-led approach that tackles online Islamophobia as a separate phenomenon.

Methodology and Findings

Recent threats, made against the former British Member of Parliament, the Respect leader Salma Yaqoob, have reinforced the problem of online anti-Muslim abuse. As noted previously, after appearing on the BBC programme *Question Time* in 2013, Salma Yaqoob tweeted the following comments to her followers: 'Apart from this threat to cut my throat by #EDL supporter (!) overwhelmed by warm response to what I said on #bbcqt.' The person arrested, in connection with the comments, Steve Littlejohn, had threatened Salma Yaqoob, stating that: 'if that salma yaqueb's there, cut her f### throat, rip weyman bennets teeth out with pliers and carve edl across all the asian scum who try and attack us' (*Birmingham Mail* 2013). This chapter aims to examine how Muslims are being viewed via one main social media platform, namely Twitter. In doing, this research, the author analysed 500 tweets and looked for patterns that were emerging about Muslim communities on this social media platform. A lot of the data collected as we shall see, was used by people to promote online hate and targeted abuse against Muslims. As a result, some of the research questions explored in this chapter included:

- How is Twitter being used to describe and view Muslims?
- What content is being used via Twitter to demonise and stereotype Muslims?
- What physical and non-physical threats are being used against Muslims via Twitter?

This study used a mixed-methodology which was part of a wider content analysis that utilised qualitative and quantitative data gathering techniques and was embedded within grounded theory. This chapter analysed and examined 500 separate tweets to try and find out how Muslims were being viewed and the way in which perpetrators of online abuse were targeting them through social media sites such as Twitter. All of the tweets were analysed between January 2013 and April 2014. As noted previously, the overwhelming number of tweets were written and posted by people in the UK, although there were some tweets from users who were based in Australia and the United States. From the data collected, the majority of tweets were posted by males (72%) in comparison to females who accounted for 28%. The chapter used three hashtags, namely; #Woolwich, #Muslim and #Islam, to note and look at patterns emerging regarding online Islamophobia on Twitter.

Following this, the author examined the tweets to try and find out how Muslims were being viewed and targeted by perpetrators of online anti-Muslim abuse. Some of the most common reappearing words used to describe Muslims in a derogatory way were also examined. This I hope will allow for further research in this area and help collect a pattern and trend about online anti-Muslim hate. Clearly there are drawbacks to using and analysing data via social media sites such as Twitter, with the obvious limit in the actual word frequency. However, this was overcome by using hashtags and taking a random sample of 500 tweets and then collating and identifying tweets, correlations and patterns that emerged.

Indeed, tweets were examined to try and understand how Muslims were being targeted by perpetrators of online abuse. Some of the most common reappearing words used to describe Muslims in a derogatory way included the words #Muslimpigs, #Muzrats, #MuslimPaedos, #Muslimterrorists, #Muslimscum and #Pisslam (see Figure 2.3 for a breakdown of the most common words used). Interestingly, Tell MAMA, which measures anti-Muslim hate attacks also examined the use of words on social media to describe Muslims from January 2013 to December 2013 and used a software system to collate high-frequency words that were directly related to anti-Muslim hate and prejudice. They also similarly, found the words Ninja, Muzrats and Paedo were being used against Muslims (Tell MAMA 2014).

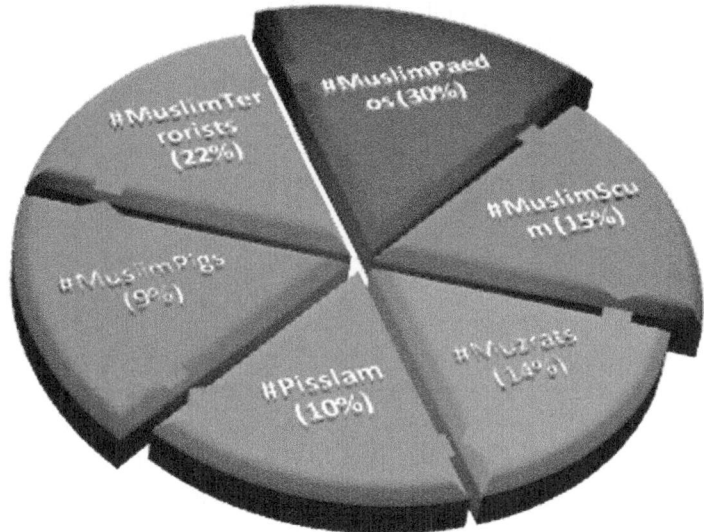

Figure 2.3 **Common reappearing words used to describe Muslims via Twitter**

After examining the 500 separate tweets and looking at the use of language to depict Muslims in a negative light, this chapter proposes a typology consisting of eight different people who are identified as online cyber trolls; i.e. people who are using social networking sites such as Twitter to produce a sustained campaign of hate against Muslim communities. Some of the examples of those tweets are grouped in Figure 2.4.

A Typology of Online Perpetrators

Over 75% of the tweets examined indicated and showed a strong and Islamophobic feeling which was used to stereotype and blame all Muslims for a particular issue which was used to justify the abuse. For example, @ensine and @seafarer1847 were open about their anger and hatred for Muslims as a result of recent cases surrounding Asian men convicted of grooming underage girls. Both those accounts used and showed related publications which were exploited in order to send out tweets that defamed and caricatured Muslims as dangerous paedophiles. Indeed, the word Muslim paedos was used up to 30% of times which does reflect and coincide with recent cases of Muslim men convicted of grooming offences (Greenwood 2013).

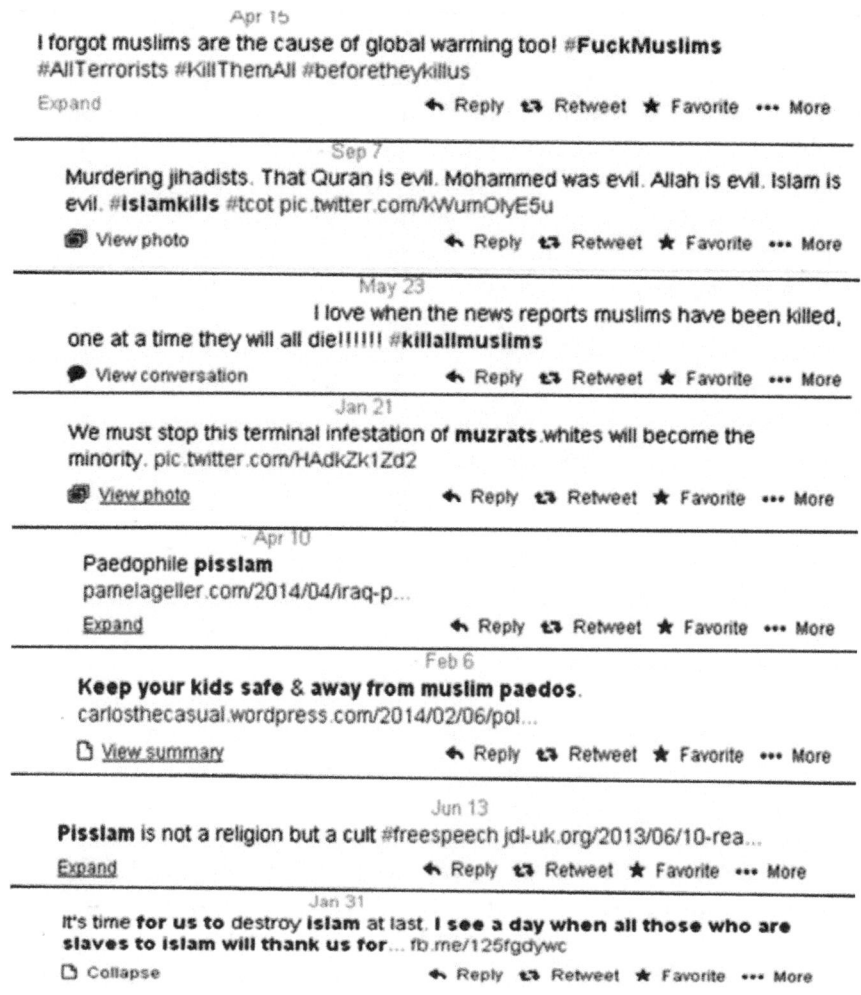

Figure 2.4 **A brief selection of tweets examined within the article**

However, in some cases, people simply used Twitter as a means to antagonise and create hostility which @ShellyMonsoon and @DeSoosider did by referring to Muslims as 'Muzrats' which is a demeaning word to describe Muslims as bacteria or a type of disease. Both people showed a sustained level of anti-Muslim abuse which was depicted through language that was hostile and offensive to Muslims. For example, @ShellyMonsoon noted how #Islamkills and 'whites will become a minority unless the Muzrats are stopped'. Interestingly, the word #Muslimterrorists also appeared high on the list of frequent words used accounting for 22%. In particular, it became part of the September 11 trending words across Twitter where Muslims were being depicted through pictures and videos as extremists and terrorists.

On the face of it, a number of offenders shared similar characteristics but were uniquely different in their approaches to targeting Muslim communities online. Using an online content behavioural offender typology, this chapter grouped the tweets together in different categories and created a typology based on the following. These are: the trawler (a person who has gone through other people's Twitter accounts to specifically target people with a Muslim connection), the apprentice (someone who is fairly new to Twitter but nonetheless has begun to target people with the help of more experienced online abusers), the disseminator (someone who has tweeted about and retweeted messages, pictures and documents of online hate that are specifically targeting Muslims), the impersonator (a person who is using a fake profile, account and images to target individuals), the accessory (a person who is joining in with other people's conversations via Twitter to target vulnerable people), the reactive (a person who following a major incident, such as Woolwich, or issues on immigration, will begin an online campaign targeting that specific group and individual), the mover (someone who regularly changes their Twitter account in order to continue targeting someone from a different profile) and finally, the professional (a person who has a huge following on Twitter and regardless of the consequences has and will launch a major campaign of hate against an individual or group of people because they are Muslim. This person will also likely to have multiple Twitter accounts all aimed at targeting Muslim communities). See the Table 2.1 below which has grouped the profile of the offender behaviour and characteristics which includes the number of cases found within the tweets examined.

At the heart of each of these different categories it became clear that the users involved had similar motivations. Some of those were based on seeking authority and power as shown by the tweets from @RestoreAust who used his Twitter account to collect and maximise influence. In such a case, this affords some people the motivation to commit the online abuse and as a result, they are able to target specific people (Iganski 2012). Figure 2.5 shows a cycle demonstrating those key characteristics and motivations of the cyber troll.

Challenges around Online Hate and Islamophobia

As noted previously, online Islamophobia is under-researched both at a policy level and an academic level, and this chapter argues that a new cyber hate policy is much needed both at government level and policing level which would be timely considering the recent spike of online anti-Muslim abuse (ACPO 2013).

Table 2.1   Typology of offender characteristics

Type	Characteristics	No. of cases
The trawler	Someone who has gone through other people's Twitter accounts to specifically target people with a Muslim connection.	57
The apprentice	A person who is fairly new to Twitter but nonetheless has begun to target people with the help of more experienced online abusers.	39
The disseminator	Someone who has tweeted about and retweeted messages, pictures and documents of online hate that are specifically targeting Muslims.	75
The impersonator	A person who is using a fake profile, account and images to target individuals.	76
The accessory	A person who is joining in with other people's conversations via Twitter to target vulnerable people.	82
The reactive	A person who following a major incident, such as Woolwich, or issues on immigration, will begin an online campaign targeting that specific group or individual.	95
The mover	Someone who regularly changes their Twitter account in order to continue targeting someone from a different profile	46
The professional	A person who has a huge following on Twitter and regardless of the consequences has and will launch a major campaign of hate against an individual or group of people because they are Muslim. This person will also have multiple Twitter accounts all aimed at targeting Muslim communities.	30

Interestingly, cyber hate has been used by the far-right and white supremacists who have used it to inflame religious and racial tensions. For example, a study for the British-based think-tank group Demos (2011) found that far-right populist movements are gaining in support across Europe and playing upon public disenfranchisement within society to promote an agenda of protecting national identity as a method to whip up online anti-Muslim hate.

The Demos study (2011) is interesting because their findings would seem to suggest that the EDL have become a web-based far-right group that is using social networking sites such as Facebook and Twitter where it has gained a core group of online sympathisers to target Muslim communities (Awan and Blakemore 2012). The Demos study found that on a national scale 72% of supporters for the EDL were under the age of 30 and 36% of people were aged between 16 and 20, thus reflecting the movement's desire to attract a 'younger' audience on social networking sites such as Facebook.

The Online Hate Prevention Institute report (2013) into online Islamophobia searched over 50 different Facebook pages and showed how online hate

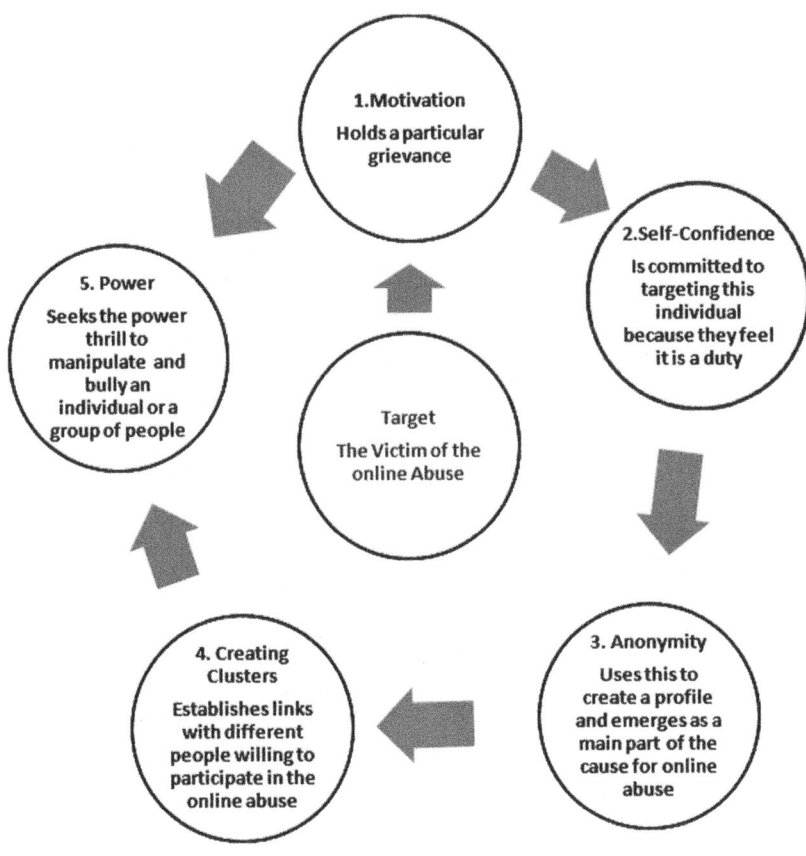

Figure 2.5   The cyber troll: A cycle of online abuse

speeches had targeted Muslims. Overall, they found 349 separate instances of online hate speeches directed against Muslims. Indeed, they also included a number of those Facebook pages that were created in order to specifically target Muslim communities. For example, they found a number of group pages that had a number of people who had visited and 'liked' certain posts and pages. For example, the 'Boycott all Halal products in Australia!' page had over 520 likes (see https://www.facebook.com/pages/boycott-all-halal-products-in-australia/171203192936626).

Furthermore, the online Facebook page 'The truth about Islam' which has over 150,000 likes (see https://www.facebook.com/TheIslamicThreat); the Islam is Evil page (418 likes) (see https://www.facebook.com/IslamIsEvil) and the Prophet Muhammad Still Burns in Hell page which has 470 likes (see   https://www.facebook.com/pages/The-Prophet-Muhammad-STILL-

Burns-In-Hell-Fire/281538198643648). This report is significant because it documents the rise of online Islamophobia post Woolwich through Facebook (see Chapter 3 for more detail).

As noted above, policing cyberspace is difficult. Indeed, Feldman et al. (2013) found that 74% of anti-Muslim prejudice occurred online, in comparison to 26% of offline incidents. Worryingly, critics argue that the difficult nature of policing cyberspace has therefore led to Muslim communities being failed by their local police forces in the UK. Indeed, Tell MAMA, which records anti-Muslim attacks, argued that not enough was being done to investigate online anti-Muslim abuse (BBC News 2013d). Another problem for the police appears to be the way in which data is recorded and collected by local police forces (see Chapter 6 for further discussion).

The problem for the police therefore is in helping to root out far-right groups and lone wolf extremists who are using social networking sites like Twitter to post malicious statements (Esposito and Kalin 2011). This realm of cyber activism used by groups like the EDL and others who are promoting online hate means the police require more people to report what they see and what they read so that they can take the necessary actions required to either remove the online hate material or in some cases arrest and charge people. At the moment those who use online hate to disguise themselves in a cloak of anonymity remain at large because they understand that unless someone reports them they can remain anonymous.

Feldman et al. (2013: 23) state that a number of online incidents reported included direct threats from burning down mosques to killing Muslim babies. They state that: 'Racist remarks were, in turn, mainly anti-Pakistani comments and references to dirt and filth. More generally there were comments accusing Muslims of rape; paedophilia; incest; interbreeding; being terrorists; and killing Jews.'

Conclusion

After examining 500 tweets regarding online anti-Muslim prejudice, this chapter found real concerns about the derogatory and systematic abuse people were suffering as a result of online abuse. The typology which was subsequently, created of online abusers shows that offenders presented some key characteristics and motivations behind their actions. The tweets examined also revealed a dark picture emerging regarding online Islamophobia on Twitter, and shows that we need to begin a process of evidence-based research that helps create a safer online space for users. The author hopes this study can be used to help examine how online hate is determined and look at more innovative ways that policy makers, the police, third sector organisations and social networking sites (such as Twitter and Facebook) examine how best to respond to online anti-Muslim hate crime. This can than result in an improved dialogue between the different stakeholders and ensure that online anti-Muslim hate incidents are taken more seriously. In particular, Twitter has been criticised for the lack of real action towards online hate and this study can shed light on some important changes they and the police can make to ensure online hate crime can be dealt with in a more efficient and proactive manner.

Further Reading

Jewkes, Y. 2007. *Crime Online*. Cullompton: Willan Publishing.
Levmore, S. and Nussbaum, M.C. 2011. *The Offensive Internet: Speech, Privacy, and Reputation*. Cambridge, MA: Harvard University Press.
Scaife, L. 2015. *Handbook of Social Media and the Law*, Abingdon: Informa Law from Routledge.

References

Allen, C. 2001. *Islamophobia in the Media since September 11th, Forum against Islamophobia and Racism*, [Online]. http://www.fairuk.org/docs/islamophobia-in-the-media-since-911-christopherallen.pdf [accessed: 26 April 2014].
Allen, C. 2010. *Islamophobia*. Farnham: Ashgate.
Allen, C. 2014. *Findings From a Pilot Study on Opposing Dudley Mosque Using Facebook Groups as Both Site and Method for Research*, Sage Open, [Online]. http://sgo.sagepub.com/content/4/1/2158244014522074.full-text.pdf+html [accessed: 15 April 2014].
Allport, G.W. 1954. *The Nature of Prejudice*. Reading, MA: Addison-Wesley.
Anti-Islam Blog 2013. [Online] Available at: http://anti--islam.blogspot.co.uk/ [accessed: 10 June 2014].
Association of Chief Police Officers, 2013. *True Vision Records*, [Online]. http://www.report-it.org.uk/true_vision_records_a_significant_weekly_reduct [accessed: 2 September 2014].
Awan, I. 2012. 'The impact of policing British Muslims: a qualitative exploration', *Journal of Policing, Intelligence and Counter-Terrorism*, 7 (1): 22–35.
Awan, I. and Blakemore, B. 2012. *Policing Cyber Hate, Cyber Threats and Cyber Terrorism*. Farnham: Ashgate.
Awan, I., Blakemore, B. and Simpson, K. 2013. 'Muslim communities' attitudes towards and recruitment into the British police service', *International Journal of Law, Crime and Justice*, 41 (4): 421–37.

BBC News, 2013a. 'Al-Rahma Islamic Centre destroyed in "hate crime" fire' [Online]. http://www.bbc.co.uk/news/uk-england-london-22785074 [accessed: 5 September 2014]

BBC News, 2013b. 'Woolwich Aftermath: Key Facts', [Online]. http://www.bbc.co.uk/news/uk-22635318 [accessed: 10 February 2014].

BBC News, 2013c. '632 anti-Muslim hate incidents recorded by Tell Mama', [Online]. http://www.bbc.co.uk/news/uk-21712826 [accessed: 2 September 2014].

BBC News, 2013d. 'Police failing to investigate anti-Muslim abuse', [Online]. Available at: http://www.bbc.co.uk/news/uk-25057246 [accessed: 10 February 2014].

BBC News, 2014. 'Ex-footballer Collymore accuses Twitter over abusive messages', [Online]. http://www.bbc.co.uk/news/uk-25838114 [accessed: 10 February 2014].

Birmingham Mail, 2013. 'Death threats made to Salma Yaqoob after Question Time appearance', *Birmingham Mail*, [Online]. http://www.birminghammail.co.uk/news/local-news/death-threats-made-muslim-politician-4219595 [accessed: 1 September 2014].

Blakemore, B. 2013. 'Extremist groups and organisations', in *Extremism, Counter-Terrorism and Policing*, edited by I. Awan and B. Blakemore, Farnham: Ashgate, 87–102.

Bowling, B. 1999. *Violent Racism: Victimisation, Policing and Social Context*. Revised edition. Oxford: Oxford University Press.

Bunglawala, I. 2012. 'Online racist abuse: we've all suffered it', *The Guardian*, [Online]. http://www.theguardian.com/commentisfree/2012/jul/11/online-racist-abuse-writers-face [accessed: 8 September 2014].

Chan, J.B.L. 2007. 'Police and new technologies', in *Handbook of Policing*, edited by T. Newburn, Cullompton: Willan Publishing.

Christopherson, K.. 2007. 'The positive and negative implications of anonymity in Internet, nobody knows you're a dog', *Computers in Human Behavior*, 23 (6), 3038–56.

Cole, J. and Cole, B. 2009. *Martyrdom: Radicalisation and Terrorist Violence Among British Muslims*, London: Pennant Books.

Coliandris, G. 2012. 'Hate in a cyber age', in *Policing Cyber Hate, Cyber Threats and Cyber Terrorism*, edited by I. Awan and B. Blakemore, Farnham: Ashgate, 75–94.

Crown Prosecution Service. 2014. *Guidelines on Prosecuting Cases involving Communications Sent via Social Media*, [Online]. Available at: http://www.cps.gov.uk/legal/a_to_c/communications_sent_via_social_media/ [accessed: 10 February 2014].

DEMOS Report, 2011. *The Rise of Populism in Europe can be traced through Online Behaviour*, [Online]. http://www.demos.co.uk/files/Demos_OSIPOP_Book-web_03.pdf?1320601634 [accessed: 20 July 2014].

Douglas, K., McGarty, C., Bliuc, A.M. and Lala, G. 2005. 'Understanding cyberhate: social competition and social creativity in online white supremacist groups', *Social Science Computer Review*, 23 (1): 68–76.

Esposito, L. J. and Kalin, I. 2011. *Islamophobia: The Challenge of Pluralism in the 21st Century*. Oxford: Oxford University Press.

Feldman, M., Littler, M., Dack, J. and Copsey, N. 2013. *Anti-Muslim Hate Crime and the Far Right*, Teeside University, [Online]. http://tellmamauk.org/wp-content/uploads/2013/07/antimuslim2.pdf [accessed: 4 September 2013].

Forum against Islamophobia and Racism, 2013. [Online] http://www.fairuk.org/introduction.htm [accessed: 10 July 2014].

Greenwood, C. 2013. 'Stop tip-toeing around race of grooming gangs, say MPs: Committee says police and prosecutors must be able to raise issue without being accused of racism', *Mail Online*, [Online]. Available at: http://www.dailymail.co.uk/news/article-2338640/Stop-tip-toeing-race-grooming-gangs-say-MPs-Committee-says-police-prosecutors-able-raise-issue-accused-racism.html [accessed: 15 April 2014].

The Guardian. 2013. 'UK Anti-Muslim hate crime soars, police figures show', [Online]. Available at: http://www.theguardian.com/society/2013/dec/27/uk-anti-muslim-hate-crime-soars [accessed:15 April 2014].

Hall, N. 2005. *Hate Crime*. Cullompton: Willan Publishing.

Hasan, M. 2012. 'We mustn't allow Muslims in public life to be silenced', *The Guardian*, [Online]. Available at: http://www.theguardian.com/commentisfree/2012/jul/08/muslims-public-life-abuse [accessed: 7 September 2013].

Iganski, P. 2012. *Hate Crime: Taking Stock: Programmes for Offenders of Hate*. Northern Ireland Association for the Care and Resettlement of Offenders, Belfast.

JihadWatch, 2013. [Online]. Available at: http://www.jihadwatch.org/ [accessed: 5 September 2014].

Larsson, G. 2007. 'Cyber-Islamophobia? The Case of WikiIslam'. *Contemporary Islam*, 1(1): 53–67.

Leveson Inquiry. 2012. *Culture, Practice and Ethics of the Press*, [Online]. http://www.levesoninquiry.org.uk/about/the-report/ [accessed: 11 February 2014].

Online Hate Prevention Centre, 2013. *Islamophobia on the Internet: The growth of online hate targeting Muslims*, [Online]. http://ohpi.org.au/islamophobia-on-the-internet-the-growth-of-online-hate-targeting-muslims/ [accessed: 10 February 2014].

Perry, B. 2001. *In the Name of Hate: Understanding Hate Crimes*. London: Routledge.

Saul, H. 2013. 'Police call home-made bomb outside Walsall's Ashia Mosque a "hate crime" and draft in counter-terror police', *The Independent*, [Online]. Available at: http://www.independent.co.uk/news/uk/crime/police-call-homemade-bomb-outside-walsalls-ashia-mosque-a-hate-crime-and-draft-in-counterterror-police-8670548.html [accessed: 4 September 2013].

Sayyed, S. and Vakil, A. 2011. *Thinking Through Islamophobia: Global Perspectives.* Hurst and Co.

Sinha, K. 2013. 'Anti-Muslim sentiments on rise in UK: British minister', *The Times of India*, [Online]. Available at: http://articles.timesofindia.indiatimes.com/2013-05-22/uk/39444735_1_muslim-women-hate-crime-sayeeda-warsi [accessed: 4 September 2013].

Raymond. T. 2012. *Xenophobia and Islamophobia in Europe*, Edinburgh University Press.

Tell MAMA, 2013. *Anti-Muslim Hate Crime.* [Online]. Available at: http://tellmamauk.org/ [accessed: 2 September 2013].

Tell MAMA, 2014. *Analysing the Lexicon of Anti-Muslim Prejudice*, [Online]. Available at: http://tellmamauk.org/analysing-the-lexicon-of-anti-muslim-prejudice/ [accessed: 10 February 2014].

True Vision, 2013. *Internet Hate Crime*, [Online]. Available at: http://www.report-it.org.uk/reporting_internet_hate_crime [accessed: 2 September 2013].

Urquhart, C. 2013. 'Attacks on Muslims soar in wake of Woolwich murder', *The Guardian*, [Online]. Available at: http://www.theguardian.com/uk/2013/may/25/woolwich-murder-attacks-on-muslims [accessed: 2 September 2014].

Waddington, P.A.J. 2010. 'An examination of hate crime'. *Police Review*, 23 April, 118 (6077): 14–15.

Wall, D. 2001. (ed.) *Crime and the Internet.* New York, Routledge.

Weaver, S. 2013. 'A rhetorical discourse analysis of online Anti-Muslim and Anti-Semitic jokes'. *Ethnic and Racial Studies.* 36 (3): 483–499.

Whine, M. 2003. 'Far right extremists on the Internet', in *Cyber Crime: Law Enforcement, Security and Surveillance in the Information Age*, edited by D. Thomas and B. Loader. London: Routledge.

Chapter 3

The Normalisation of Islamophobia through Social Media: Facebook

Andre Oboler

Introduction

The norms of society are challenged by new technologies which create new ways of perpetrating crime and avoiding detection. These types of challenges, though highlighted in terms of the internet revolution (Protocol to the Convention on Cybercrime 2003), are not unique to it and have also occurred with previous paradigm shifts such as invention of the automobile (see the case of *Brooks v US*, 267 US 432, 438–9 1925). The challenges posed by a paradigm shift in society necessitate a careful re-examination of the weight given to competing rights and interests. As with the advent of the automobile, the social media revolution may well require new treaties, laws and regulations in the pursuit of peace, order and good government.

Online vilification, bullying and incitement against individuals and groups through social media are key challenges society faces in this new social media driven world. This chapter examines the specific problem of religious vilification targeting Muslims on the social media platform Facebook. The author examined the way Facebook was being used to normalise hate against Muslims, and looked at a variety of anti-Muslim ideas that are prevalent on Facebook. Through communications promoting those ideas, we consider the way Facebook can be used to enforce the twin messages of hate speech where victims are told they are unwelcome in society, and potential supporters of the hate are told that others share their views, and that such views are acceptable (Waldron 2012).

Lack of interest from platform providers emboldens those already using platforms like Facebook to target the Muslim community. This fuels online anti-Muslim hate, but like other forms of online hate, it is unlikely to remain purely virtual. Online Islamophobia is likely to incite religious hatred and xenophobia leading to real world crimes and a rise in political extremism both on the far-right and from the radicalisation of Muslim youth in response to messages of exclusion. This is a serious problem which social media companies, governments and communities need to tackle.

The Challenge of Hate Speech

As noted in Chapter 1, hate speech is traditionally defined as speech that vilifies a protected group, or a member of a protected group, due to their group identity. What constitutes a 'protected group' varies with context, but religion is usually included. The International Covenant on Civil and Political Rights, for example, states in article 20 (2) that: 'Any advocacy of national, racial or religious hatred that constitutes incitement to discrimination, hostility or violence shall be prohibited by law' (UN General Assembly 1966).

The Harm in Hate Speech by Jeremy Waldron (2012) opens with a story of a man taking his two young children for a walk. A sign saying, 'Muslims and 9/11! Don't serve them, don't speak to them, and don't let them in' is displayed along their route. The family is Muslim, and Waldron relates how the father struggles when his daughter asks what the sign means, and instead of replying, hurries them home. Waldron's story is fictional, but highlights the nature and purpose of hate speech. Waldron's analysis demonstrates that while racism is one form of hate speech, there are others as well. Anti-Muslim bigotry is clearly a form of hate speech.

Waldron goes on to identify two dangerous messages in hate speech. These messages work to undermine the public good of an inclusive society; they do this by removing the 'assurance [of the targeted group] that there will be no need to face hostility, violence, discrimination, or exclusion by others' as they go about their daily life (ibid. 2). The first message is directed at the group being targeted and says: '[d]on't be fooled into thinking you are welcome here' (ibid. 2). The second message is aimed at the rest of society, it says, '[w]e know some of you agree that these people are not wanted here ... known that you are not alone ... there are enough of us around to make sure these people are not welcome ... [and] to draw attention to what these people are really like' (ibid. 2–3). Waldron's twin messages of hate can target any identifiable group in society. The hate may, however, take on different flavours depending on the group targeted, the reasons given for excluding them from society, and the negative stereotypes used to represent 'what these people are really like'.

The Online Hate Prevention Institute has looked at some of the ways hate against Muslims manifests in social media and has suggested that, 'content be considered anti-Muslim hate speech when, for example, it: dehumanises Muslims, stereotypes all Muslims, for example as terrorists, advocates the exclusion of Muslims from society, such as content claiming Muslims can't be a part of society; denies human rights to Muslims, holds all Muslims responsible for the acts of extremists, or applies a double standard to Muslim communities or Muslim countries, for example making demands which would not be made of other countries in similar circumstances' (Oboler 2015). This definition mirrors some of the ideas around anti-Jewish hate as seen in the Working Definition of Antisemitism (US State Department 2008).

The Challenges in Combating Anti-Muslim Hate Speech

There are three reasons why anti-Muslim hate should be considered a problem for society. One is the impact of such hate on the human rights and fundamental freedoms of individuals; another is the negative impact such hate has on the public good of an inclusive society; and a third is the fact that such hate can become a self-fulfilling prophecy contributing to the problem of violent extremism. These three groups approach the problem from different angles, and may result in different strategies and emphasis. It may also lead to a mismatch between effective response programmes, and the availability of necessary funding. For example, funding whose purpose is tackling extremism may not be available to tackle bigotry targeting Muslims, despite the fact that addressing this problem would remove a significant factor that can push some towards self radicalisation and extremism.

Combating anti-Muslim hate speech comes with a variety of challenges. One challenge, common to all hate directed against religious groups, is the need to differentiate between hate-speech targeting people who follow the religion, and criticism of the ideas and doctrine of the religion itself. Where speech targets the people on the basis of their religion it is a form of hate speech, violates those people's human rights, and ought to be condemned. Where the speech is critical of the religion itself, it is not hate speech and would usually be protected under a freedom of speech principle.

The various controversies is public discussion over cartoons of the Prophet Mohammed are in part a failure to differentiate between, on the one hand, criticism of religion and, on the other, vilification of its followers. The original controversy was provoked by a Danish newspaper, *Jyllands-Posten*, which published 12 cartoons of Mohammed on the 30 September 2005 (BBC News 2006). The initial incident has sparked a cycle of events with the publication of cartoons of Mohammed being followed by threats and violence, which were in turn followed by further publication of cartoons of Mohammed in response (*The Telegraph* 2015). Such cartoons are not in and of themselves necessarily an attack on people who are Muslim (Oboler 2015). The original Danish cartoons, however, did include an image which crosses into hate speech. The most famous of the Danish cartoons is by Kurt Westergaard and depicts Mohammed wearing a turban that morphs into a lit bomb. On the turban is the *shahada*, the Muslim declaration of faith which reads 'There is no deity but God and Mohammad is His prophet'. In this case, the imagery of Mohammed was used to represent all Muslims, and the message was that all Muslims are terrorists. We can see that the image represents Muslims generally both by the use of the Muslim declaration of faith, and by the fact that in Mohammed's time gun powder had not been invented, so the bomb is an anachronism and can't refer to Mohammed himself. The Online Hate Prevention Institute has recommended that, 'cartoons portraying Muslims through negative stereotypes, using Mohammed to symbolise all Muslims, should be considered a form of hate speech' (ibid.).

The word 'Islamophobia' itself poses another challenge as discussed in Chapter 1. While in popular usage it means hate against people who are Muslims (Oboler 2013), a valid human rights concern, its origins rest in efforts that were far broader and which stretched beyond protecting the human rights of Muslims and into infringing on the human rights of others. This overreach came from efforts, using the word Islamophobia, to create an international law basis to protect against what is sometimes called the 'defamation of Islam' (Socolovsky 2012). This concept is not based on human rights, but is about protecting religious ideas from criticism, something that fundamentally clashes with both religious freedom and freedom of speech. These efforts to protect against 'defamation of Islam' are no longer being pursued, but a person using the phrase Islamophobia to refer to hate against Muslims may receive a response about the illegitimacy of the concept of Islamophobia. This will hopefully fade in time, but in the meantime it is important that those using the term Islamophobia clearly state what they mean, and that what they mean is limited to hate against people who are Muslims.

The line between words and action can also be blurred. Efforts to prevent food manufacturers having their products certified as halal are designed to have a real impact on the ability of Muslims to live within a society. Similarly, efforts opposing the construction of mosques and Muslim schools serve to keep Muslims away from the neighbourhood. These efforts to exclude Muslims from society directly reflect the messages Waldron highlights and these campaigns are often based on anti-Muslim hate. These efforts are coordinated through social media with supporters often coming from around the world. The anti-Muslim hate campaigns have become a social movement powered by platforms like Facebook.

Anti-Muslim hate speech is a threat not only to the Muslim community, but to the broader community as well. The hate not only excludes Muslims, particularly Muslim youth, from society, but can also push them towards radicalisation and extremism. Former Attorney General of Australia, The Hon Mark Dreyfus QC MP, stated in 2013 that the issue of online hate targeting Muslims was raised with him both by Muslim community leaders and by Australia's security agencies. He explained the concern of the security agencies by warning that, 'in demeaning, threatening and generally seeking to exclude members of the Muslim community from our multicultural society, online hate increases the risk factors associated with the marginalisation and radicalisation of Muslim youth' (Dreyfus 2013). Efforts to combat anti-Muslim hate speech must be explained in these terms as well. Below the chapter explore the normalisation of hate through social media.

The Normalisation of Hate through Social Media

The problem of anti-Muslim hate speech is particularly acute online. The human rights of individuals are subjected to attack at both the individual and communal level. Facebook pages for Muslim organisations regularly receive abusive comments and posts. The message to exclude Muslims, attacking the public good of an inclusive society, is trumpeted across social media with images, videos, pages and Tweets. Anti-Muslim blogs publish libels against the Muslim community, and anyone standing up against attacks on the Muslim community, and these posts are then spread virally through multiple platforms. Online anti-Muslim hate also takes place in an environment where the recipient may be only one click away from a path towards self-radicalisation and ultimately towards violent extremism. The environment itself is therefore higher risk than many forms of offline engagement. The greatest danger, however, comes from the risk of such hate becoming normalised; this is the danger of Hate 2.0.

The combination of hate speech content and a social media platform able to take that content viral, is what creates Hate 2.0. The aim of Hate 2.0 is not only to spread the content that contains messages of hate through social media, but to also make such content appear a normal part of the online environment. If hate against a particular group is seen as just another opinion, no better or worse, for example, than having a view on a favourite football team, then such hate can be openly expressed. This embedding of the messages of hate in the fabric of the online world makes social media a place of intimidation, exclusion, and hostility for targeted groups. There is a real danger that the normalisation of attitudes of hate online will see these attitudes migrate into daily life (Oboler 2013).

The concept of Hate 2.0 is based on the idea of 'Antisemitism 2.0' first proposed in 2008 (Oboler 2008). The aim was 'to create social acceptability' for hate content, and to thereby allow the content to 'be spread, public resistance lowered, and hate networks rapidly established' (ibid.). One feature of Hate 2.0 in Facebook is that hate pages will often contain a leading sentence on their about page declaring the page to be against hate, and certainly not a hate page itself, before continuing with a statement which is blatant hate speech. This promotes the normalisation effect by arguing that the content on the page should be deemed acceptable, either because it isn't hate, or because the specific type of hate being promoted should be an exception. Like dehumanisation, where the victim group is denied basic human rights on the basis that they are considered less than human, Hate 2.0 create a slippery slope of acceptability which ultimately see hate comments calling for violence being deemed 'acceptable' within an online community.

The Online Hate Prevention Institute's 2013 report into Anti-Muslim Hate noted that a number of pages on Facebook explicitly used the Hate 2.0

formulation (Oboler 2013). One example, the page 'People against Islam' (ibid. 10), describes itself as: '[a] page that should instantly have over 1 million. No posts are to be racist, in any way. We all want islam out of our countries and need to group together for this cause'. It continues by saying, 'Use this page as the international gateway for eliminating islam [sic]. Like and share page as much as possible!' (ibid.). These statements combine an anti-hate message, 'no posts are to be racist', with a xenophobic call to expel people, and a message of genocide calling for the total elimination of the Islamic religion and culture. The page's cover image highlights that this is not about ideas, but rather about people. It contains the word 'Muslims' in bright, dripping, blood red as part of a message that 'Muslims are not a race, they are made up of many different races. Hating Muslims does not make you a racist'.

The purpose behind the Hate 2.0 approach is to make it more difficult for social media company staff to quickly reach a decision that a page should be closed. The staff are tasked with reviewing content users report for breaching community standards, but are often given mere seconds in which to make a decision. There is also a strong bias against removing content. These two factors mean a simple statement against hate may be as much as a staff member looks at before feeling confident that they can reject the hate complaint and move on to the next one. The result is that individual images or posts are more likely to be removed than entire pages dedicated to hate. Where such pages are eventually removed, it usually follows the posting, and then removal, of multiple individual items of content. The administrator of the 'People against Islam' Facebook page, for example, complained that, 'the Savages have forced FB Police to remove many of my posts how pathetic when all I do is post actual facts, there are 2 rules in our society and Pisslam is gaining the upper hand' (ibid. 11). The page had 1,168 supporters in December 2013, and despite content being removed, and as of February 2015 it was still online and had grown to 1,827 supporters. The removal of the content from a dedicated hate page, while leaving the page online to spread further hate, is not an appropriate response.

As discussed there is an important difference between criticism of ideas, including the beliefs of Islam, which must be permitted online, and attacks inciting hate against people which need to be prevented. The Community Standards and Terms of Service of platforms like Facebook are clear in prohibiting hate speech. This includes attacks on the basis of religion. The difficulty then is not is the policies, but in their implementation. The danger of Hate 2.0 is a specific threat to society. Social media companies can self-regulate to reduce the risk associated with this threat, but if they don't Governments can and must step in. As the author of this chapter warned almost five years ago, 'if companies get it wrong, if they insist on harboring hate either by rejecting valid complaints or through excessively slow response rates, it should be governments who hold them to account' (Oboler 2010a). There are a number of models for intervention which governments can examine, and some governments are now starting to investigate these. François Hollande, Interior Minister of France, has, for example, recently called for a legal framework with sanctions to make social media companies 'face up to their responsibilities' (Oboler 2010b; 2011).

The Messages of Anti-Muslim Hate

In 2013, the Online Hate Prevention Institute conducted a major study into anti-Muslim hate crime on Facebook (Oboler 2013). The resulting report examines 401 anti-Muslim items on Facebook. The items included: 349 posts, most of which involve images, 50 Facebook pages that were explicitly anti-Muslim, and 2 pages which did not direct attack Muslims but focused on attacking halal certification (ibid. 6). The report found that out of the 349 posts, there were 191 unique items, once duplicates and closely similar images were grouped together (ibid.). These images were sorted thematically and seven themes emerged. These themes were:

- Muslims as a security threat or threat to public safety (42 items);
- Muslims as a cultural threat (29 items);
- Muslims as an economic threat (11 items);
- Content dehumanising or demonising Muslims (37 items);
- Threats of violence, genocide and direct hate targeting Muslims (24 items);
- Hate targeting refugees/asylum seekers (12 items);
- Other forms of hate (36 items)

A 2014 report by the Online Hate Prevention Institute also found that while 6 of the 50 hate pages had been closed prior to the report being published, in the year since its publication only 10 additional pages were closed (Online Hate Prevention Institute 2014). Key hate images in the report were also found to still be online, often in multiple places. This longitudinal analysis indicates that Facebook is getting it wrong initially, and is systematically failing to get it right even after a significant time has elapsed.

We will now examine the themes of hate, largely based on those categories, and with examples from Facebook which can be found in the 2013 report. In this chapter the idea of 'cultural threat' and 'economic threat' have been grouped together under the concept of Muslims being 'an attack on our way of life', a broader concept which has let to events like the reclaim Australia rallies (RT 2015). Two themes which emerged from the category 'other' are also presented: the first is the idea of Muslims as manipulative and dishonest, the second relates to the use of messages which aim to undermining resistance to anti-Muslim hate. We also consider a new category of 'seeking to exclude Muslims from

47

Society' which covers the anti-halal campaign as well as efforts to prevent planning approval for new mosques, Muslim schools or other infrastructure to support the Muslim community within society. The final additional category relates to 'bigots pretending to be Muslims', this is often done as part of an effort to stir up hate against Muslims.

Each of the themes outlined reflects a significance strand of anti-Muslim hate as seen on Facebook. These themes are significant both as a way to recognise and categorise anti-Muslim hate, but also as a first step in producing counter-speech responses to challenge and undermine these messages of hate. Counter-speech is not a solution on its own, but it is one part of the response, along with efforts by platform providers to remove hate speech, and efforts by government to hold both users and potentially platform providers accountable. Whatever the approach used, recognising the hate is the first step to countering it. Further discussion of anti-Muslim hate on Facebook is covered in Chapter 10.

Presenting Muslims as Terrorists and a Threat to Public Safety

The hate theme most people will be familiar with is the portrayal of all Muslims as terrorists. In a broader context this also includes the portrayal of Muslims as violent, lawless and generally dangerous. The broadest context builds on traditional themes of racism historically directed against the black community. The fear, and resulting hatred, from the representation of Muslims as a threat to public safety is a mix of Muslims being collectively represented as 'the enemy', of Muslims being individually presented as dangerous people. The collective claim is that the Muslim community represents an organised threat to society, and the infrastructure of the Muslim community contributes to this threat. The individual claim is based on the idea that being violent is an inherent part of being Muslim. The attribution of these violent tendencies to Muslims is more like racial vilification than religious vilification, in that it seems to suggest certain characteristics are innate to Muslims. In both bases the negative message is that Muslims are a threat to life and property.

These messages of hate have a corollary, which is that those who would promote coexistence, multiculturalism and tolerance are aiding the enemy. This leads to attacks against not only the Muslim community, but also against anyone who would speak up against such attacks. This is sometimes extended to food manufacturers who are certified to produce halal food, and shops that stock halal food, as will be discussed later in this chapter.

Some representations of this theme on Facebook include: A picture of a mob attacking a car with crowbars and fire, with the text, 'how dare you people make fun of our peaceful religion'; a picture of the bombing of the Boston Marathon with the text 'it isn't Islamophobia when they really are trying to kill you'; a picture with the coexist slogan made up of the symbols of various religions with a sword slicing it in half and the message 'you can't coexist with people who want to kill you', a variant of this image adds 'foolish infidels' and a quote 'Sura 4:89 "seize them and slay them wherever you find them …"', while an accurate quote, this is taken out of context as the surrounding verses make it clear this is in the context of a war, and there are no grounds for such action when people live together in peace.

Other representations on Facebook promote the message that 'Islam is not a religion! It's the world's largest death cult'. The message that not all Muslims are terrorists is twisted in a series of messages; one declares 'not all Muslims are terrorists, but why are all terrorists Muslims?' Another says: '"Not all Muslims are terrorists" Agreed! But as long as a Muslim believes the Quoran is the word of Allah, with the right push, they are all potential candidates ….'

Cartoon images of violent Muslims, typically combined with the slogan that Islam is a religion of peace, are also common. A typical one shows a Muslim drenched in blood, holding a sword dripping with blood, standing on top of skeletons labelled 'Hindus', 'Christians', 'Pagans', 'Jews' and 'Atheists', saying 'Islam is the religion of peace. See? No one talks back!' Another example shows a rage filled Muslim with the text 'Muslim: We are peaceful, if you don't agree, we will kill you'. Other examples shows a Muslim holding a knife with the words 'Islam means peace' and below it the text 'stop means go, up means down, left means right'. A range of images promote ideas such as 'beware! Halal food funds terrorism', pictures of specific food brands that are certified halal and the text 'funding terrorism'. Also common are images from a website that documents the number of people killed of groups claiming to be Muslim, compared to the number kill by groups claiming to be from any other religion. Images promoting the idea that Muslims are terrorists or a threat to public safety are common on Facebook and make up a significant part of the anti-Muslim hate in circulation (Oboler 2013).

The Promotion of Threats and Violence Against Muslims

Most social media platforms are based in the United States and are bound to remove content which breaches US law. The very broad interpretation given by the Supreme Court to the First Amendment to the US Constitution means only 'true threats' or 'incitement' are unlawful. True threats are those 'where the speaker means to communicate a serious expression of an intent to commit an act of unlawful violence to a particular individual or group of individuals' (see *Virginia v. Black* 538 U.S. 343 2003; 359). True threats must be distinguished from hyperbole, but the law aims to protect people not only from the risk of harm, but also from the 'fear and disruption that threats of violence engender'

(Gilbert 2003). Incitement has a higher standard and only occurs when there is 'an intent to produce imminent lawless action, and a likelihood that such action will occur' (Gilbert 2003: 865–6).

Online content which is either a 'true threat' or 'incitement' under US law should be immediately removed by a platform provider based in the United States. This, however, leaves a range of content which promotes threats and violence, but in a non-specific or hyperbolic manner. Such content is still hate speech, and where a platform prohibits hate speech it will contravene a platform's terms of service and should still be removed. Action on such content is seen as less critical for platform providers as the removal is voluntary, rather than an action to mitigate the use of their platform in the commission of a crime. This can lead to less effective and slower response times.

One example of the content which falls under this category is a post that reads, 'what's red and orange and looks good on a Muslim ... . FIRE'. The comment is expressing a positive sentiment towards harm against Muslims, but it doesn't directly call for such harm to take place. Another example is a picture of a nuclear explosion with the text, 'some cancers need to be treated with radiation ... Islam is one of them'. This image glorifies the idea of genocide against Muslims. Another image shows increasing population below a heading 'Muslims in India', and decreasing population below a heading 'Indians in India', and concludes with the text, 'It's only a matter time – eugenics may be not such a bad idea after all', another example promoting genocide.

One image which meets the legal criteria for incitement was an image of a Muslim flying through the air, with a boot that has kicked them at the edge of the frame, with the text, 'Thursday is kick a Muslim in the nuts day'. The image also contains the words, 'join the fun, find a Muslamic and wallop the bastard in the balls!' The threats and incitement this form of hate speech promote are designed to make Muslims feel not only excluded from society, but also to put them in fear for their physical safety. A surprising volume of such content is either not removed, or only removed after unreasonable delay.

The Dehumanisation and Demonisation of Muslims

Dehumanisation and demonisation has long been a tool in war. As James Forsher, assistant professor of mass communications at California State University, explains, 'when you demonize, you dehumanize' and that 'when you dehumanize, it allows you to kill your enemy and no longer feel guilty about it' (James 2003). Dehumanisation and demonisation also have a long history in racism, making it easier for attacks on a target group to take place. The target group is painted as 'a serious threat to the fabric of the perpetrator society in a way which necessitates their destruction as legitimate, as necessary, and as self-defence' (Savage 2006).

The demonisation of Muslims encountered on Facebook included the literal representation of Muslims, or the source of Islam, as demonic. In one such image the devil character is handing over a Quran to a figure in green Middle Eastern dress with only their eyes showing. The text in the image reads, 'take my teachings and deceive the world with lies and deception, the very foundation of Islam'. Another image shows a demon with tattered wings emerging out of a red mist and the text, 'Mohammed created Allah in his own image, intolerant, sexist, homophobic, and violent'.

Modern forms of demonisation, showing Muslims as an evil in society, were also present. One image showed a man flicking through a book that was about 2 meters thick. The text in the image reads, 'Muslim paedophile register finished. Part 2 will be released next week'. Others draw on Nazism as the symbol of evil, showing mixtures of Nazi and Arabic symbolism; one shows Jihadists on the left, and Hitler at a Nazi parade on the right, and then a mixture of black and white Nazi parades and coloured pictures of Jihadist parades, all showing a Nazi style salute. The text above the image says, 'Find the difference' and contains an image with a blood splash, a crescent and a swastika, below the words 'the Islamofascist Crescent and Swastika'. In another example, an image with a billboard containing a woman's face, covered by a Niqab, carries the text, 'Islam is a crime against women'. Other images list a range of deviant behaviours and crimes and attribute them to Muslims in general. This is part of the negative stereotyping that forms part of the 'what these people are really like' hate speech message which Waldron (2012) describes.

When it comes to dehumanisation, one common form is to compare the Muslim women in a Niqab to rubbish. One such image shows a mother and daughter both wearing a Niqab, and on either side of them a bag of rubbish. The text reads 'I told her she had three beautiful children. She didn't have to get all pissed off and threaten me with a bomb. It was an honest mistake …' Another image shows a woman in a blue Niqab sitting next to a pile of rubbish bags, it has the text, 'Women, can't live with 'em … Can't trick the garbage man into taking 'em'.

Another form of dehumanisation is to portray Muslims as animals. One image shows a picture of two Muslim men behind the bars of a fence at the park. The image is captioned, 'If they act like animals, treat them like it' and a sign has been photo edited onto the fence reading 'Please don't feed the animals. They survive only on a diet of hate'. Another image shows a plane carrying a large wooden crate. The plane is labelled 'humans' and the crate is labelled 'Muslims'.

One of the underlying themes in the demonisation and dehumanisation of Muslims is an attempt to dismiss the human rights of some to freedom of religion by accusing the religion itself of being against human rights. The premise of the argument is that the target is evil and has therefore forfeited the right to peacefully exist in society (Oboler 2013). The messages of dehumanisation and demonisation have much in common with racist propaganda and should be treated the same way by society.

Presenting Muslims as a 'threat to our way of life'

The anti-Muslim theme which presents Muslims as a 'threat to our way of life' has been seen in three basic forms. The first is the idea that Muslims want sharia law to replace the law of the land. The second presents Muslims as a 'cultural threat' for not fitting in, and the third presents Muslims as an economic threat, and in particular as a drain on the welfare system. The imposition of sharia law, on all citizens, is seen as the likely result of a significant Muslim population in a country, and particularly if that population doesn't 'integrate' and remains a cultural threat. Integration in this sense does not mean participating in, and contributing to, society, but rather giving up Muslim values such as eating halal food.

This view of integration reflects the more extreme interpretations of the French idea of Laïcité, a form of official secularism written into French law in 1905 (Sayare 2015). Gérard Biard, Charlie Hebdo's editor-in-chief, explained his view of concept when he said, 'you're not supposed to use religion for your sense of identity, in any case not in a secular state' (ibid.). Any distinctiveness, be it in dietary requirements, dress, accommodations for prayers or holidays, or not participating in mainstream holidays, which are often Christian based, is seen as part of an attack on mainstream culture.

Attempts to integrate, while staying within Muslim values, are also seen as offense. One example of this is the strong objection to the halal certification of the iconic Australian food Vegemite, some anti-Muslim Australians find the certification symbolically offensive. Indeed, any efforts to actively participate in society are dismissed as efforts to infiltrate and sabotage mainstream culture. This is connected to the themes of Muslims as untrustworthy manipulators, and any appearance of integration or participation in multicultural activities is seen as no more than a manipulative pretence. This cultural threat argument is particularly prevalent amongst the English Defence League (EDL) and its off-shoots in other countries. It follows the traditional racist arguments of the Far Right and the associate imagery about the values of society is often linked to the crusades (Oboler 2013).

A Facebook comment from the page 'Petition to ban the Birqa in Australia' reads: 'Muslims are evil pigs who are infiltrating our Western society, so they can destroy our civilisation, our laws, and our freedoms ... They must be deported and soon!' A similar idea is reflected in a picture of the Trojan horse with the words 'Halal is a Trojan horse of Sharia law, say no to Halal, look for non-Halal'. The attack on halal food is particularly fierce, and another image is headed, 'Muslims are urged to "conquer the word" through Halal' and carries the message that, 'It is becoming apparent that halal is being used as an instrument of Islamic mission (dawa), bringing the oblivious non-Muslim world increasingly under the authority of sharia law', and that, 'a leading European Muslim cleric has urged the international Muslim community to conquer the world through the Halal movement'.

The economic threat argument is often based on the idea of Muslims as parasites living off welfare, having large families, and shifting the demographics of a country to make it more Muslim. One Facebook image, for example, shows a man with 4 women and 13 children under the title 'one Muslim family, sucking on your welfare state'. Another uses toys to represent a Muslim man and woman, a plus sign, a pile of money, an equals sign, and an angry group of protesting toys with signs such as 'Sharia law for England'. The added text on this image reads 'welfare: feeding the enemy within'. The economic argument is also used to attack halal certification, referring to it as a Muslim tax that everyone is forced to pay. In reality the cost of certification on many processed goods is less than a cent per item and had no bearing on the price (Oboler 2013).

Other examples of Muslims as a cultural threat include a picture of World War I soldiers in trench with the text, 'we paid a heavy price for your freedom, don't let Muslims take it from you!' and one showing two lists of countries and 'happy' and 'unhappy' Muslims. The second image suggests that Muslims come from countries with sharia law, where they are unhappy, then seek to change the countries they come to by introducing sharia law in an effort to make these countries more like the countries they left.

Presenting Muslims as Manipulative and Dishonest

The presentation of Muslims as manipulative and dishonest is an approach used to spread animosity against Muslims. This theme ranges from very basic images with slogans such as 'never trust a Muslim' through a variety of images referring to what is claimed to be the Muslim doctrine of Taqiyya. A number of different images use the text: 'When Muslims are few in number, "we are from the religion of peace". When Muslims are numerous, "Islam deserves special status". When Muslims outnumber those around them, "Islam or else"'. (Oboler 2015). One common image of this form is headed 'The practical application of Taqiya (deception)'.

Another image pictures a man at prayer in front of a large flag of the United States with a crescent and star superimposed on it. The text contains a heading, 'True Islam … Deceptive by nature' followed by, 'There are two forms of lying to non-believers that are permitted under certain circumstances. Taqiyya – Saying something that isn't true. Kitman – Lying by omission' (Oboler 2013).

Taqiyya is a Shia doctrine which its literal translation means is to 'to shield or to guard oneself' (Enayat 2005: 175). Under the practise of Taqiyya, Shia Muslims may pretend to be Sunni Muslims, including by following Sunni prayer rituals, jurisprudence and by directly claiming to be Sunni rather than Shia. The practice arose as means of protection from the persecution of rulers hostile to the minority Shia sect of Islam, but continues to be practised in places like Indonesia not out of fear, but as a means of establishing greater unity within the Muslim community.

Xenophobia against Muslims

As mentioned, some of the dehumanisation of Muslims uses classic racist arguments. This is also part of a broader theme of xenophobia which sees all Muslims as 'the other'. This form of hate has difficulty with the idea of locally born Muslims being equal members of society, but largely focuses on opposition to immigration of Muslims. This opposition often focuses on refugees (those who have been granted refugee status by the United Nations) and asylum seekers (those seeking to make a claim for refugee status), but when pushed, often degenerates into a general form of hatred and fear of all Muslims using other lines of argument already discussed.

One image on Facebook contains a Lego man with a belt of grenades, a gun in each hand and a Muslim-styled head covering, and reads 'Common English mistakes: using your instead of you're; using their instead of they're; allowing Muslims into the country'. Another is a picture of a wall of anti-immigration posters. One poster reads 'No welfare for asylum seekers', another says 'deport asylum seeker sexual predators', a third says 'you are entering a Sharia Free Zone', a fourth reads 'stop the illegal trade in asylum seekers' and a fifth reads 'No asylum, secure the borders, deport illegals'.

Undermining the Resistance to Hate against Muslims

An indirect form of hate involves those efforts designed to make the anti-Muslim hate more socially acceptable. These lines of argument directly contribute to the Hate 2.0 effect discussed earlier in this chapter. An example of this is the series of images on Facebook promoting the idea that Muslims are not a race, so it isn't racist to promote hate of Muslims. This is of course a false argument, one could as easily say it isn't racist to murder people at random; it may be true, but that doesn't make murder right. A twist on this theme is an image which reads 'Fighting the enemy used to be called war, now it's called racism'. This is similar to one which shows a picture of soldiers with a speech bubble reading 'we fought and died for your freedom, and you won't speak out now because you're scared of being labelled a racist?!'

Freedom of speech arguments are also twisted and abused in order to justify and defend hate speech. One image uses the messages that it isn't hate to question a religion. The image on Facebook shows four very different looking Muslims, of different ethnicities, each with the label 'Muslim' below their picture. The image is headed 'It is not racist', and below the images continues, 'to criticize a religion (so nice try)'. The problem with this image is that while it talks about 'a religion', which is a set of ideas, the images used are clearly about people not ideas.

Another image is split into two parts; on the left are various stylised images of people and the text 'people have rights', and on the right is a collection of stylised symbols of religions, political parties and ideologies, and the text 'ideas don't have rights'. Further text on the image says 'Every Ideology must be subject to open, free discussion in regard to its value or otherwise, without fear of reprisal. No exceptions. "Islamophobia" is not racism, any more than "Communistophobia" or "Fascistophobia" would be, because Islam is an *idea*, not a *race*. In a civilised society, no idea – religious, political or philosophical – can claim any special treatment, or be set beyond the reach of empirical evidence. Support free speech. Support people'. The image by itself is not hate speech, but in this instance it is used to support the page's message which reads: 'Listen up muzzies, after reading some of the lovely messages to the page I would like to explain AGAIN why criticising Islam is not racist. Maybe if you could refrain from breeding with your cousins, future generations of Muslims would find this easier to understand' (Oboler 2013: 120–31). The post is clearly bigoted, but in its references to genetics, it is also classically racist. The image posted only highlights how the comments made are an attack on people.

Other images attack the idea of moderate Muslims. One shows a huge bomb with the word Islam on it being carried by three people labelled 'Moderate' while four people and standing on each other's shoulders so the top one can reach the fuse with a lit match (ibid. 120). The message is that all Muslims are a problem. Another image suggests there are no moderate Muslims, it shows an empty street with the text 'moderate Muslims demonstrating for peace' (ibid. 131). Another says 'The only difference between a radical and a moderate Muslim is … the distance they place between themselves and the bomb'; it shows one cartoon Muslim character with a remote control bomb, and another dressed as a suicide bomber.

Another form this theme takes is that Muslims are an exception and will never fit in to a multicultural society. One image shows people of different ethnicities dancing in a circle and holding hands, the Muslim figure in the circle is wearing a suicide vest, the text reads, 'Multiculturalism – Islam will never be a part of it' (ibid. 15). Similarly, another image shows a square peg not fitting into a round hole; it reads 'the Cult of Islam has no intention of fitting in, Muslims will never become a part of civilised society' (ibid. 74).

There are also examples of cartoons of Mohammed being used to spread hate. The character of Mohammed is used in order to engage freedom of speech sympathies in light of attacks on those who have drawn such cartoons in the past. The images we refer to here, however, are specifically those where the image is not just of Mohammed, but of Mohammed as a representation of all Muslims, and where all Muslims are presented using a negative stereotype. The primary example is the now infamous Kurt Westergaard cartoon which features a picture of Mohammed with a bomb in his turban and the Muslim declaration of faith also on the turban (Oboler 2015). The Online Hate Prevention Institute has argued that 'a cartoon should not be considered hate speech merely because it depicts Mohammed', but that 'Cartoons portraying Muslims through negative stereotypes, using Mohammed to symbolise all Muslims, should be considered a form of hate speech' (ibid. 18).

Efforts aimed at undermining resistance to anti-Muslim hate make it harder for the wider public to comfortably in speaking up against hate directed against the Muslim community, or to participate in activities designed to build bridges with the Muslim community. The lack of action by Facebook in relation to the many examples found in the Online Hate Prevention Institute's report also sends a negative message that such content is acceptable. This message is reinforced each time Facebook informs people that it did not find their report to be valid.

Seeking to Exclude Muslims from Society

Another more indirect form of anti-Muslim hate seeks to exclude Muslims from society by removing or preventing the development of the infrastructure a Muslim community needs. This form of anti-Muslim hate includes attacks on the certification and stocking of halal food, as well at political action at the local government level in an effort to prevent planning approval for mosques, Muslim schools and other infrastructure needed to support a Muslim community. These efforts are largely coordinated and promoted through Facebook.

The anti-halal campaign began as astroturfing, with many fake local branches established by the same small group of people. It has, since grown into a real international online movement. The anti-halal campaign has three points of focus: the first is online negative publicity campaigns against companies and brands that are halal certified; the second is direct contact and lobby the companies; and the third is a campaign against shops that stock halal foods.

The online campaigns against halal certification have unfortunately had some small successes. In late 2014, for example, an Australian dairy company stopped certifying its products in response to such a campaign. This, however, raised the attention of their industry body, the Dairy Farmers Association. The association hit back saying that, in this case a 'small milk company, without the resources to defend themselves ... decided it's easier to walk away' and that it was 'particularly unfair to put that sort of pressure on a small, little milk company that's just trying to operate' (ABC News 2014). The association urged other companies facing such campaigns to seek help.

The anti-halal campaign is often based on the false claim that money paid for certification is used to fund terrorism, and that as a result everyone involved in the support of halal food is a material supporter of terrorism. Another argument is that the certification costs are a religious tax being imposed on non-Muslims, and are part of an effort to apply sharia law across society. The tax argument could equally be made about user forms of certification, from Kosher certification to fair trade certification, or health related certifications like Australia's 'Heart Foundation tick of approval' (Oboler 2013: 21–2). The argument only has weight if there is a real price increase.

While some certifications, like fair trade, rely on a percentage based fee, halal certification tends to be based on a fixed-cost model. The cost passed on to consumers is likely to be swamped by other fixed costs such as advertising and marketing. As the impact of a fixed cost on each item sold decrease with an increase in sales, the opening up of new markets, locally and internationally, through halal certification can actually end up reducing the ultimate costs to consumers. Given Australia's large halal export market to Asia, the tax argument has no merit.

When it comes to local government action to block planning approval for Muslim buildings, research by the Online Hate Prevention Institute has shown that such efforts may not be local at all. Research into a Facebook page called 'Stop the Mosque in Bendigo', for example, showed that only 3% of the pages supporters were actually from the city of Bendigo. In total 80% of the supporters of the page were from outside the state, and that included 14% of the page's supporters who were from outside the country (The Bendigo Mosque 2014). Media reports also highlighted how non-local anti-Muslim organisations were supporting the anti-mosque push, including with financial support, and by providing materials and information for those wanting to fight planning approvals (Johnston 2014). There are numerous 'Stop the Mosque' style pages and they have become particularly organised in Australia.

Bigots Pretending to be Muslims

False flag pages pretending to be Muslim, but taking positions designed to outrage and upset the wider community, are another form of anti-Muslim hate.

A common theme for such pages is to attack commemorations for soldiers who have died in wars. Another approach used by anti-Muslim haters is to pretend to be Muslim while engaging in explicit support for terrorism and violence. During the Lindt Café siege in Sydney in December 2014, which left four people dead, a number of pages pretending to be run by local Muslims, and expressing support for the attack, were created. These pages are designed to create a hatred and fear of the local Muslim community and to potentially spark a breakdown of public order and potentially lead to riots.

In the case of the Sydney siege, the Online Hate Prevention Institute was able to notify both police and Facebook when the pages appeared, and then advise the public to ignore the pages as they were being dealt with by authorities. This post was seen by over 260,000 people and played a significant role in preventing the situation potentially getting out of hand. False flag pages need to be rapidly exposed and removed as they can pose a real danger to public safety.

Improving Responses to Online anti-Muslim hate

The problem of anti-Muslim hate is particularly acute due to its prevalence and growth in recent years, but also due to difficulties in applying existing mechanisms against hate speech in this area. Part of the difficulty comes from the challenge of identifying what is hate speech, and what must be protected as criticism of religion. Part of the problem, however, is structural and requires legal reform both at the national level and through international treaties.

One structural problem is that anti-hate rules and systems have traditionally been based on the narrow concept of racism and xenophobia, rather than the broader concept of bigotry against a group in society. The Universal Declaration of Human Rights clearly regards religion, like race, sex, and nationality, a factor which cannot be used to limit human rights (Universal Declaration of Human Rights 1948 Art 2). There is a universal human right to teach, practice, worship and observe ones religion both in private and in public (Universal Declaration of Human Rights 1948 Art 18). Despite this, many laws and policies do not explicitly cover religion and it can be difficult to get online religious vilification removed from social media platforms.

Social media platforms such as Facebook provide an environment that supports the creation of communities, and haters take full advantage of this facility. Social media platforms also let the haters gain ready access to victims, anything with the word 'Muslim' or 'Islamic' in its name may be targeted. Despite public policies against hate speech, those responsible for enforcing community standards at Facebook appear uninterested in doing so when it comes to anti-Muslim hate. The lack of response, after 12 months, to the report by the Online Hate Prevention Institute highlights the problem.

Some online attacks require more than just the suspension of an account. It can be difficult for law enforcement to access the data, such as IP addresses, which they need to enable a prosecution. This problem is not unique to crimes against the Muslim community, but increasingly it is Muslims who are being targeted by organised online campaigns. These campaigns, which seek to exclude Muslims from society, can also spill over to the streets and pose a threat to public safety. They can also cause Muslim youth who become disillusioned, and blame society as a whole for the hate spread by anti-Muslim extremists, to look for a way to hit back. The risk of self-radicalisation of Muslim youth online, as a result of anti-Muslim hate they are exposed to, is not insignificant.

Conclusion

Anti-Muslim hate is a growing problem. This is strongly reflected on Facebook where a wide variety of hate messages are shared and spread. Within social media, such hate can be normalised creating a risk that such views will also be normalised in wider society. Social media platforms need to do more to identify and remove online hate against Muslims. Offline systems also need to be improved to deal with the worst offenders. The Muslim community has an important role to play in responding to anti-Muslim hate, but this is not solely a Muslim community problem. Anti-Muslim hate is an attack on the inclusiveness of society, on multiculturalism, and on democracy itself. It is an attack on all of us. Governments, social media platforms and community groups must act together to better tackle the problem of anti-Muslim hate speech, as well as the problem of hate speech online more generally.

Further Reading

Awan, I. 2013. *Victims of Anti-Muslim Hate*, Evidence Submitted to the APPG on Islamophobia, 11 September 2013.

Awan, I. and Blakemore, B. 2012. *Policing Cyber Hate, Cyber Threats and Cyber Terrorism*, Ashgate: Farnham.

Oboler, A. 2013. 'Islamophobia on the Internet: The growth of online hate targeting Muslims', Online Hate Prevention Institute, 2013. [Online]. Available at: http://ohpi.org.au/islamophobia-on-the-internet-the-growth-of-online-hate-targeting-muslims/ [accessed: 30 March 2015].

Oboler, A. 2015. 'Je Suis Humain: Responsible free speech in the shadow of the Charlie Hebdo murders', Online Hate Prevention Institute, 2015. [Online]. Available at: http://ohpi.org.au/jesuishumain/ [accessed: 10 February 2015].

Waldron, J. 2012. *The Harm in Hate Speech*, Cambridge, MA: Harvard University Press.

References

ABC News 2014. 'Claims Halal certification fees fund terrorism "absolutely wrong"', ABC News, 11 November 2014 [Online]. Available at: http://www.abc.net.au/news/2014–11–11/halal-terrorism-funding-claims-absolutely-wrong/5881380 [accessed: 10 February 2015].

BBC News, 2006. *Q&A: The Muhammad cartoons row*, BBC News, 7 February 2006. [Online]. Available at: http://news.bbc.co.uk/2/hi/4677976.stm [accessed: 30 March 2015].

Dreyfus, M. 2013. Statement of Support, in Andre Oboler, 'Islamophobia on the Internet: The growth of online hate targeting Muslims', Online Hate Prevention Institute. [Online]. Available at: http://ohpi.org.au/islamophobia-on-the-internet-the-growth-of-online-hate-targeting-muslims/ [accessed: 30 March 2015].

Enayat, H. 2005. *Modern Islamic Political Thought: The Response of the Shi'i and Sunni Muslims to the Twentieth Century*, new edition, London: I.B. Tauris, 175.

Gilbert, L. 2003. 'Moking George: Political Satire as True Threat in the Age of Global Terrorism', 58 *University of Miami Law Review*: 843–66.

James, M. 2003. 'Demonizing the Enemy a Hallmark of War', ABC News, Jan 29 2003 [Online]. Available at: http://abcnews.go.com/International/story?id=79071 [accessed: 10 February 2015].

Johnston, C. 2014. 'Bendigo mosque a cause celebre for right-wing outsiders', *The Age*, 28 June 2014. [Online]. Available at: http://www.theage.com.au/victoria/bendigo-mosque-a-cause-celebre-for-rightwing-outsiders-20140627-zsoft.html [accessed: 30 January 2015].

Oboler, A. 2008. Online Antisemitism 2.0. 'Social Antisemitism on the Social Web', *Post-Holocaust and Antisemitism Series, JCPA* (April 2008, No. 67).

Oboler, A. 2010a. 'Government a welcome presence in cyber regulation', *Australian Jewish News*, 27 May.

Oboler, A. 2010b. 'Time to Regulate Internet Hate with a New Approach?' *Internet Law Bulletin* 13(6).

Oboler, A. 2011. 'A legal model for government intervention to combat online hate', *Internet Law Bulletin*, 14(2).

Oboler, A. 2013. 'Islamophobia on the Internet: The growth of online hate targeting Muslims', Online Hate Prevention Institute, 2013. [Online]. Available at: http://ohpi.org.au/islamophobia-on-the-internet-the-growth-of-online-hate-targeting-muslims/ [accessed: 30 March 2015].

Oboler, A. 2015. 'Je Suis Humain: Responsible free speech in the shadow of the Charlie Hebdo murders', Online Hate Prevention Institute, 2015,

p. 28. [Online]. Available at: http://ohpi.org.au/jesuishumain/ [accessed: 10 February 2015].

Online Hate Prevention Institute, 2014. 'How Facebook responds to anti-Muslim Hate' [Online]. Available at: http://ohpi.org.au/how-facebook-responded-to-anti-muslim-hate/ [accessed: 10 February 2015].

Protocol to the Convention on cybercrime, concerning the criminalisation of acts of a racist and xenophobic nature committed through computer systems, opened for signature 28 January 2003 (entered into force 1 March 2006) ('*Additional Protocol*').

RT 2015, 'Reclaim Australia': Anti-Islam rallies provoke fear in Muslim community, *RT*, 6 April 2015. [Online[. Available at: http://rt.com/news/247037-muslims-fear-reclaim-australia/ [accessed 14 April 2015].

Savage, R. 2006. '"Vermin to be Cleared off the Face of the Earth": Perpetrator Representations of Genocide Victims as Animals', in Colin Tatz, Peter Arnold and Sandra Tatz (eds), *Genocide Perspectives III – Essays on the Holocaust and Other Genocides*. Blackheath, NSW: Brandl and Schesinger, 17–53.

Sayare, S. 2015. 'The Charlie Hebdo I Know', *The Atlantic*, 11 January 2015, [Online]. Available at: http://www.theatlantic.com/international/archive/2015/01/charlie-hebdo-secularism-religion-islam/384413/ [accessed: 10 February 2015].

Socolovsky, J. 2012. 'Islamic Nations Relinquish Demand for Defamation Laws', *Voice of America News*, 24 October 2012 [Online]. Available at: http://www.voanews.com/content/islam-un-defamation/1532871.html [accessed: 10 February 2015].

The Bendigo Mosque: 'Exporting Hate to Regional Victoria', Online Hate Prevention Institute, 24 June 2014. [Online]. Available at: http://ohpi.org.au/the-bendigo-mosque-exporting-hate-to-regional-victoria/ [accessed 30 March 2015].

The Telegraph, 2015. 'Prophet Mohammed cartoons controversy: timeline', *The Telegraph*, 13 January 2015, [Online]. Available at: http://www.telegraph.co.uk/news/worldnews/europe/france/11341599/Prophet-Muhammad-cartoons-controversy-timeline.html [accessed: 10 February 2015].

UN General Assembly, *International Covenant on Civil and Political Rights*, 16 December 1966, United Nations, Treaty Series, vol. 999, p. 171.

Universal Declaration of Human Rights, G.A. Res. 217 (III) A, U.N. Doc. A/RES/217(III) (Dec. 10, 1948) Art 2.

Universal Declaration of Human Rights, G.A. Res. 217 (III) A, U.N. Doc. A/RES/217(III) (Dec. 10, 1948) Art 18.

US State Department, 2008. *Contemporary Global Anti-Semitism: A Report Provided to the United States Congress* (2008) p. 81 [Online]. Available at: http://www.state.gov/documents/organization/102301.pdf [accessed: 10 February 2015].

Waldron, J. 2012. *The Harm in Hate Speech*, Cambridge, MA: Harvard University Press.

Chapter 4
Online Hate and Political Activist Groups

Brian Blakemore

Dissemination of anti-Islamic feelings has grown into a sophisticated movement spanning most of the developed democratic countries of the world during the decade to 2013 (Pupcenoks and McCabe 2013). The growth of this populist movement coincides with the growth in these countries of the internet as a means of living and expressing social feelings and enjoying social interaction. This chapter will consider online hate and political groups having members who are associated with expressing anti-Muslim sentiments online. Online hate is often referred to as 'trolling' and many cases of this expression of hate are reported by the media. Trolls may have many motivations including: to entertain themselves or others, an emotional impulse to express their feelings or to advance a political point of view (Bishop 2012a, 2012b). Persaud (2014) found a 'unique constellation' of 'manipulativeness, sadism and psychopathy', in trolls (see Chapter 6 for more on the psychological aspects of hate). Various examples of online hate in Britain are shown in Table 4.1 below. The punishment given to those convicted of trolling has been inconsistent and using different aspects of UK legislation, some of which predates the cyber communications and social media age. Fiyaz Mughal, director of Faith Matters addressed not punishment but prosecution and stated that; 'unless a specific threat to a specific person is made the Criminal Justice System will not respond' (*Metro* 2013: 1). More recently the UK Justice Secretary Chris Grayling suggested quadrupling the sentence for internet trolls convicted for posting abuse on Twitter, Facebook and other social media to a term of up to two years in prison (Spence 2014).

Table 4.1 shows that the legislation used and sentences handed out are quite variable. The term 'cyber hate' covers a wider range of activities other than 'trolling'. it also covers incitement to perform physical acts of hate as well as actual online harassment and abuse. The effects of cyber harassment are not always recognised, they can have significantly affect victims (McCall 2003). Basu and Jones (2007) suggest there is a real difference between cyberstalking and 'physical world' stalking. Salter and Bryden (2009) disagree arguing that online harassment is simply another aspect of the same offence, and is likely to cause an equal amount of alarm or distress as the physical equivalent.

Table 4.1   Examples of online hate and the punishment given

Troll	Posting	Punishment
Sean Duffy	Trolling Natasha Mac Bryde's memorial website.	18-weeks imprisonment.
Liam Stacey	Student posted racist remarks on Twitter.	8 weeks in prison and a ban from Swansea University Campus.
Rio Ferdinand	Referred to another black footballer, Ashley Cole, by the racist term 'choc ice'.	£45,000 fine from his professional body, the English Football Association.
Jamie Counsel and Anthony Gristock	During the UK Riots in 2011they set up Facebook pages in the heat of the moment that attempted to encourage riots in Cardiff and Swansea.	4 years and 3.5 years imprisonment respectively.
Reece Messer	Posted that Olympic Diver Tom Daley let his late father down by not winning a medal at the London Olympics.	Received a harassment warning.
Matthew Woods	Posted offensive jokes on his own personal Facebook page, concerning missing children Madeline McCann and April Jones.	12-weeks imprisonment.
Joshua Cryer	Posted several racist messages over several days about Stan Collymore, a controversial sports host and ex-footballer.	Two years' community service and ordered to pay £150 legal costs.
Azhar Ahmed	Posted on Facebook, 'all soldiers should die and go to hell'.	Fined £300 and given 240 hours of community service over a two-year period for sending a grossly offensive communication.
Lee Francis Ball	Posted abuse about his ex-girlfriend on Facebook for a period of 9 months and even arranging for cosmetic surgeons to contact her.	Two years in prison.
Jake Newsome	Posted; 'I'm glad the teacher got stabbed up. Feel sorry for the kid' following the killing of teacher Ann Maguire in her classroom.	Jake pleaded guilty to sending an offensive communication by means of an electronic device and was sentenced to 6 weeks in prison.

Source: Adapted from Bishop (2013) and Jeeves (2014).

A right-wing Dutch politician, Geert Wilders, was found not to have committed hate speech despite making comments about Muslims such as likening the Quran to Hitler's 'Mein Kampf' and demanding that there should be a stop on Muslim immigration to Holland. These comments were deemed to be protected speech as his comments were directed against the Muslim religion not against individuals or a group of people. The Dutch Supreme Court, the US Supreme

Court and the European Court of Human Rights, follow the principle that criminal law is broken only when statements incite to violence (Jolly 2011).

The British Crime Survey (now Crime Survey for England and Wales) data for 2009/10 and 2010/11 reveals that 67% of hate crime victims experience anger, 50% annoyance, 40% shock, 35% loss of confidence, 39% fear, 23% anxiety, 20% depression and 17% record difficulty sleeping (BCS 2012). Although the incidence of hate crime incidents is generally falling within England and Wales, Muslims have suffered increased hate abuse (Feldman and Littler 2014). Copsey et al. (2013) analysed the 'Tell MAMA dataset', generated over the period April 2012 – April 2013. They found that only just over one third (37%) of those reporting incidents to Tell MAMA had also reported it to the police. This is in line with the Crime Survey of England and Wales (2011/12; 2012/13) which found that only 40% of hate crime incidents are reported to the police and therefore the majority of victims will suffer in silence (CSE & W 2012 and 2013). A very high proportion (82%) of the 734 Tell MAMA self-reported hate cases were found to be online abuse (Feldman and Littler 2014). The online abuse had a similar but slightly higher percentage (45%) of abusers who were linked to far-right/new right groups such as EDL and BNP compared to those who resorted to physical abuse (40% associated with such groups). The online links to the far-right/new right were established by the abusers use of well used catch phrases previously used by the far-right organisation or by members of such organisations and or by connecting hyperlinks or hashtags to sites affiliated to far-right/new right groups.

The British government aims to give a higher priority to tackling all forms of hate crime, with a plan to 'Challenge It, Report It, Stop It' (HMG 2014). The plan is to facilitate the removal of online material that is unacceptable or illegal in collaboration with internet service providers and website hosts, develop more sever prosecution guidelines and specify such for offences on social media, and to focus on anti-Muslim hate crime, disability hate crime and extremist hate crime.

Copsey et al. (2013) categorise general characteristics about how Muslims are depicted on social media. This includes, Muslims represented as a threat because of acts of extremism and terrorist attacks on places and people, this is followed by Muslims viewed as inferior and that they cannot adhere to a set of life values and as such they should have fewer rights in society. Furthermore, their findings suggest that Muslims are viewed in the prism of punishment and are dangerous and untruthful who are an 'out group' from the rest of society; that aim to impose their way of life on the country and indeed upon the whole world.

These last three characteristics are noted by Pupcenoks and McCabe (2013) who argue that European populists do not want to recognise diversity amongst Muslims as they construct a fearsome and loathsome Muslim 'Other'. Betz

(2007) takes this argument further and states that the aims of anti-Muslim populists are the forced assimilation of Muslim communities into their own culture or the complete removal of the Muslim community from their country.

Copsey et al. (2013) also found that the majority of the anti-Muslim hate incidents were via online media (74%).

> Anti-Muslim hate crime can be motivated, as one study has noted, by political fears about Muslims as a security or terrorist threat (rather than a fear about Islam per se), and/or it might be motivated by racism (active discrimination against South Asians in particular as people associated with Islam). In reality, the distinction between race hate crime and religious hate crime can often become blurred, making conceptual and reporting clarity difficult. (Copsey et al. 2013: 6)

The Crown Prosecution Service (2012) found that most defendants in racist and or religious hate crimes committed in 2011–2012 were male (83%). They were predominately white British (73.6%) while age was not seen to be a discriminating variable. Many of those committing hate crimes are affiliated to far-right groups and the Tell MAMA data set linked 69% of online cases to such a group (Copsey et al. 2013). However Husbands (2009) points out that given the estimated levels of hate crime, taking into account the high level of under-reporting, the known extremist organisations' levels of activity is not sufficient to account for the estimated level of hate crime committed. Husbands concludes that there must be a large number of others committing hate crime beyond these organisations. These others may be lone wolves or members of ill-defined and unknown groups. This idea is supported by Iganski (2008) citing data from the Institute of Race Relations that found less that than 4% of a sample of hate cases were committed by members of extremist groups.

The murder of the off duty soldier Lee Rigby in May 2013 and the resultant high profile and prolific media reporting of this terrible hate crime caused a steep increase in anti-Muslim hate crime. For example, the Metropolitan Police Service recorded 104 anti-Muslim hate crimes in May and 108 in June 2013 (*Metro* 2013). Significantly more than the previous year's average of 28 per month, this increase was also experienced in other police services within the UK (*Metro* 2013). This was also reflected in self-reported cases to Tell MAMA with nearly four times the rate of online and offline reports in the week following the murder than in the week preceding it (Feldman and Littler 2014).

This sudden rise in hate crimes and incidents following a related high profile incident is a general phenomenon with anti-hate groups becoming more active when their perceived enemy is active or newsworthy. A more recent example is the conflict in Gaza which has resulted in a sharp increase in attacks upon Jewish targets within the UK. Pilditch lists 100 hate crime incidents and bomb threats and assaults which occurred at twice the typical rate of such activity and spikes in hate crime following this conflict were also recorded in France and Germany (Pilditch 2014).

Counter Extremist Extremism

Feldman and Littler (2014) describe the phenomena of increased incidence of retaliation against those thought to be extremist or to support extremists and those who have committed extremist acts against society. This revenge extremism against extremist groups can of course include attacks against innocent communities in which the extremists socialise and or live. This spiral of hate and fear leading to counter activism and counter attacks has been called 'cumulative extremism' and this was observed following the Bradford race riots in 2001, the London bombing attacks on 7 July 2005 (Eatwell 2006: 205), and in the counter demonstration by the 'United people of Luton' following Islam4UK's demonstration in Luton against British soldiers returning from Afghanistan in 2009 (Wardrop 2009). The Council on American Islamic Relations (2013) also reported two spikes in hate attacks on mosques in the USA; one in May 2011 following the death of Osama bin Laden and the other in August 2012 following the killing of six Sikh worshippers.

Bartlett and Birdwell (2013) recommend that to prevent far-right and Islamist 'cumulative extremism' that for a short period following any terrorist attacks that the security forces should not only pursue the terrorist but should also increase its surveillance and policing of the opposing extremist groups. They also point out that this counter extremist extremism is likely to subside to typical levels after a little time, so the phenomena is a spike of activity not a self-sustaining spiral of increasing activity from both sides. Disha, Cavendish and King (2011) found that hate crimes against Arabs and Muslims increased following the 9/11 terrorist attack. Their regression analysis suggested that counties having larger immigration levels of Arabs and Muslims experienced more hate crimes. Their study supports the idea of counter extremist extremism in the form of hate crime and that the location of such crimes is not likely to fluctuate wildly.

Some examples of online counter extremist extremism have been noted in the media. The BBC News (2014b) notes the use of direct argument and of sarcastic humour on social media by individual Muslims to create a counterweight to the use of social media to attack Muslims and Muslim values. They cite the first use of such sarcastic humour as #NotInMyName. They also describe sites which counters the claims that Muslims and the Muslim religion is intolerant and violent; one tweet that was tagged 50,000 times in a week 'Al-Qaeda, Taliban, ISIS and 9/11 … do not represent me bec my religion doesn't teach hate & murder', and secondly a tweet #MuslimApologies which stated 'Sorry for Algebra, cameras, universities, hospitals, oh and coffee too' (BBC News 2014b: 1).

This trend to counter extremist argument on social media is also evident in other languages with one French language hashtag – being accessed 5,000 times in one day. The Council on American Islamic Relations (2014) used its social media site #MuslimsThank to launch a campaign acknowledging the public support received for Muslims from those in the media. The site lists personalities, celebrities and political leaders who have defended Muslims and Islam from racism.

Political Dimensions to Hate Crime

Groups that are fundamentally concerned with nationalism and a perceived historic culture and tradition may be referred to as 'Far-Right' groups. Right wing activists fear the loss of this historic cultural and ethnic identity and fight against this perceived threat to their view of life. They see other religions, immigration, economic recession and globalisation as the enemy diluting their identity. The British Government perceives that the major threat from far-right extremism comes from unaffiliated lone agents who are disillusioned with the views of society (Home Affairs Committee 2012). A YouGov survey (2012) revealed that the majority of respondents (63%) supported reducing the numbers of Muslims coming to Britain with 49% forecasting a 'clash of civilisations' between Muslims and white Britons and that 54% were of the opinion that tensions between these groups would deteriorate.

This analysis of core values seems to be valid across Europe and beyond 'As anti-Semitism was a unifying factor for Far Right parties in the 1910s, 20s and 30s, Islamophobia has become the unifying factor in the early decades of the 21st century', according to Thomas Klau member of the European Council on Foreign Relations (*Daily Telegraph* 2011: 1). A post on Facebook showing the image of a masked German police officer giving the Nazi salute with accompanying text 'you call it freedom and tolerance. I call it a death dance for Europe. You talk of multi-cultural state. For me it is only white betrayal' (Dixon 2012: 24) speaks to this fear of loss and sense of betrayal with the government of the day. Although members of 'far-right' groups may be active in hate crimes they are not particularly active in the commission of terrorist activities as only 17 members of far-right groups have been convicted of terrorism-related offences in the UK in recent years (Goodwin and Evans 2012). However the British Government's Commons Select Committee (2012) expressed concern regarding the trend of growing support for both non-violent extremism and for more extreme and violent forms of far-right ideology. The YouGov survey carried out in the same year found that 21% of respondents aligned themselves with the values expressed by the EDL although they did not agree with the methods used by the EDL (YouGov 2012).

A second category of political groups has been identified in Europe, termed 'Populist Extremist Parties' or 'the New Right' (Bartlett et al. 2011). These groups are committed to democratic government and politics, they do not associate with existing mainstream political parties. However they are concerned with the effects of globalisation and some especially concerned with immigration (Betz 1998). They are also anti-establishment and support the rights of the working class and so have a combination of both left wing and right wing viewpoints. They too are particularly concerned with protecting their national culture and are against immigration. The YouGov (2012) survey sampled 1666 adults and found that the single most important issue facing the country at the time was the economy (60%) followed by immigration and asylum seekers (20%) while 'Muslims in Britain' was the main concern for only 3% of the responses.

Bartlett et al. (2011) found that such populist New Right activists use online social media extensively. They surveyed 10,000 online respondents across Europe and found that these digital populists are mainly young men (75% males and 63% under the age of 30). The authors concede that using an online survey may attract a disproportionally higher response rate from younger age groups. The respondents' were pessimistic regarding their country's future and were critical of the loss of control over borders and the erosion of cultural identity within the European Union. Bartlett et al. (2014) described a non-extremist digital populist movement called Moviemento 5 Stella as being generally positive towards immigration (see below) but noted that those under 30 years of age tended to be less positive on this aspect.

Bartlett et al. (2014) also found that the use of social media is fundamental to many citizens' lives with the majority of people being informed about unfolding news stories via social media rather than more established and formal media channels such as the press, television and radio. The average European citizen spends over four hours a day using the internet and across Europe there are 250 million Facebook accounts. The socialising that takes place in social media enables movements using this channel to grow rapidly and mobilise large numbers of followers and activists.

> Social media politics vary greatly, from single issue campaigns to established political party Facebook accounts with strict control over the content. But they share in common the idea of a direct, free and easy involvement (or disengagement); regular updates and information; and active participation. (Bartlett et al. 2014: 12)

Bartlett et al. (2014) cite examples such as the English Defence League in the UK, the Pirate Party in Germany, and the Occupy movement as successful manipulators of social media to achieve political and social impact in a short time period. The existing political parties may have been slow to use social media but are now trying to catch up for example the American Democratic party invested millions of dollars in the 2012 US election in social media platforms to attract supporters and votes.

Not all digital popularist movements are anti-Muslim or even concerned with Immigration and loss of identity. On such example is a relatively new movement Moviemento 5 Stella (M5S) founded in Italy who are using Facebook and attracting those who are not affiliated to traditional political parties but are mainly concerned with the economic situation (62%), unemployment (61%) and levels of taxation (43%). Bartlett et al. (2014) found members to be generally positive towards immigration and not particularly concerned with loss of identity. However, the trend to support political groups highly concerned with both the loss of their cultural and social identity and stopping immigration was made clear in the European Parliament elections in 2014 where mainly right-wing and anti-European integration groups increased their parliamentary representation from 31 to 38 MEPs. At the same time independent groups including far-right groups such as the British National Party and France's National Front accounted for 20% of the total vote increasing their representation from 29 to 109 MEPs according to the BBC News (2014).

The Hate not Hope annual 'State of hate' in the UK report for 2014 claims that groups such as the EDL and BNP became less effective in 2014 due to lack of leadership, breaking up into splinter groups and possibly the emergence of UKIP as an alternative way of expressing concerns of identity, economics and immigration. The caution that events in Europe such as the Charlie Hebdo and associated terrorist acts present a tinderbox that might inflame anti-Muslim feelings (Lowles 2015).

The English Defence League

The English Defence League (EDL) was formed in 2009 as a counter extremism reaction to an Islam4UK organised protest against British soldiers who had returned from fighting in Afghanistan (Pupcenoks and McCabe 2013). The exact size of the EDL is debated. Bird (2010) suggested it had 100,000 followers on Facebook with a hard core membership of around 10,000. However, Bartlett et al. (2011) found that the EDL is mainly a Facebook group which they estimated to have 30,000 supporters and sympathisers. This second estimate represents 0.066% of the adult population of England and Wales (ONS 2011). In the YouGov survey only 33% of respondents had heard of the English Defence League and knew what they stood for, while 42% had heard of them but were unsure of their aims and objectives. The direct support for the EDL found in the survey (YouGov 2012) was that 9% of those who had heard of the EDL (n=1282) would consider joining the EDL and only 1% considered themselves to be a member of EDL. However 3%, agreed with the values and methods of the EDL, representing nearly 1.4 million adults if the sample is representative of England and Wales, suggesting that there is potential growth for this or other groups, see Britain First below (YouGov 2012).

The EDL allows free access via social media and does not require a membership fee; this removes the normal barriers to joining a movement. Leadership by the hard core activists and founders in such an open society needs to be by persuasion and by appealing to the needs of the membership. Bartlett et al. (2011) concluded that the main focus of their extremism is driven by major concerns regarding an uncertain future, especially the lack of employment, high rates of immigration and the loss of traditional British identity. The EDL home page states that the EDL is 'not racist, not violent, no longer silent' its mission statement reveals it:

> was founded in the wake of the shocking actions of a small group of Muslim extremists who, at a homecoming parade in Luton, openly mocked the sacrifices of our service personnel without any fear of censure. Although these actions were certainly those of a minority, we believe that they reflect other forms of religiously-inspired intolerance and barbarity that are thriving amongst certain sections of the Muslim population in Britain: including, but not limited to, the denigration and oppression of women, the molestation of young children, the committing of so-called honour killings, homophobia, anti-Semitism, and continued support for those responsible for terrorist atrocities. (EDL webpage 2014)

This section of the website further states that not all Muslims are complicit or responsible for these crimes and that 'Muslims may be victims of Islamic traditions and practices' it further adds that 'radical Islam has a 'stranglehold on British Muslims' and believes that British Muslims should be able to safely demand reform of their religion'. The mission statement also maintains that sharia law is incompatible with democratic principles;

The EDL promotes the understanding of Islam and the implications for non-Muslims forced to live alongside it. Islam is not just a religious system, but a political and social ideology that seeks to dominate all non-believers and impose a harsh legal system that rejects democratic accountability and human rights. It runs counter to all that we hold dear within our British liberal democracy, and it must be prepared to change, to conform to secular, liberal ideals and laws, and to contribute to social harmony, rather than causing divisions (EDL webpage 2014).

This statement labels Islam as a whole as a totalitarian set of values and states that it is not in accord with the democratic way of western society. It also asserts the need to contest and defeat this type of religious system. The message on the website maps well with the categories given by Copsey et al. (2013) above. Within the 'Dynamic Model of Mobilization' (McAdam, Tarrow and Tilley 2001) is the requirement for successful organisations to achieve 'innovative collective action'. That is groups modify their collective behaviour to adapt to changes or developments based on their shared knowledge and the communication networks between key members of the group. Online groups have a simple and direct way of sharing knowledge and key members tend to be active on the web pages informing all members of the need to adapt. Hence online groups are well positioned to mobilise at least some of their members into action. The Tell MAMA survey (Copsey et al. 2013: 22) found that English Defence League is most associated with anti-Muslim activity citing 147 of such cases are attributable to EDL supporters whereas other activists groups were only linked in a few cases with the CXF (Combined Ex-Forces) being linked to five, the JDL (Jewish Defence League) linked to four, and the BNP to just two cases. 'The Far Right groups, particularly the EDL (English Defence League) perniciously use the internet and social media to promote vast amounts of online hate', according to Fiyaz Mughal, director of Faith Matters (*Metro* 2013: 1).

The British National Party (BNP)

The BNP was formed in 1982 from a group splitting from within the National Front organisation. It conforms to the views of the far-right and is tough on crime and punishment and asserts that its policy will reduce demand on the criminal justice system, replace criminals' human rights with victims' rights and reintroduce corporal and capital punishment (BNP 2014). However, The British National Party regards itself as being a modern and progressive democratic party and accuses traditional parties of being totalitarian and elitist demonstrated by their ignoring of the true views of the common voter.

> On immigration, on capital punishment, on the surrender of British sovereignty to the EU and in numerous other areas, democracy has been absent as Labour, Tories and Lib-Dems conspire in election after election to offer the British people no real choice on such vital issues. (BNP 2014)

The BNP is also in favour of the fullest possible devolution: a bill of rights, removing anti-discrimination legislation, the Human Rights Act and all limits on free speech other than common law protection against inciting violence. The BNP is also concerned with Immigration and the threat to British values and the British identity, it calls for deportation of illegal and criminal immigrants and drastically reducing the number of asylum seekers allowed into the country,

> Given current demographic trends, we, the indigenous British people, will become an ethnic minority in our own country well within sixty years – and most likely sooner. (BNP 2014)

The BNP has been linked with campaigns against Britain's Muslim communities. For example, following the 9/11 terrorist attacks in the USA, the BNP distributed a leaflet where the name Islam was associated with intolerance, slaughter, looting, arson and molestation. In 2004 Nick Griffin, the then leader of the BNP, referred to Islam as 'an evil, wicked faith'. Following the 7/7 London bombings the BNP again produced a leaflet showing the damage caused and suggesting that 'maybe now it's time to start listening to the BNP'. The BNP has also written on Muslim paedophile gangs and emphasised the connection between British Muslims and the heroin trade (Copsey: 12). In one campaign Nick Griffin has worked with extremists from within Sikh and Hindu communities in Britain on an anti-Muslim campaign distributing material that contained phrases such as 'Islam is the biggest threat Britain has ever faced', and 'This is our country and you [Muslims] will never take it from us' (Harris 2001: 1). The campaign was condemned by all mainstream Sikh and Muslim spokespersons and organisations.

Hope (2007) reported, in a pre EDL era, that the BNP website received more hits than all the other political parties put together following a survey by Hitwise. At this point in time the BNP received seven times more hits than Labour and three times as many as the Conservatives. The web visitors were disproportionately middle class, however this interest was not seen in election results until a little later when in 2009 the BNP held over 50 local council seats and two Members of the European Parliament, but by 2013 the BNP had only two council seats (*The Huffington Post* 2013).

Mobilisation against Islamism and the perceived threat from mass immigration have been linked to the recent pursuit of a European identity and a movement to revitalise Europe's historic Christian identity (Zuquete 2008). Far-right parties based that promote anti-Muslim ideas have gained some popularity in countries where such views were not previously thought to have any form of popular support, such as the Netherlands and Scandinavia. It is argued by anti-extremist organisation 'Hope not hate' that this global rise of Far-Right extremism has evolved into an international network of and that this network is increasing in size, with 190 different counter-jihadist groups identified (Townsend 2012). Goldberg (2006) suggests that the thought of Muslims in Europe has become one with the thought of death and cultural extinction.

These networks may operate at different levels and in different ways; the 'Hope not hate' report cites examples such as the EDL and BNP collaborating regarding standing for election in Britain to avoid splitting their vote (Communities and Local Government 2009) and a well-funded US group, the International Civil Liberties Alliance, reportedly co-ordinate individuals and groups in 20 countries online and also held a counter-jihad conference in London (Townsend 2012).

Anti-Muslim action is not limited to Western countries. In Burma there is an ongoing anti-Muslim campaign with the Buddhist monk 'The Venerable Ashin Wirathu' likening his group to the EDL. He leads the '969' campaign which promotes the boycott Islamic businesses and stop inter-faith marriage to the majority Buddhist population. Many have been killed in riots, such as 43 people in the city of Meiktila in April 2013 and a year earlier in western Myanmar, 110 people died and 120,000 people were made homeless, most of them stateless Muslims (Blake 2013).

Britain First

The Britain First group is liked by over 590,000 Facebook users (at the time of writing) (Britain First 2014) a remarkable number given that his group was only established in 2011 by former members of the BNP (BBCNews 2014c). On their webpage, the opening banner asks you to 'sign up as an activist and join the fightback!' and features a video clips such as 'BF fighting to tale our country back' one with a subtitle 'we don't need terrorist we don't need homicide bombers' and a further banner at the bottom of the webpage 'Britain First fighting for a future for British Children!' The website is a platform to join and buy merchandise emphasising union jack and Knights Templar emblems and then link to social media sites such as Facebook for constant updates and messaging.

Hate Groups in the USA

FBI Hate crime statistics (2012) did not specify online hate but did report 5,796 physical hate crime incidents involving 6,718 offences. Of these hate crime offences 3,297 were categorised as racially motivated, with the following breakdown of the races that were subject to hate incidents:

- 66.1% were motivated by anti-black bias;
- 22.4% stemmed from anti-white bias;
- 4.1% resulted from anti-Asian/Pacific Islander bias;
- 4.1% were a result of bias against groups of individuals consisting of more than one race (anti-multiple races, group);
- 3.3% were motivated by anti-American Indian/Alaskan Native bias.

The above breakdown demonstrates a very low association with races typically associated with the Muslim faith. A second breakdown categorised hate crimes believed to be motivated by anti-religious feelings. This comprised 1,166 offences with those aimed at Muslims ranked second and being considerably less than those against those of the Jewish religion:

- 59.7% were anti-Jewish;
- 12.8% were anti-Islamic;
- 7.6% were anti-multiple religions, group;
- 6.8% were anti-Catholic;
- 2.9% were anti-Protestant;
- 1.0% were anti-Atheism/Agnosticism/etc.;
- 9. 2% were anti-other (unspecified) religion. Source: FBI Hate crime statistics (2012).

Pupcenoks and Mc Cabe (2013) note that there is considerable anti-Islamic sentiment in the USA and that groups such as the Tea Party and Stop the Islamisation of America are associated with this movement. The Southern Poverty Law Centre (SPLC 2014) claims that there are 939 different hate groups active within the USA and that this has more than doubled during the first 14 years of the new millennium. They ascribe this increase to:

> anger and fear over the nation's ailing economy, an influx of non-white immigrants, and the diminishing white majority, as symbolized by the election of the nation's first African-American president …. These factors also are feeding a powerful resurgence of the antigovernment "Patriot" movement, which in the 1990s led to a string of domestic terrorist plots, including the Oklahoma City bombing. (SPLC 2014: 1)

The Council on American Islamic Relations (2013) state that they found 37 groups who are mainly concerned with generating anti-Muslim hate and a further 32 groups who as a secondary purpose regularly supports such activities. The SPLC note that anti-Muslim hate groups tended to arise after the 9/11 attacks in 2001. One example of a self-starter or lone wolf anti-Muslim was Terry Jones – a Pastor in Florida who provoked international outrage with plans to burn the Quran on the anniversary of the 9/11 attack in 2010. He freely admitted that he had never read the Quran despite his accusation that the text was 'of the devil' (Krattenmaker 2010).

Hate groups tend to describe all followers of Islam as having an alien mindset and depict these as being of lower worth than their own values. Typically they in a similar fashion to their European counterparts portray Muslims as 'irrational, intolerant and violent, and their faith is frequently depicted as sanctioning paedophilia, marital rape and child marriage' (SPLC, 2014: 1).

These groups also conform to the populist or far-right typology outlined above, in that they are highly concerned with the threat to their way of life, which they perceive to be 'the America way of life' from the Muslim faith and sharia law being practiced within the USA. Muslim values are seen as a threat to democracy and civilisation. Again Islam is portrayed by these hate groups as a single point of view rather than a spectrum of beliefs and interpretations within a religion. 'These groups generally hold that Islam has no values in common with other cultures, is inferior to the West and is a violent political ideology rather than a religion' (SPLC 2014: 1).

Storm Front

Storm Front was one of the early online political groups, having strong white nationalist policies. The website was used from 1995, only five years after the group's foundation (Swain and Nieli 2003). The website's purpose is to attract those who are driven by the fear of the loss their cultural and ethnic position. It explicitly aims to defend the white race (Daniels 2007). The group is interesting in that it has been subject to policing in several countries: Google removed its index (web address) from its search engine in both France and Germany in 2002 following legislation in these countries to ban links to websites that were deemed to be denying the holocaust or to be white supremacist. More recently (2012) in Italy not only was the website blocked but four were arrested with regard to inciting racial hatred against members of the Jewish religion (Jewish Telegraphic Agency 2012).

The Tea Party

The TeaParty.org is as its full name suggests an online party that has local activists working to promote the party's ideas and plans. It was formed in 2004 and its main policy is to reduce the scope of government control over the lives of the American citizen and to get back to the self-reliant culture and ideals of the newly freed America after gaining independence from the United Kingdom. The Tea Party too is reacting to and attempting to defend their country from perceived threats to their culture. Barreto et al. (2011: 126) stated that members, 'hold a strong sense of out-group anxiety and a concern over the social and demographic changes in America' although they are not necessarily being associated with traditional right wing parties, it also chimes with some who have strong Christian and patriotic view-points.

> We stand by the Constitution as inherently conservative. We serve as a beacon to the masses that have lost their way, a light illuminating the path to the original intentions of our Founding Fathers. We must raise a choir of voices declaring

America must stand on the values which made us great. Only then will the politically blind see and deaf hear! By joining the Tea Party, you are taking a stand for our nation. You will be upholding the grand principles set forth in the U.S. Constitution and Bill of Rights. (Teaparty.org 2014: 1)

The Tea Party lists 'non-negotiable core beliefs' that include: Illegal aliens are to be deterred and treated as criminals, policies should concentrate on domestic business, the amount of government must be curtailed, taxation should be reduced as far as possible and as a consequent government spending should be cut drastically, the English language must be core, and traditional family values are encouraged. The Tea Party campaigns against reducing border security measures and the granting of amnesties. Given that it is by its very nature anti-government it is not surprising to see it attack the US president. However, Burghart and Zeskind (2010: 64) cite one Tea Party member, Mark Williams, referring to President Obama as an 'Indonesian Muslim turned welfare thug' on his blog. Mehdi (2014 np) also cites another Tea Party member Mark Williams for his stance against the Park51 project in Manhattan which intended to include building a mosque on the site of the World Trade Centre destroyed by the 9–11 attack:

"The monument would consist of a mosque for the worship of the terrorists' monkey-god and a 'cultural centre' to propagandise for the extermination of all things not approved by their cult", wrote Mark Williams, a spokesman for the right-wing Tea Party movement, on his blog. (Mehdi 2014 np)

Similarly Burghart and Zeskind (2010) and Mehdi (2014) cite Pamela Geller a guest speaker at a Tea Party Patriots-sponsored conference, 'We are at a point of having to take a stand against all Muslims. There is no good or bad Muslim. There is [sic] only Muslims and they are embedded in our government, military and other offices … What more must we wait for to take back this country of ours …' Burghart and Zeskind (2010: 70). Geller, the co-founder of Stop Islamisation of America organisation who also argued against the building of the mosque on the world trade centre site with a blog entitled 'Monster Mosque Pushes Ahead in Shadow of World Trade Center Islamic Death and Destruction' (Mehdi 2014, np).

Conclusion

The British Government has pursued a policy of multiculturalism and inclusion, along with the development of community engagement and the Big Society. However, poor economic conditions and the perceived threats arising from globalism including the loss of identity and religious warfare fuels hate crime and hate groups are experienced across all democratic developed countries. The manifestation of hate may be in the real world or online and as the trend is for many to live more and more in the virtual world, then the relative power of online hate will increase. Hate may be associated with membership of groups or from self-start individuals but in all cases the motivation stems from perceiving threats to their way of life. Policing online crime is still in its infancy and better individual and community-based social control, including via social media and online activism, may be a first step in combating online hate. Feldman and Littler (2014) found that Britain is inclusive but despite this there is a consistent level of anti-Muslim incidents. Pupcenoks and McCabe (2013) find that the differences of perception remain and suggest that inter group conflict will continue. Digital populism can access the majority of the population in developed countries while governments generally have limited powers to curb extremist and hate messages given the need to balance freedom of speech against hate speech and the difficulties of international ownership of the World Wide Web. This allows such groups to flourish. The situation requires both the Government and society to continually address this issue.

Further Reading

Copsey, N. 2003. Extremism on the Net: The Extreme Right and the Value of the Internet. In R. Gibson, P. Nixon and S. Ward (eds), *Political Parties and the Internet: Net Gain*. London: Routledge.

Franklin, R.A. 2009. The Hate Directory (15 February, release 13.1). [Online] Available at WWW.hatedirectory.com [accessed 19 November 2014].

Jackson, P. and Gable, G. (eds) 2011. *Far-Right.Com: Nationalist Extremism on the Internet*. Ilford: Searchlight and RNM Publications.

References

Barreto, M.A., Cooper, B.L., Gonzalez, B., Parker, S. and Towler, C. 2011. The Tea Party in the Age of Obama: Mainstream Conservatism or Out-Group Anxiety? In J. Go (ed.) *Rethinking Obama (Political Power and Social Theory, Volume 22)*, Emerald Group Publishing Limited, pp. 105–37 . DOI 10.1108/S0198–8719(2011)0000022011.

Bartlett, J., Birdwell, J. and Littler, M. 2011. The New Face of Digital Populism. Demos. [Online]. Available at: http://www.demos.co.uk/publications/thenewfaceofdigitalpopulism [accessed: 5 June 2012].

Bartlett, J. and Birdwell, J. 2013. Cumulative Radicalisation between the Far-Right and Islamist Groups in the UK: A Review of Evidence, Demos, 5 Nov; [Online]. Available at: www.demos.co.uk/files/Demos%20-%20 Cumulative%20Radicalisation%20-%205%20Nov%202013.pdf pp. 8–9. [accessed: 12 June 2012].

Bartlett, J., Littler, McDonnell, M.D. and Froio, C. 2014. New Political Actors in Europe: Beppe Grillo and the M5S. Demos. [Online]. Available at: http://www. demos.co.uk/publications/newpoliticalactorsineuropebeppegrilloandthems [accessed: 11 September 2014].

Basu, S. and Jones, R. 2007. Regulating Cyberstalking. *Journal of Information, Law and Technology* 2(1).

BBC News. 2014a. Vote 2014 European Parliament results. [Online] Available at: http://www.bbc.co.uk/news/events/vote2014/eu-election-results [accessed: 9 July 2014].

BBC News. 2014b. #BBCtrending: 'Sorry for algebra', and more #MuslimApologies by BBC Trending. [Online] Available at: http://www. bbc.co.uk/news/blogs-trending-29362370 [accessed: 25 September 2014].

BBC News. 2014c. BBCtrending: The rise of Britain First online. [Online]. Available at http://www.bbc.co.uk/news/magazine-29525146 [accessed: 2 December 2014].

BCS. 2012. Smith, K. (ed.), Lader, D., Hoare, J. and Lau, I. Hate Crime, Cyber-Security and the Experience of Crime among Children. Home Office Statistical Bulletin, Supplementary Volume 3 to Crime in England and Wales 2010/11, Home Office: March, p. 22.

Betz, H. 1998. Introduction in *The New Politics of the Right: Neo-populist Parties and Movements in Established Democracies*. Edited by H. Betz and S. Immerfall. Basingstoke: Macmillan.

Betz, H. 2007. Against the Green Totalitarianism: Anti-Islamic Nativism in contemporary Right Wing Populism in Western Europe. In C.S. Liang (ed.), *Europe for the European: The Foreign and Security Policy of the Populist Right*. Burlington, VT: Ashgate.

Bird, S. 2010. We Don't Care if you call us racists. We won't be beaten into Submission, *TheTimes*, 25 October.

Bishop, J. 2011. All's WELL that ends WELL: A Comparative Analysis of the Constitutional and Administrative Frameworks of Cyberspace and the United Kingdom. In A. Dudley-Sponaugle and J. Braman (eds), *Investigating Cyber Law and Cyber Ethics: Issues, Impacts and Practices*. Hershey, PA: IGI Global.

Bishop, J. 2012a. The Psychology of Trolling and Lurking: The Role of Defriending and Gamification for Increasing Participation in Online Communities Using Seductive Narratives. In H. Li (ed.), *Virtual Community Participation and Motivation: Cross-Disciplinary Theories*. Hershey, PA: IGI Global, pp. 170–76.

Bishop, J. 2012b. Scope and limitations in the Government of Wales Act 2006 for Tackling Internet Abuses in the Form of 'Flame Trolling'. *Statute Law Review* 33 (2): 207–16.

Bishop. J. 2013. The art of trolling law enforcement: A review and model for implementing 'flame trolling' legislation enacted in Great Britain (1981–2012), *International Review of Law, Computers & Technology*, 27 (3): 301–18.

Blake, M. 2013. Right-wing Buddhist leading the campaign to force Muslims out of Burma says he wants his group 'to be like the English Defence League'. *The Daily Mail*. 31 May. [Online]. Available at: http://www.dailymail.co.uk/news/article-2333858/Right-wing-Buddhist-leading-campaign-force-Muslims-Burma-says-wants-group-like-English-Defence-League.html [accessed: 15 May 2014].

BNP. 2014. The BNP website. [Online]. Available at: http://www.bnp.org.uk/policies/. [accessed: 22 September 2014].

Britain First. 2014. [Online]. Available at: https://www.britainfirst.org/home/. [accessed: 2 December 2014].

Burghart, D. and Zeskind, L. 2010. Tea Party Nationalism: A Critical Examination of the Tea Party Movement and the Size, Scope, and Focus of Its National Factions. Institute for Research & Education on Human Rights. Special report. Kansas City, MO, pp. 1–94.

Copsey, N. 2003. Extremism on the Net: The Extreme Right and the Value of the Internet. In R. Gibson, P. Nixon and S. Ward (eds) *Political Parties and the Internet: Net Gain*. London: Routledge, pp. 218–33.

Copsey. N., Dack. J., Littler, M. and Feldman, M. 2013. *Anti-Muslim Hate Crime and the Far Right*. Centre for fascist, anti-fascist and post-fascist studies, Teeside University.

Council on American Islamic Relations. 2014. [Online]. Available at http://www.cair.com/ [accessed: 21 October 2014].

Council on American Islamic Relations. 2013. Legislating fear Islamophobia and its impact in the United states. [Online]. Available at: http://www.cair.com/islamophobia/legislating-fear-2013-report.html [accessed: 21 October 2014].

Crown Prosecution Service. 2012. Hate Crimes and Crimes Against Older People Report 2011–12 (October 2012), pp. 15–16.

CSE&W (2012 and 2013). An Overview of hate crime in England and Wales. [Online] Available at: https://www.gov.uk/government/uploads/system/uploads/attachment-data/file/266358/hate-crime-2013.pdf. [accessed: 9 September 2014].

Daniels, J. 2007. Race, Civil Rights and Hate Speech in the Digital Era. In A. Everett (ed.) *Learning Race and Ethnicity: Youth and Digital Media*. Cambridge, MA: MIT Press.

Disha, I., James C., Cavendish, J.C. and King, R.D. 2011. Historical Events and Spaces of Hate: Hate Crimes against Arabs and Muslims in Post-9/11 America. *Social Problems*, 58 (1): 21–46.

Dixon, C. 2012. Nazi salute by a policeman that shocks Germany, *Daily Express*, 24 February, p. 17.

Eatwell, R. 2006. Community Cohesion and Cumulative Extremism in Contemporary Britain. *The Political Quarterly*, 77 (2): 205.

FBI Hate crime statistics. 2012. FBI. [Online]. Available at: http://www.fbi.gov/about-us/cjis/ucr/hate-crime/2012/topic-pages/incidents-andoffenses/incidentsandoffenses_final [accessed: 27 August 2014].

Feldman, M. and Littler M. 2014. Tell MAMA Reporting 2013/14: Anti-Muslim Overview, Analysis and 'Cumulative Extremism'. Centre for Fascist, Anti-fascist and Post-fascist Studies, Teesside University July. [Online]. Available at: Tellmamauk [accessed: 10 July 2014].

Goldberg, D. T. 2006. Radical Europeanization. *Ethic and Racial Studies*, 29 (2): 345–6.

Harris, P. 2001. Hindu and Sikh extremists in link with BNP. *The Observer*. [Online]. Available at: http://www.theguardian.com/uk/2001/dec/23/race.politics [accessed: 23 September 2014].

HMG. 2014. Challenge It, Report It, Stop It: Delivering the Government's Hate Crime Action Plan, HM Government, May. [Online]. Available at: https://www.gov.uk/government/publications/hate-crime-action-plan-challenge-it-report-it-stop-it [accessed: 3 September 2014].

Home Affairs Committee. 2012. Roots of violent radicalisation. [Online]. Available at: http://www.publications.parliament.uk/pa/cm201012/cmselect/cmhaff/1446/144605.htm#a10 [accessed: 14 June 2012].

Hope, C. 2007. BNP website is the most popular in politics. *The Telegraph*. [Online]. 13 September. Available at: http://www.telegraph.co.uk/news/uknews/1562960/BNP-website-is-the-most-popular-in-politics.html [accessed: 23 September 2014].

The Huffington Post. 2013. Local Elections: BNP Down To Two Councillors, [Online]. Available at: http://www.huffingtonpost.co.uk/2013/05/03/local-elections-bnp-down-to-two-councillors_n_3208959.html? [accessed: 22 September 2014].

Husbands, C.T. 2009. Country Report Great Britain. In Bertelsmann Stiftung (ed.) *Strategies for Combating Right-Wing Extremism in Europe*. Gütersloh: Verlag Bertelsmann Stiftung, p. 264.

Iganski,P. 2008. *Hate Crime and the City*. Chicago: University of Chicago press.

Jeeves, P. 2014. Troll jailed for vile post about teacher, *Daily Express*, 5 June, p. 18.

Jewish Telegraphic Agency. 2012. Italian white supremacists arrested for inciting anti-Semitism. [Online]. Available at: http://www.jta.org/2012/11/18/

news-opinion/world/italian-white-supremacists-arrested-for-inciting-anti-semitism. [accessed: 3 December 2014].

Jolly, D. 2011. The Netherlands: Anti-Muslim Speech Is Found Offensive but Legal. *New York Times* 24 June: A6(L). [Online]. Avilable at: Infotrac Newsstand. Web. 10 Oct. 2014. http://go.galegroup.com/ps/i.do?id=GAL E%7CA259647471&v=2.1&u=glamuni&it=r&p=STND&sw=w&asid=e6 0f849344ef63af2a61cf8847ab0e6a [accessed: 1 October 2014].

Krattenmaker, T. 2010. Get to know a Muslim, rather than hate one. *USA Today*. 27 Sept: [Online] 23A. Infotrac Newsstand. Web. 10 Oct. Available at: http://go.galegroup.com/ps/i.do?id=GALE%7CA238131082&v=2.1&u= glamuni&it=r&p=STND&sw=w&asid=939531a8372d4d99b80188cdd609 cf0f. [accessed: 17 October 2014].

Lowles, N. 2015. HOPE not Hate launches 2014 'State of Hate' report. [Online]. Available at: http://www.hopenothate.org.uk/blog/nick/hope-not-hate-launches-2014-state-of-hate-report-4212 [accessed: 15 January 2015].

McAdam, D., Tarrow S. and Tilley, C. 2001. *The Dynamics of Contention*. Cambridge: Cambridge University Press.

McCall, R. 2003. Harassment and Cyberstalking: Victim access to crisis, referral and support services in Canada concepts and recommendations (5 October). [Online]. Available at: http://www.vaonline.org/ [accessed: 12 August 2014].

Mehdi, H. 2010. Fear and loathing in Manhattan: opponents of the so-called Ground Zero mosque are giving the perpetrators of the 11 September attacks exactly what they wanted: a clash of civilisations. Muslims who once walked happily on New York's streets now feel hate in the air. New Statesman. 1 Nov. [Online]. 22+. Infotrac Newsstand. Web. Available at: http://go.galegroup. com/ps/i.do?id=GALE%7CA242669675&v=2.1&u=glamuni&it=r&p= STND&sw=w&asid=cffdf295d82cf02265a1d579c995a4ba [accessed: 15 October 2014].

Metro. 2013. Anti-muslim-hate-crimes-rise-across-england-in-2013, *Metro*. [Online]. Friday 27 December. Available at: http://metro.co.uk/2013/12/27/ anti-muslim-hate-crimes-rise-across-england-in-2013–4243074/ [accessed: 9 July 2014].

ONS. 2011. How people are living in England and Wales. [Online]. Available at: http://www.ons.gov.uk/ons/rel/census/2011-census/key-statistics-and-quick-statistics-for-wards-and-output-areas-in-england-and-wales/sty-how-people-are-living-in-england-and-wales.html. [accessed: 30 September 2014].

Persuad, R. 2014. Inside the Mind of the Twitter Troll. [Online]. Available at: http:// rajpersaud.wordpress.com/2014/10/07/inside-the-mind-of-the-twitter-troll-by-raj-persaud-frcpsych-consultant-psychiatrist/ [accessed: 27 October 2014].

Pilditch, D. 2014. Gaza war Sparks UK hate crime, *Daily Express*, 8, July 28.

Pupcenoks, J. and McCabe, R. 2013. The Rise of the Fringe: Right Wing Populists, Islamists and the Politics in the UK. *Journal of Muslim Minority Affairs*, 33 (2): 171–84.

Salter, M. and Bryden, C. 2009. I can see you: Harassment and stalking on the Internet, *Information & Communications Technology Law*, 18 (2): 99–122.

Southern Poverty Law Centre. 2014. [Online]. Available at: http://www.splcenter.org/what-we-do/hate-and-extremism [accessed: 22 August 2014].

Spence, A. 2014. Internet trolls facing two years' jail in battle against 'baying cybermob', *Times*. [Online]. Available at: http://www.thetimes.co.uk/tto/news/uk/crime/article4240970.ece. [accessed: 2 October 2014].

Swain, C.M. and Nieli, R. (eds). 2003. Don Black. *Contemporary Voices of White Nationalism in America*. Cambridge: Cambridge University Press.

Teaparty.org. 2014. [Online]. Available at: http://www.teaparty.org/about-us/. [accessed: 24 September 2014].

Wardrop, M. 2009. Nine Rioters Arrested After Luton Protest Turned Violent. *The Telegraph*, 25 May.

YouGov. 2012. Survey results. [Online]. Available at: http://cdn.yougov.com/cumulus_uploads/document/h8vxb8d4l3/YG-Archive-221012-EDL-Toplines.pdf. [accessed: 30 September 2014].

Zuquete, J. P. 2008. The European Extreme Right and Islam a New Direction. *Journal of Political Ideologies*, 13 (3): 321–44.

Chapter 5

The Media Impact of Online Islamophobia: An Analysis of the Woolwich Murder

Mohammed Rahman

Crime is considered as a crucial component of the omnipresence of mass media communication (Ericson et al. 1991; Williams and Dickinson 1993; Ericson 1995; Pearson 2002). The reporting is increasingly accessed via the domain of the internet – an influential and fixed 'public sphere' (Butsch 2007) which plays a complex and contradictory role in public deliberation. The media often reports on criminality as it has the legitimate right to do so (Brookes et al. 2015). However, it is believed that the media can 'sensationalise' crime (Karatzogianni 2012) so as to create a 'moral panic' (Cohen 1972; Waddington 1986; Watney 1987; Goode and Ben-Yehuda 1994), and that this method is used as a controlling mechanism to regulate the behaviour of public. Brookes et al. highlight that crime news is not only consumed online but is 'reproduced, recycled and discussed in this digital environment', most notably through social media sites (2015: 2). Twitter and Facebook are examples of social media sites that have had significant impact upon Islamophobia.

When Allen (2012) reviewed evidence relating to the representation of Muslims and Islam in the British media, he described the impact as 'contentious' and 'debatable'. He stated that: 'research has shown that the media plays a fundamental role in the formulation and establishment of popular views and attitudes in society' (2012: 3). The print media, such as newspapers and their online duplicates, consist of periodical publication of informative articles on a wide range of topics, including crime. As newspaper companies fundamentally focus on selling newspapers to increase their profit (Beckett and Sasson 2000), a process McManus (1994) notes as 'market-driven journalism', the 'reporting of crime is, of necessity, selective' (Peelo 2005: 26). Based on this perception Buckler and Travis state that:

> news organization decisions are based on journalist and news editor perceptions of what type of stories resonate with the general public. Accordingly, the news production process becomes characterized as an exercise in market strategy

rather than a presentation of an accurate summary of local, national, and world events. (Buckler and Travis 2005: 1)

So too, it is clear that the media do not publish or broadcast every criminal act that is within the public domain, but are selective of the kinds of crimes, criminals and circumstances upon which they report. Some criminal acts are chosen over others because of their 'newsworthiness' (Brookes et al. 2015) – in other words, those aspects of a crime that journalists argue make for a good news story, a judgment which is, in turn, a product of their 'newsroom culture' (Scraton et al. 1991: 111; see also Wilson et al. 2010: 154) and that the 'pursuit of market and organizational imperatives often results in crime coverage that is disproportionate to the reality of the crime problem' (Buckler and Salanas, 2009: 719). Often this encourages 'media stereotypes', which when applied, contributes 'to the maximization of profits for the corporation' (Enteman 2011: 22). Stereotypes are ultimately used to stigmatise a particular identity. This reflection is evident in the study of Poole (2002), who reports press coverage relating to Muslims and Islam in British national newspapers had increased by approximately 270% over preceding decade, of which 91% was deemed negative. Poole's findings also reveal that 50% of all the analysed coverage referred to Muslims and/or Islam as posing a 'threat'. Furthermore, a significant majority – 84%, represented Islam and Muslims either as 'likely to cause damage or danger' or as 'operating in a time of intense difficulty of danger' (Poole 2002).

Chermak (1995) considered that news organisations assessed newsworthiness of a crime based on (i) the violent or heinous nature of the offence, (ii) demographic factors of the victim and offender (age, race, gender, income and socioeconomic status), (iii) characteristics of the incident producers (the news agency), (iv) the uniqueness of the event, and (v) event salience (for example, is the offence a local event). With Chermak's analysis in mind, it is clear as to why a crimes such as 'terrorism', would be considered newsworthy. So too, it presents the opportunity of terrorism becoming a crime that is reported disproportionality from its reality, hence resulting to oversimplified assumptions of particular identities. Since 1970, there have been 69 terrorist attacks in Great Britain involving violence or fatality (GOV.UK, 2014). Periodically there have also been prevented, failed or aborted attacks, which would also be classified under either the Prevention of Terrorism Act 1974, Terrorism Act 2000 or Terrorism Act 2006 (Terrorism Act 2006). Most recent and notable in the UK, was the horrific murder of fusilier Lee Rigby.

The Murder of Lee Rigby and the Anti-Muslim Backlash

Lee Rigby was a 25-year-old drummer who was murdered on 22 May 2013, in Woolwich, England. From Middleton, Greater Manchester, Rigby was also a machine-gunner in the 2nd Battalion of the Royal Regiment of Fusiliers and served in Cyprus, Germany and Afghanistan before working in recruitment and assisting with duties in the Tower of London. He was attacked whilst returning back to the Woolwich barracks from working at the Tower.

The attack of drummer Lee Rigby took place approximately at 14:20 in Wellington Street, near the perimeter of the Royal Artillery Barracks where Rigby was stationed. Rigby, who arrived at Woolwich Arsenal Station at 14:10, was wearing a 'Help for Heroes' hoodie, and was walking down Wellington Street towards the Barracks. He crossed the road to head towards a shop and it was then when two men, who were later identified as Michael Adebolajo and Michael Adebowale, rammed their Vauxhall Tigra car at him at a speed between 30–40 mph, subsequently knocking him onto the pavement. Adebolajo and Adebowale immediately got out the car and attacked Rigby with a knife and a meat cleaver. It was later revealed that they attempted to behead him. Instantaneously, after the attack, several witnesses shielded Rigby's lifeless body from further injury. A cub-scout leader from Cornwall by the name of Ingrid Loyau-Kennett exited from a bus with the intention of providing first aid (Hickman 2013). After discovering Rigby had died, she engaged with Adebolajo in conversation. Shortly after, Adebolajo was filmed by a bystander and said:

> The only reason we have killed this man today is because Muslims are dying daily by British soldiers. And this British soldier is one ... By Allah, we swear by the almighty Allah we will never stop fighting you until you leave us alone. So what if we want to live by the Sharia in Muslim lands? Why does that mean you must follow us and chase us and call us extremists and kill us? ... when you drop a bomb do you think it hits one person? Or rather your bomb wipes out a whole family? ... Through many passages in the (Arabic) Koran we must fight them as they fight us ... I apologise that women had to witness this today but in our lands women have to see the same. You people will never be safe. Remove your governments, they don't care about you. You think David Cameron is gonna get caught in the street when we start busting our guns? Do you think politicians are going to die? No, it's going to be the average guy, like you and your children. So get rid of them. Tell them to bring our troops back ... leave our lands and you will live in peace. (Michael Adebolajo, extract from *The Telegraph* 2013)

The above statement from Adebolajo recorded on amateur footage revealed his justification for the horrific attack, which evidently makes it an act of terrorism. Within 10–15 minutes of the attack, the Metropolitan Police had deployed unarmed and authorised firearms police officers. At that point, Adebolajo was still holding the meat cleaver whilst Adebowale was armed with a revolver. Armed police acted effectively by wounding and subsequently disarming both men by shooting at them in a total of eight times. On 19 December 2013, almost seven months after the attack, both men were found guilty of the murder. On 26 February 2014, Adebolajo and Adebowale were sentenced to life imprisonment. Adebolajo – who was considered the mastermind of the attack was given a whole life order with no parole, and the younger Adebowale was given a minimum term of 45 years in prison. In December 2014, both men lost their legal challenges against their sentences. The recorded amateur footage became a crucial asset from a 'newsworthiness' perspective, as an uncut version of the footage was circulated by ITV news in their live 6.30pm news bulletin. This caused immediate outrage from the general public, who followed up their resentment with official complaints (Halliday 2013).

Moreover, an anti-Muslim backlash occurred in the United Kingdom in the aftermath of the attack and the amateur footage broadcasted by ITV, and the subsequent newspaper publications that made reference to the footage was crucial for the increase in Islamophobic incidents (Taylor and Siddique 2013). The group 'Hope not Hate' reported that within four days of the attack, there were 200 Islamophobic incidents, including attacks on 10 mosques (Taylor and Siddique 2013). The government-funded project – Tell MAMA (Measuring anti-Muslim Attacks) – reported over 200 anti-Muslim incidents, of which included 125 internet based incidents, 17 physical attacks, and 11 attacks on mosques. Of note, three weeks after the attack, in June 2013, a senior Metropolitan Police officer confirmed an eight-fold increase of Islamophobic incidents after Mr Rigby's death, and acknowledged that actual figures may be higher due to under-reporting (Sheils 2013).

Indeed, understanding the role of the media and the subsequent 'moral panic' are important when contexualising the role of the media and the reporting of terrorist incidents. As a result, the author of this chapter embarked upon a content analysis of online newspapers which aimed to examine the use of news headlines and news coverage of the Woolwich attack, by observing a three-week data set. The three-week range started from the date of Mr Rigby's attack – 22 May 2013 up to 12 June 2013. This range was purposely considered to capture initial reporting's of the incident as it was felt that the 'newsworthiness' (Jewkes 2004) of Mr Rigby's death would be particularly high. This in turn could provide the scope for disproportionate reports. In order to search for online newspaper articles, the electronic database Nexis was used.

Nexis is an electronic database which houses all major British newspapers, including both national and regional titles, some 2,000 global newspapers, plus copies from newswires and newsletters. The terms *Woolwich*, *terrorism*, *Muslim* and *Islam* were key search terms for generating all UK regional and UK broadsheet outputs. The content analysis excluded the output of tabloid newspapers. Although they are considered to be more influential in democracy, there have been 'global debates' over their 'media standards' (Sparks and Tulloch 2000), as was felt more recently when the controversy of unethical tabloid reporting reached its peak in the UK, when the biggest selling English language newspaper in the world – the *News of the World* closed production in July 2011, following revelations of on-going phone hacking scandals. In total the search of UK broadsheet and regional newspapers generated 922 results, from which excluded all duplicates and applied the inclusion criteria – the 'custom' three-week period.

There is a clear limitation of using Nexis for this particular examination: as the program holds a restriction for searchable words, thus the accuracy of the information is not assured. However, literature based on the international analysis of terrorism highlights the tendency of terrorist cases being communicated through a variety of media outlets (Freedman and Thussu 2012) – and evidence surrounding 'newsworthiness' (Jewkes 2004) would therefore denote that cases of terrorism involving Western countries are perhaps amongst the most likely to be reported. After identifying all online newspaper sources, a coding program – Nvivo – was used to interpret the findings from the Nexis search. Nvivo is electronic based qualitative data analysis software designed for working with text or multimedia based information, where extensive analysis of small or large data volumes is required. Using Nvivo to process the outputs from Nexis allowed the possibility to create coded themes. A standard coding search revealed that amongst the most top 50 frequent terms were *Muslim*, *terrorist*, *terrorism*, *Islam* and *Islamic*. Subsequently, these five terminologies were finalised as themes for the analysis. Of note, to discover such term in the study of Islamophobia is not unusual or esoteric as the content analysis findings of Akbarzadeh and Smith identified the term 'Islamic terrorism' (2005: 23) as a key finding in their analysis of the representation of Muslims and Islam in Australian media.

Out of the total results, only a selected volume of broadsheet (four) and regional (five) newspapers (723 online newspapers) were used for the analysis, as it showed that these daily newspapers provided extensive coverage of the Woolwich attack during the chosen timeframe, and more importantly they supported the themes that emerged from the Nvivo analysis. It is important to note that this chapter does not intend to demonise the newspapers in analysis, nor does it aim to fully represent the British print media. Rather it aims to shed further light into considering how the rhetoric's used in their outputs may have influenced the how Muslims were being viewed after the murder of Lee Rigby.

Results

Based on the selected UK broadsheet and regional newspapers that gave extensive coverage to the murder of Lee Rigby and the aftermath of the attack, the search identified in total 723 online newspaper articles (see Table 5.1). In relation to the broadsheet findings, there were a total of 597 articles, with the most output from *The Telegraph* (n = 244, 40.9%), second *The Times* (n = 150, 25.1%), third *The Independent* (n = 137, 22.9%) and fourth *The Guardian* (n = 66, 11.1%). Regarding the UK regional newspapers, there were a total of 126 articles, with the most output from *The Scotsman* (n = 38, 29.5%), second *Scotland on Sunday* (n = 25, 19.4%), third *The Yorkshire Post* (n = 23, 17.8%), fourth *The Belfast Telegraph* (n = 22, 17.1%) and fifth *The Evening Standard* (n = 21, 16.3%).

Table 5.1   Total Sample of Articles

Newspapers	n	%
Broadsheet		
The Guardian	66	11.1
The Independent	137	22.9
The Telegraph	244	40.9
The Times	150	25.1
Total	**597**	**100.0**
Regional		
Belfast Telegraph	22	17.1
Evening Standard	21	16.3
Scotland on Sunday	25	19.4
The Scotsman	38	29.5
Yorkshire Post	23	17.8
Total	**126**	**100.0**
Total Sample	**723**	**100.0**

Turning to examine the term Muslim (see Table 5.2) – for broadsheet newspapers, the term was most frequent in *The Telegraph* articles (n = 444, 45%), second *The Independent* (n = 222, 22%), third *The Times* (n = 205, 21%) and fourth *The Guardian* (n = 119, 12%). In relation to regional newspapers, the term was most frequent in *Scotland on Sunday* (n = 118, 36%), second the *Evening Standard* (n = 65, 20%), third *The Scotsman* (n = 55, 17%), fourth the *Belfast Telegraph* (n = 36, 19%) and fifth, the *Yorkshire Post* (n = 30, 9%). Through analysis, it is revealed that the majority of the newspapers within the sample initially reported the Woolwich murder based around press comments from 'Muslim' community members. For instance, *The Times* and *The Telegraph* reported how the 'Muslim Council of Britain' within hours of the attack was quick to distance Islam from the incident ('Sickening, deluded and unforgivable': Horrific attack brings terror to London's streets', *The Times*, 23 May 2013; 'Woolwich attack: terrorist proclaimed 'an eye for an eye' after attack', *The Telegraph*, 24 May 2013):

Table 5.2   Total search hits of 'Muslim'

Newspapers	n	%
Broadsheet		
The Guardian	119	12
The Independent	222	22
The Telegraph	444	45
The Times	205	21
Total	**990**	**100**
Regional		
Belfast Telegraph	36	19
Evening Standard	65	20
Scotland on Sunday	118	36
The Scotsman	55	17
Yorkshire Post	30	9
Total	**304**	**100**
Overall Total	**1294**	**100**

Indeed, the British Prime Minister David Cameron revealed how: 'the strength and unity of response from Muslim community leaders' was evident shortly after chairing the emergency Cobra meeting following the murder ('Sickening, deluded and unforgivable': Horrific attack brings terror to London's streets', *The Independent*, 23 May 2013). Regional newspapers also provided coverage of Muslim community leaders from various regions condemning the attack. Coverage of such nature from newspaper outlets may be used as a 'control mechanism' (Chomsky 2008), for the attempt to alleviate any fears communities may be experiencing about reprisal attacks. This was revealed by the London Evening Standard, who considered how Muslim groups were too quick to condemn the incident without obtaining factual information, as it reports that; 'mainstream Muslim groups have been quick to condemn the killing, more so after than 7/7. But we do not know enough about their [attackers] background and influences' ('The threat from lone wolf terrorism', *London Evening Standard*, 23 May 2013). Of note, it is considered that terrorism incidents can obscure and conflate arguments that sometime lead to counter-productive assertions embedded within the narrative that some people are sympathetic to terrorism causes if they try to rationalise terrorist behaviour and do not condemn certain actions.

On the day of the attack Robinson reported on the 6.00pm BBC news bulletin that 'the attackers were of Muslim appearance' ('Woolwich attack: as it happened May 23', *The Telegraph*, 22 May 2013). Robinson later apologised (Hope 2013) after receiving public complaints recorded by media regulator Ofcom. This can be seen as the first phase of 'moral panic' within the Muslim communities, especially if the wider population are unaware of how the theological aspects of Islam are governed. Indeed, Allen found that 64% of the British public claimed that they do know about Muslims and what they do know is 'acquired through the media' (2005: 10).

Turning to analyse the terms *terrorism* and *terrorist* (see Table 5.3), for broadsheet newspapers, the terms were most frequent in *The Telegraph* articles (n = 420, 68%), second *The Times* (n = 113, 18%), third *The Guardian* (n = 48, 8%) and fourth *The Independent* (n = 40, 6%). In relation to regional newspapers, the term was most frequent in Scotland on Sunday (n = 101, 46%), second *The Scotsman* (n = 51, 23%), third the *Evening Standard* (n = 31, 14%), fourth the *Yorkshire Post* (n = 20, 9%) and fifth the *Belfast Telegraph* (n = 17, 8%).

Table 5.3   Total search hits of 'terrorism/terrorists'

Newspapers	n	%
Broadsheet		
The Guardian	48	8
The Independent	40	6
The Telegraph	420	68
The Times	113	18
Total	**621**	**100**
Regional		
Belfast Telegraph	17	8
Evening Standard	31	14
Scotland on Sunday	101	46
The Scotsman	51	23
Yorkshire Post	20	9
Total	**220**	**100**
Overall Total	**841**	**100**

Two days after the murder, *The Telegraph* headlined an article: 'Woolwich shows that Muslim leaders have learned how to respond to terrorism'. In the main body of the same article it is reported 'Muslims have had to embark on this learning curve without any help from the media'. The article ended by stating: 'Muslim leaders finally sound like they are on side. Our side' ('Woolwich shows that Muslim leaders have learned how to respond to terrorism', *The Telegraph*, 24 May 2013). Bryant and Oliver (2009) theorise how the 'media effects' of generalisation provide disproportionate and hostile social reactions to a condition, person or groups defined as 'a threat to societal values, involving stereotypical media representations and leading to demands for greater social control and creating a spiral or reaction' (Murji 2006: 251).

It is believed that the headline and the contents in the article clearly categorised the general Muslim community with acts of terrorism. In doing so, it led to 'demands for greater social control', which was clearly highlighted by various Muslim leaders condemning the attack, subsequently creating a 'spiral or reaction' (Murji 2006: 251) from far right groups like the British National Party, who to staged demonstrations under the banner 'United Against Muslim Terror' ('EDL marches on Newcastle as attacks on Muslims increase tenfold in the wake of Woolwich machete attack which killed Drummer Lee Rigby', *Independent*, 25 May 2013). Allen argues that such tactics can increase feelings of 'insecurity, suspicion and anxiety amongst non-Muslims' (2012: 10).

Analysing the terms *Islam* and *Islamic* (see Table 5.4), for broadsheet newspapers revealed yet again that the terms were most frequent in *The Telegraph* articles (n = 424, 46%), second *The Independent* (n = 274, 29%), third *The Times* (n = 158, 17%) and fourth *The Guardian* (n = 73, 8%). In relation to regional newspapers, the terms were most frequent in Scotland on Sunday articles (n = 118, 33%), second the *Evening Standard* (n = 93, 26%), third the *Belfast Telegraph* (n = 62, 18%), fourth *The Scotsman* (n = 41, 12%) and fifth, the *Yorkshire Post* (n = 40, 11%).

As highlighted above, thus far British broadsheet and regional newspaper outlets have predominantly reported the murder of Lee Rigby within a sensitive and professional manner, with the exception of a handful of articles that have publicised generalised statements of Muslim that have certainly caused forced social reactions whether in condemnation or retaliation. In relation to the analysis of the terms *Islam* and *Islamic*, it was revealed that some newspapers within the sample quoted members from a certain political backgrounds who aligned the murder with the ideology of Islam. For instance, former Prime Minister Tony Blair stated 'there is a problem within Islam' ('Tony Blair: Woolwich attack shows there is a problem "within Islam"', *The Telegraph*, 2 June 2013; 'Tony Blair: Woolwich attack shows there is a "problem within Islam"', *The Independent*, 2 June 2013).

Table 5.4   Total search hits of 'Islam/Islamic'

Newspapers	n	%
Broadsheet		
The Guardian	73	8
The Independent	274	29
The Telegraph	424	46
The Times	158	17
Total	**929**	**100**
Regional		
Belfast Telegraph	62	18
Evening Standard	93	26
Scotland on Sunday	118	33
The Scotsman	41	12
Yorkshire Post	40	11
Total	**354**	**100**
Overall Total	**1283**	**100**

Tony Blair referred to the influence of religion in violent murder. Interestingly, Tony Blair has previously referred to the role of his Christian faith in his decision to go to war in Iraq, stating that he had prayed about the issue, and said live in an interview with Michael Parkinson, broadcast on ITV1 on 4 March 2006 that God would judge him for his decision: 'I think if you have faith about these things, you realise that judgment is made by other people ... and if you believe in God, it's made by God as well' (BBC 2006). Along with Blair, former Home Secretary Jack Straw, who was also a supporter of the Iraq War, was quick to point out that the 'ideology' [of Islam] 'inspired such Stone Age savagery' ('The far right: BNP and EDL mobilise as mainstream leaders strive to contain backlash', *The Independent*, 23 May).

All of the broadsheet outlets in analysis reported that the English Defence League – a far-right anti-Muslim street protest movement in the United Kingdom, held 'Islam' accountable for the attack. Stephen Yaxley-Lennon, publicly known as Tommy Robinson – the former leader of the EDL argued that the attack was due to 'political Islam' that 'is spreading across this country'. Furthermore, Robinson argued: 'They're [Muslims] chopping our heads off. This is Islam. That's what we've seen today. They've cut one of our Army's heads off on the streets of London. Our next generation are being taught through schools that Islam is a religion of peace. It's not. It never has been. What you saw today is Islam' ('Woolwich attack: as it happened May 23', *The Telegraph*, 23 May 2013; 'Anti-Muslim reprisals after Woolwich attack', *The Guardian*, 23 May 2013; 'Two arrested after Braintree and Gillingham mosque attacks', *The Independent*, 23 May 2013; 'The Muslim Community Responds to the attack', *The Times*, 24 May 2013).

The comments made by Robinson resulted in mass demonstrations by the far-right group and subsequent fire bombings of several mosques in England ('EDL marches on Newcastle as attacks on Muslims increase tenfold in the wake of Woolwich machete attack which killed Drummer Lee Rigby', *The Independent*, 28 May 2013). Indeed, based on the ideology of the EDL and their frequent association with violence, their actions during the aftermath of the murder could to stoke up fear and hate. Crucially, as highlighted above, this was influenced by mainly broadsheet press, which undoubtedly resulted in the second, and more severe, phase of moral panic amongst Muslim communities. All the above evidence corroborates with the work of Said (1981: 56) who in his book 'Covering Islam', states that the definitions of Islam today are predominately negative.

Discussion

This chapter sets out to consider whether, and to what extent, the print media reporting the murder of Lee Rigby may have influenced the rise in fear and moral panic against Muslim communities. The discussion below will address these aims respectively. From the results, there is a clear trend of the high report activity by certain newspapers. The analysis revealed that *The Telegraph* produced the highest number of articles for all UK broadsheet newspapers by a wide margin and *The Scotsman* produced the highest number of articles for all the UK regional newspapers. Nonetheless the high outputs from the newspapers reveal how they were able to provide extensive coverage of the Woolwich incident. For instance, immediately after the attack, *The Telegraph* presented online, 'timeline' coverage of the incident, by displaying a list of events in chronological order.

Information within the timeline included images of the crime scene, reports from journalists, interviews from witnesses and passers-by, pictures of the perpetrators, amateur footage of the perpetrators and images of the victim. Due to the nature of the incident, the majority of the initial information was descriptive accounts of the event. Crucially this method of news reporting allowed readers to consume disturbing images, videos and text within one particular source. Indeed Whyte-Venables (2012) suggests audiences may interpret news as a risk signal. Psychologists and primatologists have shown that humans and apes frequently monitor the environment for information that may indicate the possibility of physical danger or threat to the individual's social position. This receptiveness to risk signals is a powerful and virtually universal survival mechanism.

While high outputs can be a form of proactive journalism, it also presents the opportunity of controversy. Some of the examples provided in the results section, displayed how comments from certain political influence may have caused the rise in fear of Islam and Muslims more generally. Not only did this cause harm and distress to Muslim communities, it also provided the opportunity for the 'stigmatisation' of media outlets.

Awan (2014) study also reveals how social networking sites such as Twitter have been used by offenders following the murder of Lee Rigby, to make direct threats against Muslim communities (BBC News 2013). Indeed the online newspaper, analysed for this study, 'reproduced, recycled and discussed' (Brookes et al. 2015: 2) their information in various digital environments, namely in popular social media sites such as Facebook and Twitter, that allow the 'sharing' of online information. The comments from former EDL leader – Tommy Robinson, who held 'Islam' accountable for the murder of Lee Rigby were publicised in articles from *The Guardian*, *The Independent*, *The Times* and *The Telegraph*. All four newspaper outlets have online 'sharing' facilities to major social media sites, thus allowing readers and subscribers to circulate articles to an uncountable online audience.

Of note, all four-broadsheet newspapers have verified Twitter accounts, containing a combination of over 6 million 'followers'. Their online accounts work on the principle of 'tweeting' articles, which arguably forms as a method of market-driven journalism (McManus 1994). Articles and website URL's of the Woolwich attack were posted, yet again revealing the 'newsworthiness' of the incident and thus enabling the majority of the British public to learn more about Muslims (Allen 2005) and potentially increasing the feelings of insecurity, suspicion and anxiety amongst non-Muslims (Allen 2012). This process of media reproduction and discussion inevitably allowed the opportunity of Islamophobic incidents as Twitter users made direct threats that included burning down mosques and killing Muslims (Feldman et al. 2013). Awan (2014) was able to capture Islamophobic tweets from several Twitter accounts that propagated violence against the Muslim population, one of which said: 'BLOW UP EVERY MOSQUE' (Anonymised user 2013). This particular tweet received the supports of 'retweets' and was also 'favourited' by other users.

In response to the question: 'Did print media influence moral panic amongst Muslim communities?' – clearly it did. As revealed, some of the print media in analysis became indirect influences for moral panic amongst Muslim communities. Within hours of the attacks, the Muslim Council of Britain was 'quick' to distance the doctrine of Islam from the incident. As reported by several regional newspapers, various Muslim community leaders on the day of the attack also condemned the incident. It is of the belief that vocal disapprovals of the attack by Muslim individuals and group were 'pressured' by reporters, a 'media effect' (Bryant and Oliver 2009) by the press so as to be able to demonstrate social control and cohesion within a volatile society.

This proved to be the case, as the stories of the attack were replicated online to social media networks, thus causing a strong backlash of Islamophobic threats and incidents. Through a substantial amount of online evidence, Awan (2014) was able to provide a typology of the characteristics of Islamophobic offenders. He considers that the majority of Twitter incidents of Islamophobia were conducted by 'the reactive' type, a person 'who is following a major incident, such as Woolwich', who will then 'begin an online campaign' (Awan 2014: 125). Below are examples of some tweets posted by 'the reactives' on the day of Lee Rigby's murder:

sick of these sand niggers thinking they can do what they want, fuck off back to your caves #letsstartracewar. (Anonymised user 2013)

That has to be enough with them Islams fuck them all back to the Middle East and let the bomb each other, They have it too good here #Pakis. (Anonymised user 2013)

A wave of 'hate crimes' began (Awan 2014) and although actual figures of anti-Muslim incidents may be unclear due to under-reporting, at least a dozen mosques were attacked. During that period, it was reported that bombs were planted in several mosques within the West Midlands, England. However it was later revealed that they were unrelated to the Woolwich incident and were planted by Pavlo Lapshyn. Lapshyn killed pensioner Mohammed Saleem on the 29 April 2013, five days after his arrival from Ukraine, and attempted three bombings on local mosques by targeting the Friday prayers of 'Jummah', which are the most populated services of the week. The first homemade bomb was laid outside a mosque in Walsall on the 21 June, which led to home evacuations. The second was planted in a mosque in Wolverhampton on the 28 June and the third was in Tipton on the 12 July (Dodd 2013).

Lapshyn has since been convicted of the murder of Mr Saleem and the explosions, and was sentenced to 40 years in prison in October 2013. Some online social media users later praised Lapshyn for his crimes and far-right ideology, hence further increasing hostility, bias and negative attitudes towards the Muslim population. Law enforcements current struggle to combat online Islamophobia (Awan, 2014) is disadvantaged by criminal legislation. McLaughlin states, 'hate crimes need to be acknowledged in criminal legislation as different because they inflict distinctive harms upon their victims as well as to society' (2006: 196). Thus, a discrete offence category would help strengthen the ongoing process of identifying of hate crime and online Islamophobia.

Conclusion

Hetherington states that 'anything which threatens people's peace, prosperity and well-being is news and likely to make headlines' (1985: 1). As revealed, the Woolwich attack momentarily threatened peace and prosperity and attracted 'newsworthiness'. The findings in this chapter indicate that the horrific murder of solider Lee Rigby caused extreme social tension in various Muslim communities, resulting to physical and violent encounters. The flexibility of the cyber-world allows instant networking opportunities, involving a large audience. In doing so, information from online newspapers was consumed by audiences that was then re-examined, reinterpreted and reaffirmed in accordance to their extreme political views. Further research needs to be conducted, with perhaps a larger data sample, but what the results currently suggest, is that, newspapers proprietors focused on selling newspapers to increase profits, also results in their contribution to online Islamophobia.

Further Reading

Awan, I. 2013. *Victims of Anti-Muslim Hate*, Evidence submitted to the APPG on Islamophobia, 11 September 2013.

Awan, I and Blakemore, B. 2013. *Extremism, Counter-Terrorism and Policing*, Ashgate: Farnham.

Grabosky, P. and Stohl, M., 2010. *Crime and Terrorism*, Sage: London.

References

Akbarzedah, S. and Smith, B. 2005. *The Representation of Islam and Muslims in the Media*, Monash University: School of Political and Social Inquiry. 23.

Allen, C. 2012. *A Review of the Evidence Relating to the Representation of Muslims and Islam in the British Media*, University of Birmingham: Institute of Applied Social Studies, School of Social Policy.

Awan, I. 2014. Islamophobia and Twitter: A Typology of Online Hate against Muslims on Social Media, *Policy and Internet*, 6(2): 115–32.

BBC News. 2006. *Blair 'prayed to God' over Iraq*. [Online]. Available at: http://news.bbc.co.uk/1/hi/uk_politics/4772142.stm [accessed: 6 November 2014].

BBC News. 2013. *632 Anti-Muslim Hate Incidents Recorded by Tell Mama*. [Online]. Available at: http://www.bbc.co.uk/news/uk-21712826 [accessed: 28 December 2014].

Beckett, K. and Sasson, T. 2000. *The Politics of Injustice: Crime and Punishment in America*, Thousand Oaks, CA: Pine Forge Press.

Brookes, M., Wilson, D., Yardley., E., Rahman, M. and Rowe, S. 2015. Faceless: High Profile Murders and Public Recognition, *Crime Media and Culture*. [Online]. Sage. 1–16.

Buckler, K. and Salinas, P. 2009. Mass media and crime and justice, in *21st Century Criminology: A Reference Handbook*, edited by Miller J.M., Thousand Oaks: Sage, pp. 711–20.

Buckler K and Travis L. 2005. Assessing the Newsworthiness of Homicide Events: An Analysis of Coverage in the Houston Chronicle, *Journal of Criminal Justice and Popular Culture*, 12 (1) 1–25.

Butsch, R. 2007. *Media and Public Spheres*, London: Palgrave Macmillan.

Chermak S. 1995. *Victims in the News: Crime and the American News Media*. Boulder, CO: Westwiew Press.

Chomsky, N. 2008 *Media Control: The Spectacular Achievements of Propaganda*, New York: Seven Stories Press.

Cohen, S. 1972. *Folk Devils and Moral Panics*, London: MacGibbon and Kee.

Dodd, V. 2013. *Pavlo Lapshyn, the 'shy' and 'polite' student turned terrorist*. [Online]. Available at: http://www.theguardian.com/uk-news/2013/oct/21/pavlo-lapshyn-ukrainian-student-terrorist [accessed: 29 December 2014].

Enteman, W. 2011. Stereotypes, the Media, and Photojournalism, in *Images that Injure: Pictorial Stereotypes in the Media*, edited by S. Ross and P. Lester, California: ABC-CLIO Publications.

Ericson, R. 1995. *Crime and the Media*, Aldershot: Dartmouth.

Ericson R., Baranek P. and Chan J. 1991. *Representing Crime: Crime, Law and Justice in the News Media*, Toronto: Toronto University Press.

Feldman, M., Littler, M., Dack, J. and Copsey, N. 2013. Anti-Muslim Hate Crime and the Far Right. Teeside University. [Online]. Available at: http://tellmamauk.org/wp content/uploads/2013/07/antimuslim2.pdf [accessed: 31 March 2015].

Freedman, D. and Thussu, D. 2012. *Media and Terrorism Global Perspectives*, London: Sage.

Goode, E. and Ben-Yehuda, N. 1994. *Moral Panics: The Social Construction of Deviance*, Oxford: Blackwell.

GOV.UK 2015. *Terrorism and national emergences*. Available at: https://www.gov.uk/terrorism-national-emergency/terrorism-threat-levels [accessed: 29 December 2014].

Halliday, J. 2013. *Woolwich attack video: TV broadcasts prompt 800 complaints The Guardian, Thursday 23 May 2013*. [Online]. Available at: http://www.theguardian.com/media/2013/may/23/woolwich-attack-video-tv-complaints [accessed: 12 November 2013].

Hetherington A. 1985. *News, Newspapers and Television*. London: Macmillan.

Hickman, L. 2013. *Woolwich attack witness Ingrid Loyau-Kennett: 'I feel like a fraud'.* [Online]. Available at: http://www.theguardian.com/uk/2013/may/27/woolwich-witness-ingrid-loyau-kennett [accessed: 19 December 2014].

Hope, C. 2013. *Nick Robinson says sorry for saying suspected Woolwich killers were 'of Muslim appearance'.* [Online]. Available at: http://www.telegraph.co.uk/news/politics/10076799/Nick-Robinson-says-sorry-for-saying-suspected-Woolwich-killers-were-of-Muslim-appearance.html [accessed: 12 December 2014].

Jewkes, Y. 2004. *Crime and Media,* London: Sage.

Karatzogianni, A. 2012. *War and Violence in the Media: Five Disciplinary Lenses (Media, War and Security),* London: Routledge.

McLaughlin, E. 2006. 'Hate Crime', in *The Sage Dictionary of Criminology,* McLaughlin. E. and Muncie, J., London: Sage, 194–6.

McManus, J.H. 1994. *Market-driven Journalism,* Thousand Oaks, CA: Sage Publishers.

Peelo, M. 2005. Crime and the media: Public narratives and private consumption, in *Questioning Crime Criminology,* edited by M. Peelo and K. Soothill, Cullompton: Willan, pp. 20–39.

Peelo, M., Francis., B. Soothill, K., Pearson, J. and Ackerley, E. 2004. Newspaper reporting and the public construction of homicide. *British Journal of Criminology,* 44: 256–75.

Poole, E. 2002. *Reporting Islam: Media Representations of British Muslims,* London: I.B.Tauris.

Said, E. 1981. *Covering Islam,* London: Routledge.

Scraton P., Sim, J. and Skidmore P. 1991. *Prisons Under Protest,* Buckingham: Open University Press.

Sheils, J. 2013. *Fire at London Islamic school: four teenagers arrested as police step up security.* [Online]. Available at: http://www.standard.co.uk/news/london/fire-at-london-islamic-school-four-teenagers-arrested-as-police-step-up-security-8651586.html?origin=internalSearch [accessed: 26 December 2014].

Sparkes, C. and Tulloch, J. 2000. *Tabloid Tales: Global Debates over Media Standards (Critical Media Studies: Institutions, Politics and Culture),* New York: Rowman & Littlefield.

Taylor, M. and Siddique, H. 2013. *Woolwich Murder: 200 Islamophobic Incidents since Lee Rigby killing.* [Online]. Available at: http://www.theguardian.com/uk/2013/may/28/woolwich-murder-200-islamophobic-incidences [accessed: 25 December 2014].

The Telegraph. 2013. *Woolwich attack: The terrorist's rant.* [Online]. Available at: http://www.telegraph.co.uk/news/uknews/terrorism-in-the-uk/10075488/Woolwich-attack-the-terrorists-rant.html [accessed: 27 December 2014].

The Terrorism Act. 2000. *Terrorism: Interpretation.* [Online]. Available at: http://www.legislation.gov.uk/ukpga/2000/11/section/1 [accessed: 11 October 2013].

Waddington, P.A.J. 1986. Mugging as a moral panic: A question of proportion, *British Journal of Sociology*, 32(2): 245–99.

Watney, S. 1987. *Policing Desire: Pornography, Aids and the Media*, London: Methuen.

Whyte-Venables, J. 2012. *What is News?* London: Willow Publishing.

Williams, P. and Dickinson, J. 1993. Fear of crime: Read all about it. *British Journal of Criminology*, 33(1): 33–56.

Wilson, D., Tolputt, H., Howe, N. and Kemp, D. 2010. When serial killers go unseen: The case of Trevor Joseph Hardy. *Crime Media Culture*, 6(2): 153–67.

Chapter 6
The Psychology of Online Islamophobia

Jane Prince

In this chapter, we will consider the motivations and behaviours of members of online hate groups, focusing on Islamophobic groups, and consider the ways in which such groups are established and maintained, their role in aggressive actions and the psychological implications for their targets. The anonymity of the net is both an advantage and a disadvantage for hate groups; identification of individuals is difficult, hence criminal offences may be committed with a perceived lessened chance of being brought to justice, even when there is a will so to do. Identifying and stopping those inciting violence is problematic in part because of a reluctance on the parts of governments to interfere with websites (such interference running counter to the democratic notion of freedom of expression) and also because the geography of the internet makes identifying an authority/government with the legal power to take action can be difficult. The geography of the internet lends itself to mobility with easy moves between hosting sites. This mobility combined with a lack of a means of identifying an individual who does not wish to be identified is a factor which facilitates the escalation of Islamophobic communication on hate sites (Douglas and McGarty 2002).

Social Identity Theory (Tajfel and Turner 1979) and the SIDE model of social de-individuation in web-mediated communications (Spears, Postmes, Lea and Wolpert 2002) will be used as a framework for exploring research into on-line hate groups including white supremacist groups. The chapter will consider the establishment and maintenance of such groups and their influence on the attitudes and behaviours of wider non-Islamic communities. Levels of advocacy for acts of violence will be considered within a framework of social hostility demonstrated by the hate-group to the out-group. Strategies for promoting activism and hostility against out groups will be discussed (e.g. Douglas, McGarty, Bliuc and Lala 2005). The implications of the existence of such groups for the psychological wellbeing and the behaviour of targeted groups will also be considered; there are conflicting views about the implications of being targets of hate groups (Lerner 2010; Hashemi-Najafabadi 2010) while others argue that such experiences mobilise Muslims for faith-based separatist political activism (Howard 2010).

The chapter will conclude by discussing the implications of the internet for the development and maintenance of hostile attitudes and behaviours and how, within internet communities, hate-groups might be challenged on a psychological level. We start with a caveat relating to definition and terminology; the use of the term Islamophobia can be problematic for psychologists as it carries connotations of a (treatable) mental health problem; some might argue that the underlying mental processes reflect a cognitive bias rather than a phobia and this is indeed the focus of the majority of the research discussed here. However though we continue to use the term Islamophobia as encompassing both these approaches it is helpful to consider what the term phobia implies, not least because within understanding of the meaning of 'phobia' lie possibilities for challenging Islamophobia.

A phobia is an anxiety disorder involving a persistent fear of an object, place or situation disproportional to the threat or danger posed by the object of the fear. According to the diagnostic criteria laid out in DSM-5 (APA 2013) the person who has the phobia will go to great lengths to avoid the object of the fear and experience great distress if it is encountered. These irrational fears and reactions must result in interference with social and work life to meet the DSM-5 criteria. Under DSM-5, for a diagnosis to be made, the anxiety must be 'out of proportion' to the threat considering the environment and situation. A person who has a specific phobia disorder experiences significant and persistent fear when in the presence of, or anticipating the presence of, the object of fear, which may be an object, place or situation. Exposure to the phobic stimulus provokes an immediate anxiety response, although the person recognises that the fear is out of proportion and the avoidance, anxious anticipation or distress in the feared situation interferes significantly with the person's normal routine functioning, or social activities or relationships. It can be possible to identify such responses in assertions made in discussion groups in relation to anti-Islamic sentiment. That said, an alternative view of Islamophobia is that it is a simple manifestation of hatred or out-group hostility and should best be considered and addressed within that framework. The following post (posted on the website Stormfront, a hate website directed at, amongst others, UK residents) stated:

> "Islamic doll" for children launched in Britain with no FACE in line with Muslim rules on depiction of prophet's companions. Featureless doll with no eyes, nose or lips produced for Muslim children. It complies with Muslim teachings that living things should not be created. Doll took 4 years to design and is aimed at children in strict Muslim homes. Has been designed by Ridhwana B, a former

Lancashire school teacher. "Deeni doll" is being sold for £25 and is marketed as "Shariah (sic) compliant".

and drew the following response:

Totally incompatible with our culture. However, a doll without a face is better than one with an Asian or Middle-Eastern face. Yuuuck. (See https://www.stormfront.org/forum/t1078536/ accessed 17 December 2014)

An article in *The Guardian* newspaper published in April 2014 (http://www.the guardian.com/world/2014/apr/18/hate-crime-murders-website-stormfront-report accessed 18 April 2014) implicated the Stormfront website in more than a 100 hate crime murders; these were mainly in the USA. The article suggested that one of the functions of the website was to provide a community for people who commit hate crimes against religious and ethnic minorities. While there is no incitement to kill or maim specifically contained in this post, the assumption firstly that Asian or Middle Eastern faces are too offensive for anyone to wish to view them and secondly that the idea of a doll portraying specific physical characteristics which might typify a particular group is 'incompatible with our culture' does illustrate the strength of anti-Islamic feeling and hatred displayed on this site. The comment reflects a clear concept of the other as being anyone who is not white northern European. It also reflects a clear hostility to that 'other'.

The question of the origins of such attitudes and of the perception of the holder that it is appropriate to express them is not one that can be answered easily. What is more certain is that one attraction of such sites is that allow the actualisation of ideas and attitudes which may have operated on an implicit level prior to the user accessing the hate-site. These sites are not easy to find; their location is mobile and details passed by word of mouth from insiders, as indeed are many websites devoted to activities which have the potential to cause harm to others. Hence it is reasonable to assume that a user would be likely to be actively seeking out such sites. While initially these sites may serve to satisfy the interest of a user, they also consolidate implicit attitudes which may not have previously had an opportunity for explicit expression.

Social Influence and Group-based Identities; A Framework For Islamophobia

Many years of research into aspects of social influence particularly in relation to implicit attitudes indicate that humans are very sensitive to the thoughts and attitudes of others and modify their own behaviours in line with these. This includes at times masking attitudes which may not be seen as desirable to others in the group. Stangor and Leary (2006) studied the ways in which knowledge about the prevalent attitudes within a group impacted on individual's attitudes. They found that by manipulating the apparent feelings of other group members to a stigmatised group (by manipulating what the research participants 'saw' of those expressed attitudes) the prejudice of those participants could be altered. When participants were led to believe their fellow group members were not prejudiced, their own expression of prejudiced attitudes became less hostile and conversely, when they believed others in the group were very hostile to the stigmatised group their own expressed negative attitudes increased in number and intensity. These changes operate through participants selectively focusing on information consistent with the perceived views of other group members. So the attitudes of others effectively shape both what we say and also what we perceive and remember about out-groups. This in turn impacts on implicit attitudes, those orientations which we do not state explicitly but which shape our responses. Research has indicated that being shown recordings of others exhibiting nonverbal behaviours which indicate dislike of a minority group (such as looking away or yawning when a minority group member is talking or doing something or nodding agreement when a negative comment is made about that group) is sufficient to trigger a pairing of that minority group with negative characteristics (Weisbuch and Ambady 2009).

It is clear that when individuals are exposed to negative attitudes to an outgroup from other group members, even if they themselves are not participating in any discussion or activity, then they will develop more stigmatising attitudes to that group. The distinction between implicit and explicit attitudes is important; experimental measures of implicit attitudes usually involve taking measures of response times in categorising target group members in terms of both negative and positive qualities (Greenwald, McGhee and Schwartz 1998). Nonverbal behaviours are indicators of implicit attitudes and are harder to control than verbal behaviours (Castelli et al. 2012) and may be a way of identifying those potentially at risk of becoming involved with Islamophobic hate groups on line. We will return to this issue of identifying those at risk of participating in Islamophobic activities below.

The concept of a group based identity is core in developing an understanding of the formation of hostility to groups other than the protagonists own, and to the development of Islamophobic online groups. Tajfel and Turner (1979) argued that identity derives to a large extent from group membership (whether that group be family, an ethnic group, a religious group or any other) and that an individual's identity develops through a process of social categorisation, that is allocating self and others into social groups, us and them, in-groups and out-groups. The fundamental core of social identity theory is the assertion that members of in-groups will seek to elevate the status of their own group through valorisation of that group and through belittling, hostility and criticism towards the out-group.

The process of establishing group membership is one of three-stages; first is the process of categorisation, secondly the process of social identification and finally that of social comparison. If we can categorise people into a particular group then we can draw inferences about their characteristics, qualities and general merits; it is a cognitively advantageous process (and one which is essential to everyday functioning) to be able to use categories or stereotypes to classify people and situations as this enables us to deal more rapidly with actions relating to them. Categorisation tells us about ourselves (for example, what we must support because we are Catholic, or Hungarian or a soldier) and what we should do; group norms are used as reference points to guide behaviour but for this guidance to operate we need to be able to categorise both ourselves and others. It is during the second stage, that of social identification, that we adopt the identity of the group into which we have categorised ourselves; there is an emotional significance to the group membership and it is here that self-esteem becomes entwined with continuing membership of that group.

The third stage is social comparison; once we have categorised ourselves as group members then to maintain self-esteem we need to compare ourselves with out-groups. This comparison includes consideration of group qualities (those positive things the group members have in common), group resources and group rewards. The process of social comparison makes it inevitable that resource allocation will be seen as unfair (Tajfel 1979), by definition the in-group has the highest qualities and hence deserves more than the out-group. Thus humans are predisposed to find unequal distribution of rewards and resources fair – as long as our own in-group is well rewarded.

This is a critical part of SIT as once groups see themselves as different, members inevitably develop out-group hostility either because there is competition for resources or as a result of competing identities. While a person may belong to many different groups these cannot be mutually conflicting. If they are conflicting the individual experiences dissonance and moves away from one group. Empirical support for Social Identity Theory is strong (for example, Hopkins and Reicher 1996, Lalonde 2002) and derives from both observation of real-life behaviour and empirical laboratory investigation (Tajfel 1982) and quasi-experiments such as Sherif's (1966) Robbers Cave study. It is important to note that in-group membership is a real and active part of the person's identity; manipulation therefore of in-and out-group characteristics can be used to promote actions hostile to the out-group and it is this manipulation, the emphasising of in-and out-group differences and entitlements which can facilitate the development of online hate communities where nothing is tangible and false representations of reality can be presented as fact. The process of out-group derogation legitimises the victimisation of others.

In Sherif's Robbers Cave study, in which children who were previously unknown to each other were taken to summer camp and arbitrarily assigned to groups for activities as is normal in such camps, it was found that the children developed an in-group pride coupled with an aggressive stance towards the other group which manifested itself in hate words, abuse, dislike and eventually physical violence. This was without any other communality between the boys in each group – no shared interests, religion, values or background. Sherif's initial and disturbing discovery that simply creating two groups and placing them in competition with each other led to animosity far beyond low-level rivalry with the potential for genuine hatred was further developed by Tajfel (1970) in his concept of minimal groups.

Tajfel argued that all that was need to create in-group pride and out-group hostility was for people to be told they were members of a group; the group did not have to be based around any specific interest or value system. In a series of studies involving the creation of artificial groups based on very unimportant distinctions (in one study he assigned boys to groups based on their alleged expressed preferences for contemporary art in a forced choice task) he found that not only did being assigned to a group lead to individuals identifying with that group but that one of the manifestations of that identification was a hostility to out-groups which led the focus of decision-making to be what would most disadvantage that out-group rather than what would most privilege the in-group. By merely being a group member, our cognitive, emotional and evaluative processes develop a tendency to orientate round that group, to seek to maintain it and to privilege it over any out-groups. It can be seen then that incorporating potential activists into a group requires only to identify an out-group and to identify a common organising characteristic for the in-group. For hate groups this is done through the identification of a perceived privilege the out-group has over in-group members. This might be civic (for example, perceived preferential treatment given to a particular religious group), economic (financial benefits including things such as housing accruing) or even status-oriented (members of that group have all the power). The British hate-group, the English Defence League, focuses on recruiting working class, white English males usually) living in areas of economic and social deprivation; it focuses its communications on mythical accounts of the material wealth (for example, housing cars, jobs) offered by the British state to undeserving immigrants. The Swedish National Democrats, an extreme right-wing group, focuses on similar issues and also on the 'privileges' given to homosexuals in Sweden (Lagerlof 2004). Such groups are using the net not just to present their view but to actively recruit new members.

The role of the print media in the development of negative attitudes to minority groups is important as discussed in Chapter 5. Since the 1980s the Glasgow Media Group (e.g. Philo, Bryant and Donald 2013, Glasgow Media Group cooperative 1982) has monitored the way the print media has been manipulated to create hostility to specific groups whether they be groups of workers, political groups, pressure groups such as the Hillsborough Justice campaign, or religious or ethnic groups. The goal of the print media here is to create the in-group – out-group tension which can legitimise engagement in hate-group activities through the creation of false impressions relating to perceived advantages experienced by the out-group. The availability and anonymity of the internet allows implicit negative attitudes to translate into explicitly expressed hate speech and encouragement to action.

Douglas, McGarty, Bliuc and Lala (2005) explored the ways in which online supremacist groups developed strategies to enhance their own member's status and undermined the status of out-groups. They focused on white supremacist hate groups as being the most common cyber hate group, noting that while such groups operated to an extent outside any legal imperatives restricting the advocating of violence they would still position themselves as legitimate and justified in their stance. Thus within Tajfel's Social Identity Theory approach their focus is on both defining their own groups members as morally superior and to an extent 'victims' of an unjust system while addressing the negative qualities of out groups. In Islamophobic groups this entails a focus (usually inaccurate) on stereotypical aspects of Islam whether these be associated with specific religious practices, social behaviours or physical appearance. The focus according to Douglas et al. is on maintaining the high-status position of the supremacist group through the use of socially creative strategies to maintain a positive group identity and more importantly to enhance distinctiveness. The term socially creative should not be seen as having any positive connotations. Rather it refers to the use of unusual and non-normal comparison dimensions to maintain a group's superiority.

The example from Stormfront referred to earlier describing the Islamic doll is an example of social creativity; this is not a common dimension through which Islamic and non-Islamic groups are usually compared. It serves a purpose of identifying a 'threat' to a dominant (and by implication desirable) group by a group apparently following a senseless and harmful agenda. A good example of a socially creative strategy widely employed by racist and Islamophobic groups is that of identifying benefits which the out-group enjoys to the detriment of the in-group culture; claims that non-Christian religious groups had forced the renaming of Christmas as Winterval have provided stories in popular media over the past decade and used by anti-Islamic groups as proof that Muslim groups had an influence denied to the Christian majority, without any evidence that this had ever happened. Socially creative strategies are used by hate group websites to redefine the out-group's inferiority. This is the case whether or not the hate group sees their status as secure although where such a group perceives their relative advantage as being under threat they may resort to specific socially creative strategies to resist the change as well as engaging in social conflict strategies (Haslam 2001). These operate in tandem; the conflict strategies allow the incitement of aggression and violence will the creativity strategies allow for the identification of a range of dimensions where the distinctiveness between the groups is accentuated.

In online groups it has been generally held that a mediating factor in aggressive communication or flaming has been the anonymity and lack of accountability of the communicator (Joinson 2003); however some studies focusing specifically on hate groups in online communication have found that there is increased aggression shown when the communicator is identifiable to like-minded individuals (Douglas and McCarty 2002). The SIDE (social identity de-individuation effects) model (Reicher, Spears and Postmes 1995) predicts this. While early studies of computer mediated communication focused primarily on the lack of visual and other social cues (for example, Social Presence Theory: Short, Williams and Christie 1976) more recently research has concentrated on the role of de-individuation effects (for example, Sproull and Kiesler 1986) and research using the SIDE model to predict hostile behaviour. The research provides considerable insight into the nature of cyber hate. De-individuation theory proposes that during CMC individuals become less likely to monitor their own behaviour and less inhibited and hence more prone to impulsive behaviour such as flaming and cyber hate (Douglas and McGarty 2001). In a series of studies Douglas and McGarty attempted to extend existing theorising about hate-communications via CMC by applying the strategic aspect of SIDE. In particular they found that when in-group members were identifiable to an in-group audience they were more likely to produce generalisations in line with in-group norms when describing an out-group audience than if they were not being monitored by their in-group. In other words when what they were saying could be known to members of their 'group' they would use more stereotypical attitudes to the out-group. This has particular salience for understanding cyber hate; if it is believed that communication is being monitored by an in-group member then hate speech and negative stereotypes and hostile expressions (to the out group) will be more likely.

Identifiability brings about a stronger awareness of accountability to and motivation towards the group's norms. Douglas et al. (2005) noted that while the members of white supremacist groups they studied may not have known the specific identity of any of their fellow members they had a clear idea of their audience. In their study they identified 43 hate group sites and rated their content for advocacy of violence, advocacy of conflict and for social creativity. They also noted whether the websites were anonymous or not. An example of social creativity they found was one which suggested that as no one race is superior then social integration and immigration threatened all racial groups and hence should be completely stopped, a perspective echoing the arguments for Apartheid in South Africa which repeated the mantra of Separate Development while in practice legitimising the suppression and exploitation of the majority Black population. They found that levels of social creativity on the websites were higher than levels of encouragement of violence or conflict and that identifiability did not have any effect on the communication strategy (creativity, violence or conflict). They suggested that their findings supported the finding of others that communication which emphasised potential threat from an out-group resulted in a greater level of commitment to group action regardless of the level of commitment to a group. Thus the Stormfront Islamic doll narrative, while seemingly irrelevant to central issues in the debates round Islam, serves the function of identifying a threat to everyday practices in the UK and valorising readers to an increasing level of commitment to Islamophobic action. It changes the focus of attention from seeing Islam as a religion to focusing on it as threat to 'our' children and their everyday lives.

Duffy (2003) has suggested a different way of reading the internet communications of hate groups; she refers to Symbolic Convergence Theory and proposes that one of the functions of the messages is to create a context – a story – which allows the writer to plant in the mind of any reader, however hesitant, the idea that what is written has an element of truth. According to Matsuda et al. (1993) reporting research into the psychology of religious and race hate, one effect of hate propaganda is to infuse the reader with the belief in the underlying truth of the propaganda. They do this, according to Duffy, through evoking themes of fairness, justice and morality in support of their beliefs and creating narratives which are polemical rather than evidence based to illustrate their points.

Islamophobia and Personality

If the power of the medium of the internet for explaining the development and maintenance of Islamophobic attitudes is best explained through theories developed from social identity theories what explanations does psychology have at the individual level for the development of Islamophobia? Gottschalk and Greenberg (2008) propose that the dominant reaction by non-Muslims to Islam is one of fear. It is important to make a distinction between fear and associated constructs such as prejudice. Fear has distinct components and any fear system must allow for appraisal (cognitive) components (Lazarus 1991) and strategies to avoid threat whether to physical or emotional well-being. Fear underpins intergroup reactions (Lee, Short, Yeh, Reid, Gibbons and Campbell 2013) and hence understanding fear responses may provide insight into the factors motivating people to engage with Islamophobic websites. Lee et al. have devised a measure for assessing Islamophobia which is unique in its focus on Islam rather than having measures related to race or ethnicity as earlier measures have done (e.g. the Anti-Muslim Prejudice scale: cited in Park, Felix and Lee

2007) and the Cristian-Muslim Implicit Association Test (Rowan, Franklin and Cotton 2005) often treating Arab ethnicity and Muslim faith as being identical.

They focus on measures of cognitive Islamophobia, the cognitive appraisal associated with monitoring and processing information relating to threat and Affective Behavioural Islamophobia, the response domain of the fear system which activates responses geared to avoiding potential threat. The two factors are highly positively correlated. For example feelings of discomfort when speaking with a Muslim (CI) and avoidance-related actions such as avoiding contact with Muslims (ABI) would lead to actions directed at escaping a situation when confronted with social or work situations entailing contact with Muslims. Lee et al. (2009) have found that the feelings of avoidance of contact with Muslims is associated (they believe causally) with a diminished sympathy for their suffering even when that suffering is a consequence of something over which they have no control (as is manifested in attitudes to Syrian refugees fleeing the civil war in that country in 2014); this suggests that the two components of the fear response can each act on each other, with cognitions driving emotional responses and associated behaviours and also behaviour (desire to avoid contact) driving cognitions.

Lee et al. (2009) report on their research in which an existing scale they had developed, with established reliability and validity, the Islamophobia Scale (Lee, Gibbons, Thompson and Timani, 2009) is tested more robustly for construct validity and for the extent to which it can predict associated behaviours and hence its predictive validity. The measure was found to have test-retest reliability and hence temporal validity, measuring Islamophobia consistently over time. They also found a correlation with other core measures in psychology, namely modern racism (MR, characterised by prejudice towards a wide range of minorities) and to religious fundamentalism (RF, a belief that one's own religion is the sole container for truth about God and the phenomenology of human existence). Associated with high RF scores are high scores for dogmatism and inflexibility. Lee et al. (2009) also found a negative correlation between scores on the Islamophobia Scale and three of the Big Five (Costa and McCrae 1992) personality factors. The Big Five are the five factors which have been found in almost all research on personality; they are openness, conscientiousness, extraversion, agreeableness and emotional stability. Individuals with low scores on openness and on agreeableness were found to have higher scores on Islamophobia and emotional stability was also found to correlate negatively with Islamophobia. People who are emotionally unstable tend to be very sensitive to negative signals in the environment and have fearful responses. Openness is a liking for and engagement with new experiences, ideas and events while agreeableness reflects individual differences in a general preference for harmony, agreeable people being the types who get along with others and who show consideration, trust and kindness.

The identification of key psychological constructs which have been demonstrated to be associated with Islamophobia and the development of an Islamophobia Scale which can be relatively easily administered and which has predictive validity may be the key to both the development of research programmes leading to a better understanding of the dynamics of Islamophobia. It may also hold the key to developing preventative strategies for segments of the population at risk in situations where there might be a need to predict emotional responses and behaviour towards Muslims.

Much of the research on hate groups and Islamophobia assumes a universality in the social group basis for out-group prejudice; indeed Social Identity Theory is proposed as a universal. However there are differences in the level of expressed Islamophobia or anti-Islamic sentiments in different western countries and it is worthwhile considering if such differences might constitute a base for a better understanding of Islamophobia and more effective ways of both challenging it and dealing with its consequences. One of the difficulties in comparing levels of anti-Islamic sentiment across countries is that different measures are used in different countries and by different researchers; indeed, in one study (Fetzer and Soper 2003) different measures were used to assess anti-Islamic sentiments in the different countries studied so no proper comparison of countries could be made. Savelkoul, Scheepers, Van der Veld and Hagendoorn (2012) compared the extent to which anti-Islamic sentiments pervade different countries in the West; they found differences in the expression of anti-Islamic sentiment with higher levels found in the Netherlands and Germany and lower levels in the UK and the USA. Their sample drew on data from the Pew Global Attitudes Survey (2005) conducted in 17 countries including seven Western non-Muslim countries (those listed above plus Spain, Canada and France).

The researchers focused on the seven Western countries; they attributed negative attitudes to Muslims as being associated with higher levels of unemployment and with higher proportions of Muslims in the population; they also noted that the level of education of the Muslim population within a country could also be a factor with lower levels of education associated with more negative attitudes. A different perspective was taken by Hodl (2010) who studied the characteristics of Islamophobia in Austria; he too noted that publically expressed anti-Islamic sentiments were rarer in Austria than in the Netherlands and that they typically were less frequent than in other western European countries. The Muslim population of Vienna, about 130,000 (8%) in 2005, were living throughout the city in contrast with the situation in Paris where the Muslim population were concentrated in certain poor suburbs. However Hodl noted that the anti-immigration rhetoric in Austria in the early years of the 21st century differed from that in the rest of Europe as it was directed against all foreigners rather than against Muslims. From about 2007 onwards media pressure, driven by and stimulating an anxiety about Islamic extremism, led to increasing levels of negative coverage of Islam in the media and the emergence of Islamophobia in the broader public manifesting itself in ant-Islamic chapters in school textbooks, hostility to female teachers wearing the headscarf in school and a developing Islamophobic movement. The common element to all these manifestations of Islamophobia is an appeal to in-group pride and value and denigration of out-groups. There is evidence of unity between hate-groups in different countries accessing and sharing materials via web-based sites as noted above.

Perceptions of Muslims

One question which does not receive sufficient attention in the literature is how Muslims perceive the attitudes of others towards them and how they view attempts to manage intergroup relations. Hopkins and Kahani-Hopkins (2006) proposed that British Muslims construe the dynamics of Islamophobia in one of two very different ways and their choice of perspective has a profound impact on their approach to intergroup contact. Working within the paradigm of social identity theory, Hopkins and Kahani-Hopkins explored understanding of ways of reducing intergroup hostility via contact. Pettigrew and Tropp (2006) reported a meta-analysis of psychological research which indicated that while contact had an impact on intergroup perceptions the change was primarily amongst the attitudes of the majority group. There was no literature on the use of web-based contact to facilitate the contact and the study looked at broad attitudes to Muslims rather than Islamophobia. In addition there is very little research into how Muslims perceive hostile attitudes to them as the focus of research is on Muslims as objects of discrimination rather than as active partners in an intergroup dynamic. It is noted that when contact studies are evaluated, the change in perceptions of the majority towards the minority group is taken as an indicator of the success of the intervention (Buttny and Williams 2000; Pettigrew and Tropp 2000) and the views of the minority ignored.

For example Buttny and Williams reported minority participants stating that they valued being respected more than being liked by a majority group. Respect means moving away from discriminatory practices in areas such as employment, education and health care and vulnerability to physical assault (Ansari 2004) and can involve demands for legal changes such as protection from incitement to hatred on the grounds of religion. As discussed earlier, the conflation of religion and ethnicity proved problematic for those experiencing Islamophobia.

Hopkins and Kahani-Hopkins note that in their study both perspectives shared some common ground with each other. Both groups possessed beliefs which can be summarised as thinking Muslims should maintain their

114

own identity and distinctiveness while achieving parity with the majority (a social competition strategy) and neither thought strategies of individualism or passing (Tajfel 1981) would be acceptable or helpful in achieving their goals. However they did differ in the way they thought of Islamophobia and appropriate strategies for challenging it. One perspective had as a definition of Islamophobia an account which made a distinction between legitimate and illegitimate criticisms of Muslim practices. Illegitimate or closed criticisms included those associated with a tendency to reject any Muslim criticism of the West and to focus on the view that Islam was not a genuine faith but a tool for political and military advantage. Open or legitimate views implied that disagreement with Islam could go hand in glove with attempts to eliminate discrimination and exclusion. This perspective also argues that Islamophobic perceptions were supported by assumptions that relations between Islam and the west as being inevitably antagonistic and proposed that the way to improve experience of Muslims would involve challenging these assumptions with an emphasis on Islam and the West as having mutually positive influences.

The alternative view identified was that Islamophobia was essentially a hatred of truth, part of an eternal conflict between truth and falsehood, right and wrong and people belonged to one of two groups, those who recognised that Allah was the one God and those who did not. Within this perspective the prejudice experienced by Muslims is a continuation of the sorrows experienced by generations who had, since the beginning of time, recognised God's truth. There was little point in maintaining any social relationship as, by definition, non-believers were aggressive in their challenges to God's truths and attempting intergroup contact would simply make Muslims more vulnerable. One of the ways in which this was manifested was a failure to recognise Islam-as-religion as being the core of identity; rather people were evaluated in terms of their ethnic or racial origins which was a way of distracting attention from the core of Islamophobia which was hostility to the Islamic faith.

The two perspectives imply radically different approaches to the value of intergroup contact as a means of challenging prejudice. From the first perspective, any contact between in-group and out-group would serve to better understand Islam, reduce Islamophobia and enhance the lived experiences of Muslims in the UK; from the second perspective contact with non-Muslims could do nothing but serve the interest of a society which persecuted the Islamic identity. Hopkins and Kahani-Hopkins note that the findings of their research carry implications for how to initiate challenges to Islamophobia. It has long been a central argument of social identity theory that in order to challenge discrimination the discriminated-against group must develop a group identity and elevate the status of that identity. This was part of the process of challenging stigma and prejudice against African-Americans in the 1960s (Sitkoff 1993). Hopkins and Hakani-Hopkins note:

we need to appreciate its theorization of intergroup relations and its account of the role of identity processes in reproducing and resisting oppression. And once this is done, it is clear that a minority's caution about contact may not be best construed in terms of generic identity processes but may be better explained through participants 'theories of social and political organization (and change). (pp. 261–2)

In the US, there is a similar lack of psychological research on the effects of Islamophobia on Muslims as has been noted in Europe. Some effort has been made however to overview the available research literature and to identify psychological methodologies which could be put in place in order to gauge the experiences of Muslims in their everyday experiences. Amer and Bagasra (2013) noted that a quarter of the papers published were in counselling and mental health journals and fewer than a fifth were in social psychology journals. Moreover the majority of the mental health papers focused on orienting clinical psychologists to the demographic and cultural characteristics of Muslims rather than on the health problems of Muslims per se. They argued that, while the development of culturally sensitive research instruments was essential, what was needed even more was a focus on Muslims as the central participants in any research supposedly about on their identities and their experiences of prejudice and Islamophobia, rather than the focus on them as some third party object.

Research carried out with participants in Iran and Egypt suggests the internet can offer users the opportunity to engage in developing social groups and social identities and engage in group based actions. Lerner (2010) argues that the successful integration of social movements and the internet involves, when functioning at its best a dynamic in which groups have both a real world and a cyber-based presence. Lerner investigated the potential of the web as a platform for Islamic activism supporting human rights and civil liberties noting that the web could be used to inspire sympathisers to take direct political action. As such the force of the web is to draw together individuals to challenge injustice, prejudice and Islamophobia rather than to promote hatred as in the Islamophobic websites. She notes the role played by the web in social movements inside Iran and Egypt and in particular the development of communities of bloggers in Farsi (known as Weblogistan) providing a serious source of information and organisation for all its users.

The monitoring and censorship of the internet varies from place to place; in an environment which is often viewed as free and without borders in fact some governments deny access and impose severe censorship on users. Lerner notes the availability to the Iranian government of powers of censorship and imposition of exclusion on some users; such access to 'censorship' does not seem to extend in the West to the closing down of websites which promote hatred and Islamophobia – or this may reflect a political unwillingness to intervene. Too

116

many people see online hate crimes as being somehow victimless (Reed 2009) or in any case of unidentifiable origin. Reed describes using online gaming, similar to some of the games developed by World of Warcraft, to explore intergroup hostility and what is understood by incitement to hate. He notes that one problem facing anyone seeking to exclude hate websites is a problem of definition; at what point does a site's communications become hate crimes rather than merely elevating the salient status of the in-group. He argues that since we all occupy multiple identity positions there is always overlap between them and it is not always straightforward to identify a crossing point at which moment communication should be censored. This is not a chapter intended to focus on the policing of Islamophobic sites but any psychological perspective on web-based Islamophobia based on Social Identity Theory cannot deny the conceptual problem of managing identity transitions online and questioning at what point a group-based identity moves to become a hating identity and how this can be addressed.

Perry and Olsson (2009) address some of the issues associated with managing online Islamophobic websites. They note that the development of the internet has facilitated the development of an international, borderless collective identity of Islamophobia, leading to the emergence of what they call a 'global racist subculture' (p. 185). They note the legal dilemmas which confront those seeking to close down web-sites promoting religious hatred; it is possible to use the techniques of the many governments who deny access to a large proportion of websites (see the example of Iran referred to above) but the democratic imperative makes this unacceptable (western governments claim to value freedom of speech and expression, and hence are unwilling to implement a legal means of denying this) and on the whole the ISPs are left to police their own websites either proactively or, more usually, in response to complaints from other users. The result according to Perry and Olsson is that cyber hate groups are free to disseminate their views and instructions in a largely uncontrolled medium. This has allowed the hate movements to reinvent themselves as dynamic and virile collectives. The crux of the problem of hate groups is the failure to respond to them either at a national or a global level.

Conclusion

A phobia is an irrational fear which is debilitating to possess. Within the framework of that definition Islamophobia is well named; it may be rational to be fearful of specific individuals who may be Muslim or Christian or Buddhist or Jewish or an atheist, but to be fearful of and hostile to a whole religious group is not rational. The power of online hate groups can be explained in terms of the saliency of group membership and group identity for the individual; the identification of a psychometric 'profile' for Islamophobia (with the development of a specialist personality measure) which includes fearfulness as one of its elements reinforces the appropriateness of the use of the term phobia.

The psychometric measure predicts Islamophobics to be fearful, closed to new ideas and lacking in empathy and concern for others. While whole populations cannot be screened for risk personality traits the identification of such characteristics may lead to the development of interventions which may be better tailored to challenge Islamophobics via the website communications and outside these. The real dangers of Islamophobia operate on the physical and psychological level; on the psychological it can make targets feel vulnerable and exposed and this may affect contacts being made between Muslims and non-Muslims. On the physical level the fact that hate sites attempt to propagandise and valorise readers to participate in aggressions against Muslims generates a risk to individual Muslims – or people taken for Muslims – but also to the whole population. The border-free domain of the internet allows for international collaboration in establishing and maintaining hate-sites and poses a challenge for those who wish to eliminate such sites while at the same time maintaining democratic principles of free expression. An understanding of the connection between group and personal identities, of the dynamics underpinning group identities, of the personality characteristics of particular groups of individuals can all contribute to understanding the development and impact of on-line Islamophobia and this will lead in turn to its being challenged and its influence diminished if not eliminated.

Further Reading

Benski, T. and Fisher, E. 2014. *Internet and Emotions*, London: Routledge.

Citron, D.K. 2014. *Hate Crimes in Cyberspace*, Cambridge, MA: Harvard University Press.

Joinson, A., McKenna, K., Postmes, T and Reips, U-R. (eds). 2007. *Oxford Handbook of Internet Psychology*, Oxford: Oxford University Press.

References

Amer, M. and Bagasra, A. 2013. Psychological research with Muslim Americans in the age of Islamophobia: Trends, challenges and recommendations, *American Psychologist*, 68 (3), 134–44.

American Psychiatric Association. 2013. *Diagnostic and Statistical Manual of Mental Disorders* (5th ed) Washington, DC: Author.

Ansari, H. 2004. *The Infidel Within: Muslims in Britain since 1800*, London: Hurst.

Buttny, R. and Williams, P. 2000. Demanding respect: The uses of reported speech in discursive constructions of interracial contact, *Discourse and Society*, 11, 109–33.

Costa, P. and McCrae, R. 1992. *Revised NEO Personality Inventory (NEO-PI-R) and NEO Five-Factor Inventory (NEO-FFI) Manual*, Odessa, Florida: Psychological Assessment Resource.

Douglas, K. and McGarty, C. 2001. Identifiability and self-presentation: Computer-mediated communication and intergroup interaction, *British Journal of Social Psychology*, 40, 399–416.

Douglas, K. and McGarty, C. 2002. Internet identifiability and beyond: A model of the effects of identifiability on communicative behaviour, *Group Dynamics*. 6, 17–26.

Douglas, K., McGarty, C., Bliuc, A. and Lala, G. 2005. Understanding cyberhate, *Social Sciences Computer Review*, 23 (1), 68–76.

Duffy, M. 2003. Web of Hate: A fantasy theme analysis of the rhetorical vision of hate groups online, *Journal of Communication Inquiry*, 27 (3), 291–312.

Fetzer, J. and Soper, J.C. 2003. *Muslims and the State in Britain, France and Germany*, Cambridge: Cambridge University Press.

Glasgow University Media Group. 1982. *Really Bad News*, Worthing: Littlehampton Press.

Gottschalk, P. and Greenberg, P. 2008. *Islamophobia: Making Muslims the Enemy*, Lanham: Rowman & Littlefield.

Hashemi-Najafabadi, S. 2010. Has the information revolution in Muslim societies created new publics? *Muslim World Journal of Human Rights*. Volume 7, Issue 1, article 4 ISSN (Online) 1554–4419, accessed 28/2/2014.

Haslam, S. 2001. *Psychology in Organizations: The Social Identity Approach*, London: Sage.

Herrera, M. 2012. Youth and citizenship in the digital age: A view from Egypt, *Harvard Educational Review*, 82 (3), 333–51.

Hodl, K. 2010. Islamophobia in Austria: The recent emergence of anti-Muslim sentiments in the country, *Journal of Muslim Minority Affairs*, 30 (4), 443–56.

Hopkins, N. and Kerani-Hopkins, V. 2006. Minority group members' theories of intergroup contact: a case study of British Muslims' conceptualizations of 'Islamophobia' and social change, *British Journal of Social Psychology*, 45, 245–62.

Hopkins, N. and Reicher, S. 1996. The construction of social categories and the processes of social change: Arguing about national identities, in G. Breakwell and E. Lyons (eds), *Changing European Identities* (pp. 69–93), Oxford: Butterworth Heinemann.

Howard, P. 2010. *The Digital Origins of Dictatorship and Democracy*, Oxford: Oxford University Press.

Joinson, A. 2003. *Understanding the Psychology of Internet Behaviour*, Basingstoke: Palgrave Macmillan.

Lalonde, R. 2002. Testing the social identity inter-group differentiation hypothesis: 'We're not American eh!'. *British Journal of Social Psychology*, 41 (December), 611–30.

Lazarus, R. 1991. Progress on a cognitive-motivational-relational theory of emotion, *American Psychologist*, 46 (8), 819–34.

Lee, S., Gibbons, J., Thompson, J. and Timani, H. 2009. The Islamophobia scale: Instrument development and initial validation, *International Journal for the Psychology of Religion*, 19, 92–105.

Lee, S., Short, S., Yeh, R., Reid, C. Gibbons, J. and Campbell, M. 2013. Fear of Muslims: Psychometric Evaluation of the Islamophobia Scale, *Psychology of Religion and Spirituality*, advance online publication. Doi: 10.1037/a0032117.

Lerner, M. 2010. Connecting the Actual with the Virtual: the internet and social movement theory in the Muslim World, *Journal of Muslim Minority Affairs*, 30 (4) 555–74.

Matsuda, M., Lawrence, C., Delgado, R. and Crenshaw, K. 1993. *Words That Wound: Critical Race Theory, Assaultive Speech and the First Amendment*, Boulder: Westview Press.

Park, J., Felix, K. and Lee, G. 2007. Implicit attitudes towards Arab-Muslims and the moderating effect of social information, *Basic and Applied Social Psychology*, 29, 35–45.

Perry, B. and Olsson, P. 2009. Cyberhate: The globalization of hate, *Information and Communications Technology Law*, 18 (2), 185–99.

Pettigrew, T. and Tropp, L. 2000. Does intergroup contact reduce prejudice? Recent meta-analytic findings, in Oskamp, S. (ed.) *Reducing Prejudice and Discrimination* (pp. 93–114), Mahwah, NJ: Erlbaum.

Pettigrew, T. and Tropp, L. 2006. A meta-analytic test of intergroup contact theory, *Journal of Personality and Social Psychology*, 90 (5), 751–83.

PEW global attitudes survey: Islamic Extremism: common concern for Muslim and Western publics. 2005. Washington: PEW Research Center.

Philo, G., Briant, E. and Donald, P. 2013. *Bad News for Refugees*, London: Pluto Press.

Reed, C. 2009. The challenge of hate speech online, *Information and Communication Technology Law*, 18 (2), 79–82.

Reicher, S., Spears, R. and Postmes, T. 1995. A social identity model of deindividuation phenomena, *European Review of Social Psychology*, 6, 161–97.

Rowatt, W., Franklin, L. and Cotton, M. 2005. Patterns and personality correlates of implicit and explicit attitudes towards Christians and Muslims, *Journal for the Scientific Study of Religion*, 44, 29–43.

Savelkoul, M., Scheepers, P., Van der Veld, W. and Kagendoorn, L. 2012. Comparing levels of anti-Muslim attitudes across western countries, *Qualitative Quantitative*, 46, 1617–24.

Sherif, M. 1966. *Group Conflict and Cooperation*. London; Routledge & Kegan Paul.

Short, J. Williams, E. and Christie, B. 1976. *The Social Psychology of Telecommunications*, London: Wiley.

Sitkoff, H. 1993. *The Struggle for Black Equality 1954–1992*, New York: Hill and Wang.

Spears, R., Postmes, T., Lea, M. and Wolbert, A. 2002. The power of influence and the influence of power in virtual groups: A SIDE look at CMC and the Internet. *The Journal of Social Issues*, 58, 91–108.

Sproull, L. and Kiesler, S. 1991. Computers, networks and work, *Scientific American*, September, 84–91.

Stormfront. 2004. Is your website in the Hate Directory? [Online]. Available at: https://www.stormfront.org/forum/t125037/ [accessed: 24 September 2014].

Tajfel, H. 1970. Experiments in intergroup discrimination. *Scientific American*, 223, 96–102.

Tajfel, H. 1981. *Human Groups and Social Categories*, Cambridge: Cambridge University Press.

Tajfel, H. and Turner, J. 1979. An Integrative Theory of intergroup conflict, in Austin, W. and Worchel, S. (eds) *The Social Psychology of Intergroup Relations* (pp. 33–47), Monterey: Brooks Cole.

Chapter 7
Legislation and International Frameworks tackling Online Islamophobia

Ewan Kirk

Introduction

Laws governing Islamophobic behaviour range across a number of different areas, and the legal regime in place has different aspects to it. The criminal law is heavily involved, with laws concerning religious hatred and harassment, as well as specific offences regarding online communications. Where such activities take place in the online environment, then additional considerations regarding international law and choice of law are also relevant if the parties involved engage in activities across international borders. Rather than being a coherent set of rules, the law therefore appears to be a disjointed mix of different rules which can be applied to the specific circumstances of online activity, which is designed to promote hatred, and in a religious context (Awan 2013).

Additionally, there are a range of media which may be used in an Islamophobic way, and therefore cause issues online. There are social media sites such as Facebook and Twitter, where users can very easily publish statements to a wide audience or target an individual or group just as easily (see Chapter 2). There are websites and blogs that can be used by individuals as a sort of online platform for their views. There are also sites such as YouTube or Vimeo that allow videos to be uploaded and shared. The only limit to the potential materials that can be uploaded or posted is whether there is online space to host it. This diversity of media also presents a challenge in dealing with Islamaphobic behaviour (Awan and Blakemore 2012).

This chapter intends to examine laws from all of these areas, in order to illustrate the type of sanctions available against persons engaged in Islamophobic activities online. There are a number of criminal offences which apply more generally to Islamophobic behaviour or harassment of people generally, and we will need to look at these in depth as well as any factors which will come into play because of the online context. As well as outlining the laws that affect this subject, it is also necessary to examine the guidance from the CPS regarding this area because of the complex combination of laws involved (Yar 2006).

In addition, there is a civil law dimension to consider. As the internet is essentially privately owned space, and therefore effectively run by companies at the user end of the spectrum, it is also necessary to consider steps which can be taken in a civil law context to combat unlawful activities online. These tend to be rooted not in the law, but in the behaviour of the hosts of information, the internet service providers. Finally, the influence of international law will be discussed. The laws on protection for religions vary greatly between different states, and therefore although the UN has become involved in discussions regarding a law which would defend religions against such attacks, this is part of a framework only, rather than an international law setting a uniform standard.

Specific Crime on Religious Hatred

A major area of legislation is with regard to crimes of hate. Stirring up hatred towards a section of the community in the UK is part of public order legislation, and deals specifically with incidences where there is incitement to stir up hatred in others towards members of that community. As much Islamophobic action has been aimed specifically at encouraging this sentiment in others, or involving others in their Islamophobic views, this is an important part of the law which can protect against Islamophobic actions. An individual can therefore be directly prosecuted under laws designed to protect those who follow religious beliefs (or in fact those whose view is to deliberately follow no religion at all).

Historically in the UK equality legislation has tended to focus upon hatred against races rather than religions. The main problem identified with this approach has been where racial groups have also been directly associated with particular religions, they enjoy indirect protection of the laws on racial hatred that other religious groups not specifically associated with an ethnic group were not (Olivia 2007). Therefore Sikhs and Jews as ethnic groups were protected by the law, whereas other religious groups such as Muslims were not, although Christians enjoyed some protection through the UK laws on Blasphemy. The Public Order Act 1986 originally only referred to racial hatred, and criminalising acts which might fall into this category. Part III of this Act made it illegal for anyone to use insulting, threatening or abusive words, behaviour or displays of written material which intends to stir up *racial* hatred (s.18 Public Order Act 1986). Therefore as such, the law did not cover groups which could not be 'defined by reference to colour, race, nationality (including citizenship) or ethnic or national origins' (s.17 Public Order Act 1986). We can see this point also discussed in the case of *Mandla v Dowell-Lee* ([1982] UKHL 7) where the court was required to define Sikhs as an ethnic group in order for them to be covered by the provisions of the Race Relations Act 1976 (now repealed by the Equality Act 2010).

This therefore left religious groups, defined not by nationality or ethnicity, outside of any protection by the criminal law, with only Christianity being given any protection through the common law offence of Blasphemy recognised in English law, although this has now been abolished (Common law Blasphemy was abolished by the Criminal Justice and Immigration Act 2008). This changed in 2006 with the introduction of a new part to the Public Order Act 1986 by the Racial and Religious Hatred Act 2006. Part IIIA was added to the Public Order Act in order to include incitement to religious hatred into the offences under the Act. Section 29B of the Act states:

> A person who uses threatening words or behaviour, or displays any written material which is threatening, is guilty of an offence if he intends thereby to stir up religious hatred. (Public Order Act 1986, c.64, s.29B, inserted by the Racial and Religious Hatred Act 2006, s.1 Schedule)

Furthermore, behaviour covered by the offence is also covered in s.29C to s.29F. The extent to which these sections of the Public Order Act extend the law on hate speech to hatred against religious groups however, is limited by the fact that they require two things. Firstly, the words or behaviour used, or the materials distributed must be 'threatening' (Wall 2001). This is narrower than other parts of the Public Order Act, for example racial hatred can be threatening, abusive or insulting and fall within the provisions of the Act (Public Order Act 1986, c.64, s.18). The consequence of this is that anything which is considered to be abusive or insulting is by inference permitted, and therefore there is considerable scope in regards to hate speech against Muslims that would still be permitted without any criminal offence having been committed (Perry 2001). The distinction between what is and is not covered appears to be with regard to the consequences of the actions involved. Threats go beyond the verbal assault one would associate with insults or abuse of a verbal or written nature. Although distressing, such things would not normally lead onto a person feeling fear of physical attack, whereas threatening words or behaviour would be associated with an individual's fear of imminent attack.

In this context, 'threatening' is therefore given an everyday meaning (Jeremy 2007). Lord Reid in *DPP v Clarke* (*Director of Public Prosecutions v Clarke* (1991) 94 Cr App R 359) commented that words such as 'threatening' should be construed within limits recognised by the ordinary person. However this restriction is with justification. The legislation appears to be trying to navigate the distinction between words or actions which may result in a person feeling individually threatened, and maintaining the notion of freedom of speech and the freedom to voice opinions and criticisms of religions of whatever type in a multicultural, multi-faith society such as the UK. To have allowed the words 'abusive' and 'insulting' would have placed a further restriction upon freedom of speech, which was seen as too great a restriction in a multi-faith society. This is further reinforced by the provision in s.29J:

> Nothing in this Part shall be read or given effect in a way which prohibits or restricts discussion, criticism or expressions of antipathy, dislike, ridicule, insult or abuse of particular religions or the beliefs or practices of their adherents, or of any other belief system or the beliefs or practices of its adherents, or proselytising or urging adherents of a different religion or belief system to cease practising their religion or belief system. (Public Order Act 1986, c.64, s.29J, inserted by the Racial and Religious Hatred Act 2006, s.1 Schedule)

Thus it can be seen that the distinction is drawn – religions can be challenged, whereas followers of those religions must be allowed to freely practice their religion without fear for their own safety. This is where followers of any religion may disagree with the provisions of the Act as it still allows a range of negative expression which they may find intolerable when applied to their religion, however it is this that ensures that the Act does not limit the rights in freedom of expression to allow criticism of someone because of the religion they follow (Waldrum 2013).

Secondly, the offence requires intent, establishing a need to show the *mens rea* of the offence in order for prosecution to be successful. Intent to incite others to hatred of a person based upon their religion would therefore satisfy this part of the requirement. Lack of intent, if it can be proved, would therefore defeat an accusation here. This is an important aspect of the offence as it rules out the possibility of an individual carrying out these acts recklessly being guilty of the offence.

Also, the *actus reus* is made out in terms of the effect, or potential effect that the words or actions have. In that way, it would appear clear that where statements made are not accessible by those that the hate-speaker would seek to incite, then the offence cannot be made out. What this shows therefore is that this part of the offence is less about what the alleged victim feels about the statement, and more to do with whether the actions carried out could lead to others being incited (Chakraborti and Garland 2009). The third point concerns the scope of what is covered by s.29B and can be seen in the wording of s.29A:

> In this Part "religious hatred" means hatred against a group of persons defined by reference to religious belief or lack of religious belief. (Public Order Act 1986, c.64, s.29A, inserted by the Racial and Religious Hatred Act 2006, s.1 Schedule)

From this, there is one clear distinction in terms of where this law applies; it is about hatred directed at people based upon their religious belief, and not against the religion itself. This is why anything said in private, in a situation where there is no-one of that particular religion who may feel threatened by it, is not covered by the Act. Therefore the aspect of free speech which allows criticism, parody, insult or abuse of a religious belief remains unaffected.

Application of this Offence to the Online Context

The wording in Part IIIA is deliberately broad and therefore is a good example of legislation which can cover both online and offline activity equally well. S.29B (above) makes no mention of the requirement to be in the presence of the victim, and there is no requirement of the medium by which an individual communicates in order to commit the offence. S.29B is most appropriately applied to hate speech online – the communication either verbally or in writing with others in order to incite religious hatred. However there are other sections which may be relevant to online behaviour and are also worth mentioning. S.29C covers publication of written material, and again online 'publication' (e.g. placing upon a website) would therefore come under this provision. Running a website or a blog with content that is considered threatening, which deliberately incites religious hatred, would complete the offence.

Also, s.29E (distributing, showing or playing a recording) would also be as relevant in the online context as this would also cover anything presented online in audio or video format as well. Placing recordings on an online video site such as YouTube or Vimeo, or video blogging would therefore be caught by this section. Ordinarily the offence would not be committed where the behaviour considered as inciting *was* taking place in a person's home, or not in the presence of anyone who might feel threatened by it. However, in order to ensure that the activities of a person sat alone at their computer in their own home do not fall outside the scope of the Act, it should also be pointed out that if the speech, written material is available to others, then this does still mean that it is covered by the Act. Much of this sort of activity, where taking place, for example, on internet forums and in a situation of anonymity, might be considered to be private, but its accessibility to the general public therefore means that it would be an offence (Chan 2007).

Application of the Religious Hatred Offence

One of the things that should be borne in mind regarding the offences in Part IIIA of the Public Order Act is the restrictive terminology used here, and this has been identified as a weakness (Olivia 2007). The requirement of intent and also the restriction of the offence to threats rather than also incorporating abuse and insults, as in Part III regarding racial hatred, demonstrate the limited capacity of this offence to have a significant effect. In addition to this, the effect of s.29J limits this offence further, and therefore on its own the religious hatred laws do not appear to be enough to tackle the issue of online religious hatred such as that seen in Islamophobic behaviour except in the most extreme circumstances.

Human Rights Considerations

When considering a topic such as this, it is also important to consider the human rights issues. The impact of the law in this area has to be carefully balanced with Freedom of Speech under Article 10 of the European Convention on Human Rights. Therefore the offences laid down in the 2006 Act have to be carefully balanced with freedom of speech as understood in the ECHR. This is partially dealt with in the distinction mentioned earlier regarding the difference between criticism or attacks on a specific religion, and threats or attacks against those persons who follow that religion. Taking into account the text of s.29J mentioned above, the distinction here should be reasonably clear, and the point made by the ECHR in *Otto-Preminger-Institute v Austria* (1994 19 EHRR 737) was that criticism of religion is to be expected in a free society. This distinction appears to be drawn along the lines of whether it is the religion which is being subjected to criticism or attack, or whether its followers are being threatened because of their adherence to the religion in question. S.29J's wording tries to make this distinction.

Religiously Aggravated Offences

As well as the religious hatred law, there are also provisions for augmenting the sentences handed out to those found guilty of other offences where they have been aggravated by racial or religious factors. This is contained in the Crime and Disorder Act 1998, and was originally intended to cover racial factors only, but has been subsequently expanded to include religious factors too (Amendment by the Anti-terrorism, Crime and Security Act 2001, s.39). The key with such offences is that the 'basic' offence must first be established. It is only once this has happened that the aggravating factor can then be added. Under s.28, hostility is the defining characteristic which indicates the racial or religious aggravating factor if:

a. At the time of the offence (or shortly before or after), the offender demonstrates to the victim hostility based on the victim's membership (or presumed membership) of a racial or religious group; or

b. The offence is motivated wholly or partly by hostility towards members of a racial or religious group based on their membership (or presumed membership) of that group (Crime and Disorder Act 1998, c.37, s.28 (1)).

It is demonstration of hostility or motivation by hostility that therefore establishes the aggravation. Guidance from the Crown Prosecution Service (Racist and Religious Crime: Legal Guidance 2010) indicates that demonstration of hostility is much easier to establish than motivation by hostility, presumably because the former is more easily objectively observed. Part II also lists a number of offences in s.29–32. The most relevant here is contained in s.31, which deals with public order offences such as harassment. This has one major advantage in that the strict and precise language of Part IIIA of the Public Order Act is not also to be found here, and therefore a lower threshold needs to be achieved in order to show the offence. So for example, in s.31, religious aggravation can be added to s.4A and s.5, regarding the offence of harassment. S.31 also covers actions where there is fear or provocation of violence in the commission of the offence. In addition, s.4 deals with threats of violence, but is phrased to include abusive and insulting words as found in the wording in Part III regarding racial hatred. However, it is assumed that because this contradicts the later law that the 'abusive and insulting' aspect of the law does not apply.

Crimes Related to Harassment

Also outside of the specific offence of inciting religious hatred, it may be possible to apply laws aimed specifically at preventing harassment. If the behaviour concerned does not fall within the strict boundaries of the religious hatred offence, but if behaviour is persistent and is considered to be harassment, then it may fall under the provisions of the law, and may also be considered to be religiously aggravated as mentioned above (Allport 1954).

The Protection from Harassment Act 1997, s.1 states:

1. A person must not pursue a course of conduct –
   a. which amounts to harassment of another, and
   b. which he knows or ought to know amounts to harassment of the other (Protection from Harassment Act 1997, c.40, s.1(1)).

Although admittedly not aimed specifically at the type of activity discussed in this chapter, it does nevertheless provide a possible avenue of action in situations where there is harassment of another online, for example internet 'trolling', where the activity becomes persistent and repeated. The offence itself has been described as being by necessity technologically neutral and therefore something which can be applied to harassing conduct both offline and online, rather than separate offences (Geach and Haralambous 2009).

When seen in combination with the religious aggravation discussed above, it can be seen how harassment offences can therefore be useful in dealing with Islamophobic abuse perpetrated against individuals. The harassment offence gives a basis for tackling the behaviour, and the punishment available for such activity can therefore be augmented by the provisions of the Crime and Disorder Act as discussed.

Specific Offences Concerning Online Activity

In addition to this, the Malicious Communications Act 1998 s.1(1) contains an offence of 'sending letters, etc. with intent to cause distress and anxiety'. S.1(1) was amended in 2001 by the Criminal Justice and Police Act to include indecent, grossly offensive, threatening or false information by 'letter, electronic communication or article of any description' (Malicious Communications Act 1988, c.27, s.1(1), as amended by the Criminal Justice and Police Act 2001, s.43(1)(a). Originally intended for an age before the Internet, this Act has, since the amendment, therefore also incorporated online activity, and as with other areas, with broad and neutral language which allows it to cover activities carried out online, including social media.

The Malicious Communications Act may also prove to be more effective in tackling harassment via the internet due to a further amendment which, at the time of writing, is still yet to be enacted. Clause 27 of the Criminal Justice and Courts Bill 2015 will increase the maximum penalties for offences under s.1 of the Malicious Communications Act to two years. Those campaigning for tougher punishments for 'trolling' behaviour have generally welcomed this.

Finally, the Communications Act 2003 also provides for a very similar offence in s.127. On the face of it, this appears to be almost identical to the offences already discussed, covering the sending of material that is 'grossly offensive ... indecent, obscene or [of a] menacing character' (Communications Act 2003, c.21, s.127(1)(a). However this offence concerns the act of using a public electronic communications network in committing the offence, unlike the other offences mentioned earlier which can be committed by way of private communications. In *DPP v Collins* (2006 UKHL 40) Lord Bingham commented that the focus of the offence was not on protecting individuals from harm, but preventing the public communications networks from being used to send such messages. As such, the offence is committed by the *actus reus* of sending the message on a public network.

Application of these Offences to the Online Environment

So far the offences discussed have been those which apply generally to religious hatred or religiously aggravation. There is no mention of the online environment or how they are to be applied to them. This is mainly because the UK's approach to such offences has been that of technological neutrality (Whine 2006). This has advantages in that there do not need to be specific offences applied to the online environment, something which can be complicated to define where technology is constantly moving forward and new systems and methods of communication are constantly being introduced.

However, it also has disadvantages where, without specific examples of where the law has been applied to online activity, it is difficult to anticipate how the law can be applied. Also, the main concern about the application of what are seen as 'real world' laws to cyberspace is evidential – the Internet is often anonymous, with comments and activity difficult to attribute to identifiable 'real world' individuals. An additional concern has been with regard to the international nature of the Internet, and the way in which activity will transcend borders where laws will not. The pursuit and prosecution of offenders who reside in other countries presents difficulties where they are perpetrating offences which apply in the UK.

International Law and Jurisdictional Issues

The biggest issue presented by the use of the internet in offences such as those we have discussed is that of jurisdiction. The internet allows international access to information anywhere in the world (subject to any local blocking regulations) and therefore the likelihood of the alleged perpetrator being outside of the reach of the courts is quite high. The same rules apply as do for any other type of criminal or illegal activity – an individual who is outside of the jurisdiction of the courts is outside of the reach of punishment.

The unusual issue that online activity presents is that the activity itself may be physically located on a computer in another country but is accessible in the UK. This therefore presents particular problems to law enforcement bodies who wish to prosecute any of the offences mentioned above. With regard to civil law issues such as intellectual property infringements, the approach has been that if information is accessible in a particular country, then it is subject to the laws of that country, and therefore this has been the basis of actions for infringement of that intellectual property.

This has carried over generally into civil law and contractual disputes, see for example several cases which dealt with this in the context of the Brussels I regulation, which governs choice of law for civil law disputes in the EU (see for example Case C-441/13 *Pez Hejduk v Energie Agentur.NRW GmbH* [2015] All ER (D) 161 and *Pinckney v KDG Mediatech AG* [2013] All ER (D) 49). These cases both discussed whether infringements were actionable in the jurisdiction where they were hosted on the internet outside the country in question, but were nevertheless accessible there. The law in this area has also gone as far as to say that this is the case even where it is not possible to establish the location of the alleged infringer (Case C-292/10 *G v de Visser* [2012] 3 WLR 1523).

This principle has also been applied to the criminal law, and an example which can be directly applied to the religious hatred offences discussed above. *R v Sheppard and Whittle* (2010 EWCA Crim 65) was a case involving persons prosecuted for incitement to racial hatred with anti-Semitic information they posted online. It was argued by the defence that the offence was not committed in the UK as the server upon which the information was placed was in the US, and the information in question did not breach laws regarding freedom of speech there. The court disagreed with this argument, and based its decision upon the access of that information in the UK, and therefore the effective 'publication' of material in the UK contrary to the offence of incitement to racial hatred in the Public Order Act 1986. Arguably, within the limits discussed above, this would also apply to the religious hatred offence within the same Act (Awan and Blakemore 2012).

The only other limitation to this would be with regard to successful prosecution of individuals relying upon them being physically within the jurisdiction in the same way that this would apply to any other offence, and where this is not the case would rely upon relevant extradition treaties to bring the individual to justice. The approach of international law has been that of standard setting and encouragement of nation states in developing their own laws to tackle issues of religious intolerance. Under the umbrella of the UN, the International Covenant on Civil and Political Rights provides a clear mandate to States regarding dealing with this issue. Such considerations do of course involve the interaction between freedom of expression and freedom of religion. These are contained in Article 18 and 19 of the Covenant, and both have restrictions placed upon them. For example freedom of expression under Article 19 is 'subject to certain restrictions, but these shall only be such as are provided by law and are necessary ... for the respect of the rights ... of others' (International Covenant on Civil and Political Rights, Art. 19(3)(a)). Similarly, the freedom of religion in Article 18 provides that '[n]o one shall be subject to coercion which would impair his freedom to have or to adopt a religion or belief of his choice' (Ibid., Art 18(2)). This is key because like the religious hatred laws in the UK, it outlaws behaviour which would be considered to be threatening towards someone on the basis of their religion.

There are restrictions in Article 18 (3) that this freedom 'may be subject only to such limitations as are prescribed by law and are necessary to protect public safety, order, health, or morals or the fundamental rights and freedoms of others'. These two rights are therefore intended to exist in a framework whereby there are limitations to avoid problems of overlap between the two. The area of the Covenant which has most direct relevance to the prohibition of Islamophobic behaviour is that contained in Article 20, which states that 'Any advocacy of national, racial or religious hatred that constitutes incitement to discrimination, hostility or violence shall be prohibited by law' (Ibid., Art. 20(2)). Interestingly, this goes beyond the threats required by UK law, and refers to 'discrimination' and 'hostility', which on their ordinary meaning provide a broader range of potential situations which could be covered.

CPS Guidance on Offences Including Aggravating Factors of Anti-Religious Activity

The Crown Prosecution Service's guidelines regarding the application of the offences discussed above underlines the seriousness of these offences as well as providing some useful information regarding their interpretation. CPS guidance indicates that the religiously aggravated offences and how they are applied is important for a number of reasons (Racist and Religious Crime: Legal Guidance 2010). Firstly, the penalty applied, and also the issue of which court the offence will be tried in become important. The aggravating factor may result in the offence becoming one which is triable either way, as opposed to summary offences.

Secondly, the guidance also points out the general duty on criminal courts to treat an offence more seriously if there is a racial or religiously aggravating factor to the circumstances (Criminal Justice Act 2003, c.44, s.145). Such treatment would therefore inform sentencing for that offence, within the envelope of the sentencing tariff. With regard to the religious hatred offences under the 2006 Act (discussed above), guidance from the CPS also underlines the sensitive nature of prosecuting such offences. Rather than being dealt with regionally by CPS offices, allegations of such offences have to be referred to the Special Crime and Counter Terrorism Division (SCCTD) to be dealt with by them. As such, decisions on proceeding with such prosecutions will be taken by those with specialist experience of the type of offence, something which is important because of the sensitive nature, and also because of the difficulty in establishing a successful case because of the very high standard applied to the offence. It should also be referred to the Attorney General, who must give consent for the prosecution before it goes ahead. All of this demonstrates that such prosecutions are not commonplace, are carefully applied and extremely careful consideration will be given before proceeding. However this does mean there is a risk of action only being taken in situations where clear evidence and very high level of probability of success is present.

Liability of Internet Service Providers in relation to Islamophobic Activity

In situations where written material or audio-visual material are posted online, or communications take place online, an alternative or addition to pursuing the offender using the law can also be the involvement of internet service providers (ISPs). This can be useful because as an immediate measure, material can be taken down by the ISP and therefore further incitement or harassment can be avoided. This is commonly based upon ISPs own terms of service rather than the law itself, however ISPs in jurisdictions such as the US where free speech laws are broad in application will often take action only in the face of a court order requiring them to do so. Nevertheless, where other types of offences have been involved, for example child pornography, then ISPs have faced a law which requires them to take the material down or face being complicit and therefore held liable for its continued presence on the Internet.

The basis for ISP action to take down material is rooted in the case of *Godfrey v Demon Internet* (2001 QB 201) where it was established that an ISP does not have a defence in law if they do not take down defamatory or false information within a reasonable time of having been given notice of the material. This is now something that can be found in the e-commerce regulations, and balances the position of ISPs who are not engaged in editorial activity with the content of their sites, with the need for them to act responsibly to take down inappropriate material where necessary. In this way it therefore gives a means whereby ISPs can ensure that they will not run into liability problems, whilst at the same time giving a complainant the ability to get offensive material or material which incites religious hatred removed.

This does have its limitations; however, in the *Sheppard and Whittle* case, the ISP in question was hosting the material on their servers in the US, in a system where the laws on racially motivated hate speech are somewhat different than they are here in the UK. The US Constitution's much wider approach to freedom of speech has meant that what would be considered illegal in the UK is not in the US, and therefore any attempt to get the ISP involved in any early take-down of material is likely to be unsuccessful.

Conclusion

The legal challenge to Islamophobic behaviour under UK law faces a number of issues that have been highlighted here. The law regarding religions itself is fairly controversial in that the approach has been to recognise the multicultural nature of the UK, and therefore the need to be neutral in regard to the treatment of different religions. Now that the blasphemy laws have been repealed, no one religion is intended to have particular status above others, and the religious hatred laws are intended to provide parity in that regard. The passage of the Racial and Religious Hatred Act 2006 was not without controversy, and has been restricted from its original position of parity with racial hatred laws. This is mitigated somewhat by the fact that some of the more general offences, in the area of harassment and also regarding abuse of telecommunications systems can provide some extra protection from those who use the internet to 'troll' or incite hatred against people on the grounds of their religion, and so does provide some extra protection.

However, the internet provides its own jurisdictional challenges regarding the enforcement of these laws. There is variance between countries as to how much protection is given to religions, from the very low level of protection in the US due to the strength of the freedom of speech laws, to other nations which have specific blasphemy laws, including some states where the predominant religion is Islam. The UN has attempted to provide a lead on these issues, although as we have seen, even the UK does not necessarily live up to the aims of the International Covenant discussed earlier. Criminal laws remain an issue for each individual country, and although there are solutions to Internet-only problems of where offences or civil infringements happen, these will still be subject to real-world problems of bringing people to justice only if they are physically within the jurisdiction unless suitable extradition arrangements are in place.

Further Reading

Awan, I and Blakemore, B. 2013. *Extremism, Counter-Terrorism and Policing*, Farnham: Ashgate.

Bowling, B. 1999. *Violent Racism: Victimisation, Policing and Social Context*. Revised Edition. Oxford: Oxford University Press.

References

Allport, G.W. 1954. *The Nature of Prejudice*, Reading, MA: Addison-Wesley.

Awan, I. 2013. Twitter has become a virtual wild wild west for online abuse, Tell MAMA, [Online]. Available at: http://tellmamauk.org/twitter-has-become-the-virtual-wild-wild-west-for-online-anti-muslim-abuse-says-imran-awan/ [accessed: 10 February 2015].

Awan, I and Blakemore, B. 2012. *Policing Cyber Hate, Cyber Threats and Cyber Terrorism*, Farnham: Ashgate.

Chakraborti, N. and Garland, J. 2009. *Hate Crime: Impact, Causes and Responses*, London: Sage Publications.

Chan, J.B.L. 2007. 'Police and new technologies', in *Handbook of Policing*, edited by Tim Newburn. Cullompton: Willan Publishing.

Geach, N. and Haralambous, N. 2009. 'Regulating Harassment: is the law fit for the social networking age?' *Journal of Criminal Law*, 73(3), 241–57 at 246.

Jeremy, A. 2007. 'Practical Implications of the enactment of the Racial and Religious Hatred Act 2006', *Ecclesiastical Law Journal*, 9(2), 187–201.

Olivia, J.G. 2007. 'The legal protection of believers and beliefs in the United Kingdom', *Ecclesiastical Law Journal*, 9(1), 66–86 at 80.

Perry, B (2001). *In the Name of Hate: Understanding Hate Crimes*, London: Routledge.

Racist and Religious Crime: Legal Guidance http://www.cps.gov.uk/legal/p_to_r/racist_and_religious_crime/.

Waldrum, H. 2013. Twitter rolls out 'report abuse' button for individual tweets: will you use it? [Online] Available at: http://www.theguardian.com/technology/blog/2013/aug/30/twitter-report-abusebutton [accessed: 5 September 2014].

Wall, D. 2001. (ed.) *Crime and the Internet*, NY, Routledge.

Whine, M. 2006. 'Cyberhate, anti-Semitism and counter legislation', *Communications Law*, 11(4), 124–31 at 127.

Yar. M. 2006. *Cybercrime and Society*, London, Sage Publications.

Chapter 8
Policing Anti-Muslim Hate Crime on the Internet

Imran Awan

The racist murder of Stephen Lawrence, raised a number of questions with regards the manner in which the police deal with hate crime. In particular, the police have been labelled as being passive and not doing enough to help protect victims of hate crime (Bowling 1999). This view is reinforced after a series of prominent cases, revealed how victims of hate crime reported these incidents to the police and witnessed very little action take place. Indeed, in 2007 Fiona Pilkington set her vehicle on fire, killing both her and her 18-year-old daughter, Francecca Hardwick. An inquest would later find how both Pilkington and her daughter were 'prisoners' in their home, as a group of youths had targeted them with a campaign of abuse and hate, which included throwing stones and objects at their home. This form of offline and online hate crime has prompted real issues and concerns with regards to how the police tackle hate crime, as a jury found that the police had contributed towards their death, as they failed to respond to the family's concerns.

The incident also revealed the impact and damage of hate crime upon victims and the subsequent issues about a lack of trust between the police and victims of hate crime, more generally. Coliandris argues (2012: 75) that it also shows: 'the serious consequences which can flow from the convergence of what Pilkington (2010) terms 'age-old habits' (for 'teenage pranks') and the 'huge social power' of new information and communication technologies (ICTs)'. Bowling (1999) argues that the police in such instances fail to categorise and differentiate between what are 'low level' and 'high level' hate crimes, which often can lead to them making mistakes and errors. Bowling (1999) argues that this forms part of the hierarchy of 'police relevance' which often involves categorising hate crime as less of a priority due to police culture.

Indeed, with the emergence of new technology and the power of the internet, the way in which hate crime occurs online is also now a policing priority. The Woolwich attack in South-east London, for example revealed a significant increase in anti-Muslim abuse online and crucially a number of organisations such as Tell MAMA have argued that the police have been 'failing' to investigate the hundreds of cases of anti-Muslim hate messages that are reported to them on the Internet. As noted in Chapter 1, Tell MAMA was established to provide a national referral mechanism for anti-Muslim hate crime. Through the use of webpage and telephone service, it provides a crucial service to all sections of the Muslim community. Alongside organisations such as Tell MAMA, the police are also meant to be working in partnership with wider third party reporting organisations that can help provide a key focus to Muslim victims and also provide an effective partnership to areas where victims have experienced anti-Muslim hostility.

Tell MAMA argue that in the majority of cases they report to the police, they have had a response from the police with regard to only 70 cases (at the time of writing). Currently, after recording details of abuse, Tell MAMA will report these cases directly to the Association of Chief Police Officer's (ACPO) hate crime reporting system. Fiyaz Mughal, who is the Director of Tell MAMA, stated that: 'There have been numerous occasions where we have sent information about direct threats to mosques, which frankly we haven't heard anything about ... It is worrying for us, given that the number of call-backs and subsequently the number of investigations that have moved forward have been extremely small in comparison to the volume of hate crimes we have sent in to police forces' (BBC News 2013).

In one of the case studies cited by Tell MAMA, in a BBC 5 Live investigation into police reporting of online anti-Muslim abuse in 2013, a 25-year-old woman was repeatedly targeted by a man who had posted a photograph of her on Twitter and called her an 'ugly Pakistani'. Subsequently, a number of these individual followers had commented on her appearance, which included racist language in many of the subsequent messages that followed. The threats included those from an English Defence League sympathiser who made the case that he '... lives very close to her'. However, after reporting the incident to the police it became apparent that she felt demoralised and angry as the police response was poor. She stated that:

> I made a statement and the police said it was quite difficult to do anything because it's quite difficult to prosecute someone when it comes to online abuse ... They told me the evidence was no longer there, that it was difficult to identify who he was and there was just so much online abuse. The police said they'd be in touch but that was a week ago and I still haven't heard anything. (BBC News 2013)

In another case reported to Tell MAMA the victim of online anti-Muslim abuse stated that:

> I feel like it has been a waste of time reporting to the police, unless your life was at serious risk, as the whole process can seem a useless exercise when the police inform you that they can't trace who is behind the account and that it could be

his associates? You feel like what's the point! Just proves to me the police do not have the technology to deal with online trolls and the aftercare support can be isolating.

This chapter examines some of these important issues with regards policing hate crime and the impact upon the wider community, the underreporting of hate crime and the complex nature of the web, that makes it extremely difficult to police.

Policing Online Hate Crime

As noted above, hate crime and the manner in which the police deal with it, has historically consisted of problematic associations between what is low-level and high-level hate crime (Iganski 2010). Chakraborti and Garland (2009) argue that hate crime can be categorised in the manner in which victims report hate crime from low-level racist harassment (for example, incidents such as verbal and racist abuse) to 'high-level' hate crime incidents (such as physical assaults) (Chakraborti and Garland 2009: 34). They argue that this allows for a drip-drip effect which begins as minor low-level hate incidents but these can quickly escalate into more serious high-level hate incidents, which can have a significant impact upon the victims that are targeted (Home Office 2010).

Indeed, cyber hate issues have often been used and described as being 'low-level' incidents, where the language includes abusive comments and not actual cyber violence. However, the nature of cyber violence does require it to be considered an important area of investigation within the field of hate crime studies. Thurlow et al. (2009) identifies four key categories of 'cyber violence' (cited in Coliandris 2012: 84). These include: online and offline abuse, cyber stalking, online harassment, and harmful images and text.

Policing cyberspace has often been left to the police services, however increasingly within this digital age, when it comes to tackling wider hate crime, this has often been controlled by a wider and more complex system of 'plural policing', that involves a wider number of stakeholders and partners who are working together to police the internet (Crawford 2007). This involves the use of both the public and voluntary stakeholders and organisations who are working together to police cyber hate. According to Coliandris (2012: 86) however these initiatives do come with dangers. He states that: 'These arrangements have been institutionalised with mixed results across the UK on a statutory footing through landmark law reforms such as the Crime and Disorder Act of 1998. Over the past decade or so, a range of issues to do with UK statutory partnerships have been identified which suggest less than optimal working relations and conditions'.

Furthermore, Coliandris and Rogers (2008) argue that a number of other problems emerge because of the problems around cyber policing and partnership work. They argue that where there are issues about intelligence-gathering and a lack of resources in dealing with crime prevention, this can lead to mixed results when confronting online hate crime. Whine (2003) argues that policing cyberspace is therefore problematic because the police have to ensure that they balance the right to free speech and at the same time be able to act when an offence has been committed. Moreover, there are problems about understanding the correct jurisdiction for which the offence has been committed. Indeed, Coliandris (2012: 89) argues that: 'The defining features of the Internet are, after all, its dynamic, borderless, networked and globalised character and for some, the defining property of the Internet is its commitment to, and opportunities for, open and unregulated speech.'

Wall (2001) goes further and argues that policing cyberspace has also meant a public form of policing it which is done through a level of understanding with regards ISPs and state-funded organisations. Within this space, the international problems around jurisdiction mean that the police therefore have to work a number of different partners such as the internet companies when challenging online hate crime. Inevitably, this also creates problems because different countries will have different legislation and rules around social media and hate crime. This is important because in countries such as the United States, the First Amendment provides protection of freedom of speech (Henry 2009).

Despite this, freedom of speech is not an absolute right, as one of the leading cases in the UK (*R v Shepherd and Whittle* [2010] EWCA Crim 65) has identified. In this case, two white supremacists had disseminated racist and hostile material over the internet and were convicted of publishing racially inflammatory material. Interestingly, both men argued that because the material was hosted by a server in the United States that they were subject to United States jurisdiction and not UK legislation. The Court of Appeal, however rejected this argument on the basis that as long as the material was intending to stir up racial hatred then it could be deemed an offence despite the server being located in a different country (Smith 2010).

Clearly, these issues do pose a number of transnational challenges and Coliandris argues that one way of effectively overcoming these is through the use of problem-orientated policing (POP) which was developed by Herman Goldstein (1990) in the United States. POP is a method of policing used, whereby the police take a proactive role in identifying, understanding and responding to problems in the community including those potentially in virtual communities. Unlike other models of policing it is proactive as opposed to incident-led or reactive forms of policing (Bullock et al. 2006). Furthermore, it also helps identify recurrent problems, identifying points of intervention and implementing and devising new initiatives. John Eck and William Spelman

(1987) gave the approach more focus with the SARA model which helps to identify and specify the problem at hand and analyse, in this case the (hate crime data) to understand why the problem is occurring and thus help and develop when and where responses would be best implemented. The SARA model therefore involves in practical steps, scanning (for regular problems/patterns), analysis (for causes/reasons), responding (developing intervention) and the assessment (outcomes). This is a useful way of policing cyber hate as it allows the police to use intelligence, intervention and implementation as a means to identify and root out online hate speech.

Coliandris (2012: 89) argues that:

> Essentially, POP requires a fundamental orientation towards deeper problems rather than individual incidents, and calls for a renewed emphasis on the mobilisation of police and community resources in an effort to reduce demands on policing and to deliver longer-lasting solutions, education, active risk assessment/management), intelligence-led policing, partnership working, and situational and social-oriented preventive approaches …. Cyber hate regulation will also require authorities to respond creatively and flexibly: as discussed, the form and dynamics of hate crime are constantly shifting and authorities will be required to adapt positively to emerging new threats and opportunities.

Chan (2007) makes the case that policing cyberspace, therefore requires flexibility and a move away of traditional policing methods. Indeed, it does appear that as the internet remains unregulated that this does pose significant challenges ahead. Thus, it does appear that policing the internet and online hate crime, requires innovative ways of tackling online hate and ensuring that communities feel safe in reporting incidents to the police.

Policing Online Victimisation

Cyber hate has been used historically, by the far-right and white supremacists, who have used it to inflame religious and racial tensions (see Chapter 4). A study for the think-tank group Demos (2011) has found that far right populist movements are gaining in support across Europe and playing upon a small perception of public disenfranchisement within society to promote an agenda of protecting national identity as a method to whip up online anti-Muslim hate. The Demos study (2011) is important, because their findings would seem to suggest that groups such as the EDL, have become a web based far-right group that is using social networking sites such as Facebook and Twitter where it has gained a large group of online sympathisers to target Muslim communities. Interestingly, Feldman et al. (2013) data set from Tell MAMA showed that US anti-Islamist activists Pamela Geller,

Robert Spencer and Tommy Robinson had all been reported to Tell MAMA for online abusive comments against Muslim communities.

As discussed previously, a number of these cases reported to the police include examples where people have made malicious comments via social networking sites such as Twitter and Facebook. Many of the cases have led to people being arrested, detained and charged as noted in Chapter 1 for offences relating to religious hatred and inciting racial hatred which is an offence under the Public Order Act. These comments made online are extremely damaging and have the ability to ignite further racial divisions and can be divisive for issues of multiculturalism and diversity.

The problem for the police therefore is helping root out online far-right groups and lone wolf extremists who are using social networking sites like Twitter and Facebook to post malicious statements. This realm of cyber activism used by groups like the EDL and others who are promoting online hate means the police require more people to report what they see and what they read so that they can take the necessary actions required to either remove the online hate material or in some cases arrest and charge people. At the moment those who use online hate to disguise themselves in a cloak of anonymity remain at large because they understand that unless someone reports them they can remain anonymous. As noted previously, people can be prosecuted for online hate crime under the Communications Act if it is deemed to be inciting racial or religious hatred. The Crown Prosecution Service has also published guidelines with regards this and recently published a higher threshold for prosecutions on social media (see Chapter 7). This threshold means that messages of online hate must involve a 'credible threat' and not simply be offensive, shocking or disturbing' (Crown Prosecution Service guidelines 2014).

As noted previously, the impact of online hate crime can be immense and as a result the College of Policing has published new guidelines with regards internet hate crime which may help to address some of those wider concerns. Feldman et al. (2013: 23) found that women who were responsible for 18% of online incidents also had links with the EDL. They found that a number of the incidents reported included direct threats from burning down mosques to killing Muslim babies. They state that: 'Racist remarks were, in turn, mainly anti-Pakistani comments and references to dirt and filth. More generally there were comments accusing Muslims of rape; paedophilia; incest; interbreeding; being terrorists; and killing Jews.' Accordingly cyber hate can take many forms. The report by Feldman et al. (2013) highlights these representations of 'cyber violence'. Below is a direct set of quotes taken from the Feldman et al. (2013: 25–26) report regarding online anti-Muslim abuse:

'Just pour pigs blood in every reservoir in Britain, the whole land will be tainted, good bye muzzrats!' EDL Yorkshire Ref. 308.

'Have you seen the price of meat? And Muslim babies are so plentiful! Sharia allows sodomising babies! #EDL' Ref. 370.

'There is no such thing as a moderate Muslim. They are all nutjobs because they are animals'. 'Tommy Robinson' Ref. 313.

'Hope your mosque has fire insurance Muslim immigrant cunt. Fried halal'. 'You raped British women and children. Now you can pay'. EDL Ref. 29343.

The above examples show that online comments are contributing towards the stigmatisation and the 'othering' of Muslim communities. However, both offline and online incidents can also have a similar pattern and a trend, which is based primarily on the perpetrator using abusive language to pose real offline threats against Muslim communities (Awan and Blakemore 2012). Therefore the above incidents clearly show that online hate crime committed against Muslim communities in this instance can have a detrimental impact upon the governments social and community cohesion strategy as well as a more personal impact on the victims and the families affected by such measures. The online prejudice and discrimination paradigm is used by perpetrators who will involve swearing and racist language as a means to target a particular group.

This online element is also used by perpetrators where statements and messages which are prejudicial are used to target a particular group or person. This is often personified by racist jokes and stereotypical 'banter'. If these incidents go unchecked, physical attacks can also take place and could culminate from extreme online prejudice and discrimination which are intertwined together. Indeed, this type of negativity can also lead to an escalation of online abuse and the normalisation of such behaviour through likes and retweets via social media sites such as Twitter and Facebook. Below the chapter will examine the issue of reporting online abuse from Muslim communities and why issues of a lack of trust with the police and Muslim community may also have an impact on reporting online Muslim Communities.

Policing Hate Crime, Communities and Trust

One of the major issues of cyber hate is the role of the police in dealing with an increasing complex arena that allows many people to remain anonymous and is based in many cases on a person's personal fortitude and courage to come forward and report such incidents. Tell MAMA (2013) for example actively encourages people to report these incidents in particular from the Muslim community who at many times may feel stigmatised from reporting such incidents because of 'fear' of what the community might think. Apart from these problems, the role of the police in dealing with hate incidents offline will also have an impact on how incidents are reported online. For example, public perception of the police in tackling offline hate crime has had a significant impact upon police and Muslim community relations.

Historically, the policing of ethnic minorities have often been tainted by allegations of policing by stereotypes that include racial prejudice and racial discrimination of Black and Asian men. Bowling (1999) argues that this can be traced back to historical issues such as the 1981 Brixton riots which have led to a legacy of mistrust. Following the 9/11 attacks the risk is that those stereotypes have re-emerged with 'over policing' of Muslim communities, who are increasingly viewed with suspicion. This intensified with cases such as Rizwaan Sabir. Sabir, a student at the University of Nottingham, was arrested by the police for downloading an al-Qaeda training manual but released without charge. After winning damages of £20,000 from Nottinghamshire police, Sabir said: 'I was very, very lucky in the sense that I was released without charge because I was innocent in the first place ...' (cited by Jones in *The Guardian* 2011).

The Sabir case highlights how, post-9/11, the police need to be very careful about how they deal with counter-terrorism cases because old stereotypes may re-emerge and may have a wider impact upon how Muslim communities report online abuse. Indeed, in a joint study I conducted regarding policing and Muslim community relations, we found that often participants would describe the police as being 'racist', 'heavy-handed', 'unprofessional' and having a 'lack of communication and community skills'. This in turn resulted in the Muslim community not reporting crime to the police because they felt a sense of mistrust (Awan et al. 2013).

Furthermore, victims' lack trust and confidence in the police could be due to racist stereotyping at the hands of police and also traumatic events that may have occurred. Indeed, Awan et al.'s (2013) study of Muslim community perceptions of the police also found real issues of a lack of trust of the police service and also the view that individual experiences with the police shaped that mistrust and were some reasons why they felt not comfortable reporting abuse to the police. Counter-terrorism policing operations also appeared to have a significant impact on the Muslim community's perception of the police service. For example, in Birmingham, the local community and area had been making headline news in the wake of controversial counter-terrorism arrests. Project Champion and the installation of secret CCTV cameras to effectively ring fence the Muslim community in predominately Muslim areas in Birmingham and monitor their movements was an additional reason why the community was distrustful of the police (Awan 2012).

As previously discussed hate crimes have been identified as both 'low level' and 'high level' priority incidents. Indeed, evidence shows that because cyber hate incidents are not reported regularly to the police, there remains a problem in the actual data and its reliability when examining online anti-Muslim abuse. By this the author suspects that the actual number of online incidents is much higher but because of under-reporting we do not have the exact true figures. This is intensified because at times people are not aware when an online hate crime offence has been committed or in some cases decide to report the online abuse to a different company and not the police (Chakraborti and Garland 2009). Moreover, even if such cases are reported to the police, it is acknowledged that they do have limited resources, and in many cases tracking this crime can have many problems from both a jurisdictional point of view with internet service providers, to the role of free speech and the issue of online hate crime protocol. Below the chapter will examine the new College of Policing strategy and guidelines with regards online hate crime.

Policing Strategy for Online Hate Crime

The ACPO and the new College of Policing have now established new guidelines and rules with regards online hate crime and operational guidance for police officers who must respond to online hate crime. The guidelines are important as they replace the old hate crime manual that was published in 2005 and work alongside the new national policing hate crime strategy. As noted in chapter one, religious hate crime is where: 'Any criminal offence which is perceived, by the victim or any other person, to be motivated by a hostility or prejudice based on a person's religion or perceived religion.' The College of Policing guidance makes it clear that far-right extremists pose major challenges for the police. The College of Policing guidance (2014: 39) states that:

> The emergence of the English Defence League and similar groups has highlighted the animosity towards Islam and Muslims that exists in the UK. The mass killings carried out by right-wing extremist Anders Breivik in 2011 in Norway were evidence of how such bigotry can escalate into violence if left unchecked. Breivik had many extremist views but foremost in his bigotry was his objection to Islam and Muslims.

Police forces in England, Wales and Northern Ireland have recorded 636 anti-Muslim hate crimes in 2011 (total 1, 829 recorded religious hate crimes) (College of Policing guidelines 2014). However, as noted above a number of these hate crimes do go unreported. ACPO acknowledge that some of the reasons for why people do not report these incidents are because of issues of trust between the police and communities. There may of course other barriers that need to be dismantled such as fear of being victims of hate crime and in some cases victims not knowing what might constitute a hate crime.

The new operational guidance for hate crime against Muslim communities also states that:

> The police need to understand the nature of the problems faced by communities and to build relationships with them which give victims the confidence to report crimes. It is also important that hate crime trends are recognised and shared locally. Measuring anti-Muslim hate crime in isolation, without considering other motivations such as race, will give only a limited picture of the risks to local communities and their needs. (The College of Policing guidance 2014: 40)

As noted above, the police face major challenges in tackling online hate crime as offenders can in many cases simply delete messages or change accounts. The police acknowledge that there response to online hate crime has been in some cases 'erratic' and 'problematic'. The guidelines state (2014: 115) that: '... there have been many more occasions where victims have had poor responses from the police and have been left frustrated by their unwillingness to deal with the incident.' This sense of frustration can lead to problematic problems with how cyber hate material can be removed. As noted above, this is increasingly difficult when examining issues of jurisdiction and policing online hate crime.

The College of Policing operational guidance (2014: 115) states that:

> ... Although hate mail is still sent through the postal system, the majority of it is now sent by email, social networks, instant messaging and open-source websites. The internet also allows an individual to take on a new and anonymous identity, and to bypass traditional editorial controls, to share their views with millions.

Inevitably, this can lead to problems in how social media can be used by 'cyber mobs' and those who aim to target individuals with the rise in online hate messages. Indeed, a number of these offenders are able to use a false identity and use the power of the internet to amplify there messages of hate though a quick and easy mode of online hate. Despite these challenges there remain real problems with regards online hate crime legislation (discussed in Chapter 7).

According to the new guidance, if police officers receive any complaints regardless of what medium of online space they have suffered, they must deal with it as a hate crime. As well as recording a potential hate crime, the police must also ensure that all victims are treated with respect and dignity. The role of the police therefore is multi-faceted and includes bringing offenders to justice and at the same time reducing fear and helping restore community trust.

According to the new guidance given to police officers, the police must take the following operational steps, if an online hate crime is reported. These steps include:

- Establishing the nature of the complaint;
- Establishing on which online platform the abuse occurred;
- Identifying possible criminal offences;
- Making sure all evidence is secured;
- Preventing further use of device by which the online abuse occurred;
- To examine the audit trail where the online abuse occurred;
- To determine the time, date and geographic place of origin. (The College of Policing guidance 2014: 116)

Police forces in England and Wales, can also work and liaise closely with internet service providers which can often help them trace and track down where the online hate has appeared. As the new guidelines state (2014: 117) that: 'Wherever the computer or the individual is located, there will be an electronic audit trail that will have significant evidential value.' As noted above, this can be very important, especially where the police require information from different service providers based in different jurisdictions. Interestingly, the guidance also alerts police towards understanding the impact of online hate upon communities.

A number of the online hate messages can have individuals posing real threats and also warning of violent offline attacks and action against Muslim communities. It is important in such instances to ensure that many offenders who are posting this online hate messages to then escalate this type of behaviour and tackle the risk posed. The police are also working very closely with the Home Office to ensure that there is a national response towards cyber hate. A lot of this work is done closely with the True Vision website which considers the following key information:

- Consider the online hate material and offences caused;
- To keep the victim informed about the investigation;
- To keep the victim informed about any action the police need to take;
- To contact the ISP, so that offenders can be identified;
- To identify the location of where the offence has been committed;
- Where evidence is available, to be able to prosecute the offender. (The College of Policing guidance 2014: 118)

Clearly, whilst operationally the police are involved in a range of strategies at combatting online hate crime, there are also a range of things which they will not consider, due to limitations in policy and also the reactive focus of the True Vision website which like Tell MAMA are recording systems for online hate and are therefore not preventative in nature.

Conclusion

Policing online anti-Muslim hate crime is a complex problem and one that requires a wide range of partners working together alongside the police in order to best challenge and confront those issues. As noted above, this includes work alongside third party reporting groups, the CPS, the police and equality units. Sadly, it does appear that where there are issues of mistrust between the police and communities, then people are less likely to report online hate crime to the police. In the UK, a person is entitled to the right to freedom of thought and religion. With this in mind, people are entitled to follow their religious practices without fear of being victims of hate crime. At the moment, victims of hate crime however can feel a sense of fear and apprehension (Chakraborti and Garland 2009). Currently, the new guidance operational policing guidelines on online hate crime are welcomed and it is hoped that this will give police forces a clearer and stronger direction with regards cyber hate. Ultimately, the victims of hate crime are the most important people when it comes to dealing with online hate crime. Whilst policing online anti-Muslim hate crime has come a long way, there are still clearly questions about how we can effectively police cyberspace and ensure victim's rights are protected.

Further Reading

Chakraborti, N. and Garland, J. (2014) (eds) *Responding to Hate Crime: The Case for Connecting Policy and Research*, Bristol: The Policy Press.

Jewkes, Y. 2010. Public Policing and the Internet', in *Handbook of Internet Crime*, edited by Y. Jewkes and M. Yar. Cullompton: Willan.

Jewkes, Y. and Leukfeldt, R. 2012. Policing Cyber Crime, in *Cyber Safety: an Introduction*, edited by R. Leukfeldt and W. Stol. Utrecht: Eleven Publishing.

Jewkes, Y. and Yar, M. 2010. The Internet, Cybercrime, and the Challenges of the 21st Century, in *Handbook of Internet Crime*, edited by Y. Jewkes and M. Yar. Cullompton: Willan.

References

Awan, I. 2012. The Impact of Policing British Muslims: A Qualitative Exploration, *Journal of Policing, Intelligence and Counter-terrorism*, 7 (1): 22–35.

Awan, I. and Blakemore, B. 2012. *Policing Cyber Hate, Cyber Threats and Cyber Terrorism*, Farnham: Ashgate.

Awan, I., Blakemore, B. and Simpson, K. 2013. Muslim Communities Attitudes towards and recruitment into the British Police Service, *International Journal of Law, Crime and Justice*, 41 (4): 421–37.

BBC News, 2013. Police 'failing to investigate anti-Muslim abuse', [Online]. Available at: http://www.bbc.co.uk/news/uk-25057246 [accessed: 14 January 2015].

Bowling, B. 1999. *Violent Racism: Victimisation, Policing and Social Context*. Revised Edition. Oxford: Oxford University Press.

Bullock, K., Erol, R. and Tilley, N. 2006. *Problem-Oriented Policing and Partnerships: Implementing an Evidence-Based Approach to Crime Reduction*, Cullompton: Willan Publishing.

Chan, J.B.L. 2007. Police and New Technologies, in *Handbook of Policing*, edited by T. Newburn, Cullompton: Willan Publishing, 655–79.

Chakraborti, N. and Garland, J. 2009. *Hate Crime: Impact, Causes and Responses*, London: Sage Publications.

Coliandris, G. 2012. Hate in a Cyber Age, in *Policing Cyber Hate, Cyber Threats and Cyber Terrorism*, edited by I. Awan and B. Blakemore, Farnham: Ashgate, 75–94.

Crawford, A. 2007. The Pattern of Policing in the UK: Policing beyond the Police, in *Handbook of Policing*, edited by T. Newburn, Cullompton: Willan, 136–68.

Crown Prosecution Service, 2014. Guidelines on prosecuting cases involving communications sent via social media [Online]. Available at: http://www.cps.gov.uk/legal/a_to_c/communications_sent_via_social_media/ [accessed: 10 January 2015].

DEMOS Report. 2011. The Rise of Populism in Europe can be traced through Online Behaviour, [Online] Available at: http://www.demos.co.uk/files/Demos_OSIPOP_Book-web_03.pdf?1320601634 [accessed: 20 July 2014].

Eck, John E. and William Spelman. 1987. *Problem solving: Problem-oriented policing in Newport News*, Washington, DC: Police Executive Research Forum.

Feldman, M., Littler, M., Dack, J. and Copsey, N. 2013. Anti-Muslim Hate Crime and the Far Right, Teeside University, [Online]. Available at: http://tellmamauk.org/wpcontent/uploads/2013/07/antimuslim2.pdf [accessed: 4 September 2013].

Henry, J.S. 2009. Beyond Free Speech: Novel Approaches to Hate on the Internet in the United States. *Information & Communications Technology Law*. [Online]. 18 (2): 235–51. Available at: http://www.informaworld.com/smpp/content~content=a912572577~db=all~jumptype=rss [accessed: 28 September 2014].

Home Office. 2010. *Cyber Crime Strategy*. Cm. 7842. London: TSO.

Iganski, P. 2010. Hate crime, in *Handbook on Crime*, edited by F. Brookman, M. Maguire, H. Pierpoint and T. Bennett, Cullompton: Willan Publishing, 351–65.

Jones, S. 2011. Student in Al Qaida raid paid £20,000 by police, *The Guardian*, [Online]. Available at: http://www.theguardian.com/uk/2011/sep/14/police-pay-student-damages-al-qaida [accessed: 22 August 2014].

MailOnline, 2012. Cyber-sleuth Noel traces 'he needs to die' Facebook troll … and offers to pay for his studies, [Online]. Available at: http://www.dailymail.co.uk/tvshowbiz/article-2123384/Cyber-sleuthNoel-traces-needs-die-Facebook-troll-offers-pay-studies.html [accessed: 22 June 2014].

Smith, G. 2010. Race hate website conviction upheld where server sited in USA, Bird & Bird, [Online]. Available at: http://www.twobirds.com/en/news/articles/2012/race-hate-website--usa-050510 [accessed: 14 January 2015].

Tell MAMA (Measuring Anti-Muslim Attacks), 2013. Anti-Muslim Hate Crime, [Online] Available at: http://tellmamauk.org/ [accessed: 2 September 2014].

The College of Policing, 2014. Hate Crime Operational Guidance, [Online]. Available at: http://report-it.org.uk/files/hate_crime_operational_guidance.pdf [accessed: 14 January 2015].

Thurlow, C., Lengel, L. and Tomic, A. 2009. *Computer Mediated Communication: Social Interaction and the Internet*, London: Sage.

Wall, D. 2001. *Crime and the Internet*, London: Routledge.

Whine, M. 2003. Far right extremists on the Internet, in *CyberCrime: Law Enforcement, Security and Surveillance in the Information Age*, edited by D. Thomas and B.D. Loader, London: Routledge, 234–50.

Chapter 9

The Experiences of Victims of Online Islamophobia

Jeane Gerard and Kate Whitfield

Following the murder of Lee Rigby in Woolwich, South East London, in May 2013, Feldman and Littler (2014) reported an increase in online victimisation against Muslims. Michael Adebowale and his accomplice, Michael Adebolajo, targeted the young British soldier and ran over him with their car, before attacking him with a meat cleaver and knives in the street. According to Awan (2014) this horrific attack fuelled both online and offline Islamophobia, with physical attacks on the Muslim community (for example, the bombing of a mosque) and electronic aggression through forums such as Facebook and Twitter.

Islamophobia and Islamophobia-related incidents are not a new phenomenon, but have taken a variety of forms at different times, whilst fulfilling multiple functions (Richardson 2004). Additionally, Islamophobia can be exacerbated by a number of contextual factors. Indeed, it has been recognised that the daily lives of Muslims in the United States of America (USA) have been affected by an increase in discrimination in both public and private places due to their perceived religious affiliation (Barkdull et al. 2011). This chapter will consider trolling and online Islamophobia, as well as provide an overview of the impact of online victimisation and, more specifically, anti-Muslim abuse.

Online Victimisation through Trolling

The occurrence of trolling has been on the rise across online forums and Facebook pages, with abusive comments being very close to hate speech (BBC News 2014). *The Oxford Dictionary* (2015, para. 1) defines trolling as making 'a deliberately offensive or provocative online posting with the aim of upsetting someone or eliciting an angry response from them'. It is not a behaviour that is viewed lightly and can result in a prison sentence. For example, Sean Duffy was jailed for 18 weeks following his actions of posting offensive messages on tribute pages for young people who had committed suicide (BBC News 2014).

However, according to Philips (2012), there is no agreed definition of the concept of trolling, which in the past has included a variety of behaviours, ranging from harmless pranks to defamation and cyberbullying. The term can be dated back to the 1990s, where 'to troll' referred to disrupting the conversation on a discussion board by posting incendiary comments. This could be either for the perpetrator's own amusement or because they wished to initiate some form of conflict. Philips (2012) suggests that a troll is difficult to distinguish from people who are racist, sexist, or simply ignorant. Nevertheless, they can be recognised by sometimes including subtle references to trolling so that other like-minded trolls may notice these references and respond accordingly to them.

In a study where the meaning of trolling was extracted from discussions in a number of online forums, Hardaker (2010) found that a troll is considered by users to be an online forum user who creates a genuine image of wanting to belong to, and participate in, a particular forum. This may include communicating false and disingenuous messages, while the true motive is to create a disturbance in the forum and initiate or aggravate conflict for no real reason other than personal entertainment. According to Hardaker (2010), there are four potential responses to trolling. First, it can be prevented from progressing if others correctly perceive the troll's intentions and do not react to their messages. Secondly, it can be countered from succeeding if others correctly perceive the troll's objectives, but respond to their messages in a way that thwarts these original intentions. Thirdly, it can fail if the plans of the troll are not noticed by the other users and they do not respond to the inflammatory messages. Finally, it can be successful if the forum's users trust the troll's messages and are provoked into providing a genuine response. It is worth noting that forum users can also 'mock troll', which is where they may pretend to troll by writing provocative messages, but their aim is to use these messages to encourage user cohesion within the forum (Hardaker 2010). Herring, et al. (2002, p. 372) illustrate the purpose of trolling by citing a forum user called Andrew, who states, 'The object of recreational trolling is to sit back and laugh at all those gullible idiots that will believe *anything*'. This declaration shows that the intent of a troll is to disrupt the ongoing conversation in such a way that it may lead to an extended aggravated argument (Herring et al. 2002).

The Impact of Online Victimisation and Trolling

Hate comments found on the internet can impact negatively on the victims and their families, and can be both upsetting and frightening (Bunglawala, 2012 cited in Awan, 2014). Indeed, as expected in the Sean Duffy case, the last thing families and friends who set up tribute pages after the loss of a loved one want is to receive abuse from anybody. A number of cases of online victimisation have been found on Facebook pages that were set up in memory of individuals. In these cases, victims were mocked and abused. For example, the Facebook memorial page of Georgia Varley (aged 16), who died after falling under a train in Liverpool in October 2011, was taken down after derogatory messages were left by trolls (BBC News 2011a). Members of Parliament (MP) have reacted with shock and disgust to similar attacks, such as conservative MP Karen Bradley, who found a Facebook page with graphic pictures and abuse relating to the accidental death of Hayley Bates, who died in a car crash in Stoke-on-Trent (BBC News 2011b). Victims of this online abuse and their family members need to be protected from these cruel behaviours.

Similar to cyberbullying, trolling cannot be contained in a particular area of the world and is an international phenomenon. In 2006, in Missouri (USA), Megan Meier committed suicide after being bullied online in MySpace by her neighbour (see Chapter 10 for further discussion of case studies of cyber bullying). The offender, Lori Drew, was later acquitted of unauthorised computer use. Freedom of speech, which is protected by the first amendment of the USA Constitution, makes arresting and punishing online offenders very difficult (BBC News 2014).

It has been suggested that the behaviour of offenders who target their victims through the internet can be viewed as 'normal' by the offenders. This is due to the feeling of anonymity that the online environment provides (Douglas et al. 2005 cited in Awan, 2014). According to Christopherson (2007), there are two types of anonymity, namely, technical anonymity and social anonymity. Technical anonymity refers to the removal of information that enables identifying the author, while social anonymity relates to the perception of anonymity due to the lack of cues regarding the author's identity. The internet can be perceived as a safe environment that allows online offenders to attack the social or political beliefs of others in order to improve their own self-esteem or sense of patriotism (Awan 2014). Additionally, these offenders are also aware that they are protected by their anonymity and the low rate of reporting online abuse (Awan 2014). The feeling of anonymity that is observed in online abuse is not dissimilar from some of the concepts contained in Zimbardo's (1969) theory of deindividuation. Zimbardo (1969) suggests that the anonymity provided by large groups generates a state of deindividuation, where the individual loses self-awareness. As a result of this loss of self-awareness, the individual may be more inclined to get involved with antisocial behaviours. When examining this process in the online environment, Spears and Lea (1994) refined Zimbardo's (1969) theory and developed the social identity model of deindividuation effects (SIDE) theory. This theory advocates that the occurrence of anti-normative behaviour is mainly due to specific conditions encountered in social situations, for example, social identity and visual anonymity. Abusive behaviour or non-abusive behaviour depends on how the individual decides to use the anonymity provided by the internet (Spears and Lea 1994).

According to Christopherson (2007), SIDE theory includes two components regarding the use and effect of anonymity in online settings. Firstly, there is a cognitive component that focuses on the mediating effect of anonymity on group dynamics and individual behaviour, as well as how an individual identifies with a group. Secondly, there is a strategic component that considers the intentional use of anonymity for an individual's purposes that outweighs the benefits allowed by anonymity. Christopherson (2007, p. 3051) asserts that 'SIDE theory is arguably the most influential and current theory of anonymity and interpersonal interaction in computer-mediated communication to date. Most researchers, that investigate issues of anonymity on the internet, use SIDE theory as a template for explaining their results'. Online forums can be used by members of minority groups to share information, experience a sense of belonging, and provide mutual support (Herring, et al., 2002). However, Herring, et al. (2002 p. 371) state that these online forums, despite giving the illusion of security and privacy, 'can be accessed by individuals hostile to the purpose of the forums, actively seeking to disrupt and undermine them'.

The Impact of Online Islamophobia

The term 'Islamophobia' emerged in Great Britain in the early 1990s, where it was defined as an intense fear or dislike of Muslims (Barkdull, et al., 2011). According to Semati (2010) Islamophobia can be viewed as an ideological response that assigns the blame of any controversies in society to Islam, such as those following the terrorist attacks that occurred on 11 September 2001. In the United Kingdom (UK), any offences committed as a result of Islamophobia can be regarded as hate crime. The British Crime Survey (2009–2011) suggests that hate crime has a greater detrimental impact on the well-being of victims than non-hate crime. The range of emotions experienced by victims of hate crime includes anger, annoyance, shock, fear, loss of confidence, anxiety and depression (Allen, Isakjee and Young 2013).

Modern society and the extensive use of the internet and social media have opened a door for online hate. A range of terms have been used to describe online anti-Muslim abuse, such as cyber harassment, -abuse, -threats and -hate (Awan 2014). However, there is very little literature available on online Islamophobia, both at an academic level and at policy level. Awan (2014) therefore recommends a separate definition for this relatively new phenomenon. He defines online Islamophobia as 'prejudice that targets a victim in order to provoke, cause hostility and promote intolerance through means of harassment, stalking, abuse, incitement, threatening behaviour, bullying and intimidation of the person or persons, via all platforms of social media' (Awan 2014, p. 122). Cases of cyberhate usually include harassment, abuse and incitement on a range of social networking sites (for example, Facebook, Twitter, Bebo and MySpace), but can also occur in blogs and chat rooms (Copsey, et al. 2013).

The Tell MAMA project was established in 2012 and models the work of community security trusts that specifically monitor anti-Semitic incidents. The Tell MAMA service enables victims of anti-Muslim abuse across England and Wales to report the abuse they have experienced (Copsey et al. 2013). It is also a public service for measuring and monitoring anti-Muslim attacks. When exploring the incidence of online Islamophobia, they recorded 599 cases of reported online abuse that occurred between 1 May 2013 and 28 February 2014, with an increase of nearly four times more online and offline reports in the week following the murder of Lee Rigby (Feldman and Littler 2014). However, it is worth noting that the rate of reporting online victimisation is low. This may be due to a lack of awareness of whether or not an online offence has been committed (Awan 2014). It could also be a result of fear of further victimisation, non-disclosure by victims in repeated cases of abuse, or the victim's perception that the police lack the resources to effectively help them (Feldman and Littler 2014).

Online abuse accounted for 82% of the cases recorded by the Tell MAMA project in 2013–2014, with the majority representing anti-Muslim abuse (for example, threats, abuse and dissemination of anti-Muslim literature). Additionally, Feldman and Littler (2014) suggest that the many of the victims of online Islamophobia tend to be female. This might be due to women having a greater willingness to report abuse. In offline cases, it may also be a result of their greater visibility owing to items of clothing (for example, the hijab).

Shortly after the murder of Lee Rigby, 11 attacks on mosques were confirmed. These ranged from graffiti to arson, through to bombing and throwing stones, all of which impacted on the feeling of safety within the Muslim community (*The Guardian* 2013). Fiyaz Mughal, the director Faith Matters, was interviewed by *The Guardian*, and argued that these attacks directed at different institutions affect hundreds of people and are responsible for Muslims feeling threatened with regard to their identity. Additionally, Mughal points out that online abuse should not be underestimated, as it can lead to offline attacks (*The Guardian* 2013). Dr Leon Moosavi, a sociologist specialising in Islamophobia studies at the University of Liverpool, was also interviewed by *The Guardian*, and stated that online Islamophobia should be monitored as it hurts people and can lead to hate crime and discrimination (*The Guardian* 2013).

A number of British citizens appear to have a negative view of Islam and Muslim communities. Indeed, a BBC survey of 1,000 young people, aged 18–24 years old, showed that 27% of the sample did not trust Muslims and felt that the country would benefit from fewer Muslims in it. Additionally, 44% of the sample considered Muslims not to have the same values as the rest of the British population, and 60% of the sample thought British citizens hold a negative image of Muslims (*Daily Mail* Online 2013a). According to Akeela Ahmed, who represents a cross-government working group on anti-Muslim hatred, young people should mix with Muslims at a local level and work on collaborative projects to dispel any prejudices held (*Daily Mail* Online 2013a). The government has blamed the negative media coverage of Muslims for encouraging anti-Islam attitudes (*Daily Mail* Online 2013a). However, Allen (2001) asserts that the media are not the cause of Islamophobia, but they do have an indirect effect on it by indiscriminately disseminating descriptions of extremists as if they were the norm.

When violent attacks perpetrated in the name of Islam receive a lot of media coverage, anxiety in the Muslim community tends to increase, as backlashes may occur. There are several examples of this, such as the attack on a mosque in Rotherham after the beheading of David Haines by Islamic State militants, and attacks on mosques after the terrorist incidents on 11 September 2001. Backlashes usually tend to target buildings and women wearing the hijab. As a result of these backlashes, fear of retaliation rises when radical extremists kill new victims (*The Guardian* 2014). In addition to the fear of retaliation, victims of Islamophobia are concerned that the police may not respond based on their testimony (*The Guardian* 2013). Even when anti-Muslim incidents are not violent, they create a sense of fear in the Muslim community (The Guardian 2013).

In qualitative research exploring the experiences of Muslims in four Western countries after the 11 September 2001 terrorist attacks, participants reported that they feared for the safety of Muslim women and girls (Barkdull et al. 2011). This is because Muslim women and girls are the primary targets of anti-Muslim hate (Allen et al. 2013). In reaction to this fear, many women and girls stopped going to public places and isolated themselves socially. Additionally, some women stopped wearing the hijab in public places, as it highlighted that they were Muslim (Barkdull et al., 2011). According to Abu-Ras and Suarez (2011), the avoidance of public places and social isolation aims to protect victims from repeated abuse. However, it also has a negative impact, as it separates victims from social support. As a result of these life changes, women are also more likely to report lower self-esteem and lower self-confidence than men (Abu-Ras and Suarez 2011).

The Experiences of Victims who Report Online and Offline Islamophobia

In the US, after the terrorist attacks on 11 September 2001, Muslims reported higher rates of post-traumatic stress disorder, anxiety and depression in comparison to non-Muslims. It was found that Muslims had to not only live with their own sorrow after the terrorist attacks, but also the additional fear of suffering discrimination (Rippy and Newman 2006; Khalid 2007: both cited in Barkdull et al., 2011). Research conducted by Barkdull et al. (2011) found that life as a Muslim after the 11 September 2001 terrorist attacks changed drastically for the Australian, Canadian and North American participants in their sample. Similar to individuals from other faiths, innocent Muslims were also wounded as a result of these events. However, they additionally suffered discrimination and harassment in the wake of the attacks (Abu-Ras and Suarez 2011). As Barkdull, et al. (2011, p. 144) state, 'Normal psychological and emotional responses to witnessing a traumatic event were quickly heightened by the realisation of Muslims that they were suddenly regarded by many non-Muslims with suspicion, fear, or anger and might find themselves vulnerable to an anti-Muslim backlash, particularly in the immediate aftermath of the attacks'. Additionally, the study's participants reported verbal harassment (for example, racial slurs and being called a terrorist) and being rejected by their non-Muslim friends (Barkdull, et al., 2011). Discrimination when travelling was also experienced, such as being thoroughly searched and scrutinised by government officials at airports. Further discrimination was encountered at the workplace, where participants lost their jobs, were excluded from job interviews, were alienated by their colleagues, or lost business from non-Muslim customers (Barkdull, et al., 2011).

Other abusive experiences were reported following the 11 September 2001 terrorist attacks. Indeed, the Islamic Human Rights Commission (2002) logged 674 cases, including discrimination, harassment and violence, with the majority of cases (that is 344 cases) being serious violent crimes. They were able to divide the 674 cases into four categories based on the nature of the abuse experienced. These categories were: verbal and written abuse, discrimination, psychological harassment and pressure, and serious crimes of violence (Islamic Human Rights Commission 2002).

Verbal and written abuse included receiving malicious telephone calls and death threats. For example, in one case, a family received threatening letters telling them to either leave where they live or be killed. A few days later, the father in the family was stabbed. Although the family were re-housed after the attack, a week later another threatening letter was received at their new address. The letter suggested that the next attack would be fatal (Islamic Human Rights Commission 2002).

Discrimination refers to the loss of customers by Muslim-run businesses since the 11 September 2001 terrorist attacks. Psychological harassment and pressure encompasses verbal abuse, discrimination and bullying against children at school. For example, there were cases where Muslim children were told by non-Muslim children that they could no longer play together because they were Muslim. This resulted in Muslim children feeling isolated (Islamic Human Rights Commission 2002). Serious crimes of violence included throwing alcohol at victims, assaulting victims at clubs and pulling off individuals' headscarves (Islamic Human Rights Commission, 2002). Allen, et al. (2013 p. 17) describe the experience of Rachael, a 28-year-old white British Muslim, who was the victim of violent crime:

> Pregnant at the time, Rachael recalled how on the day of the incident she had gone to the bank and felt dizzy and near to collapse. Her husband came to collect her in his car but when they returned to their house, there was a man in a car parked across their drive. Getting out of the car, she says she went up to the driver and asked him to move so that they could get onto their drive. Refusing to move, the other driver became extremely aggressive and kept shouting: "Thing […] Get this thing away from me". The "thing" was of course Rachael. Becoming increasingly agitated, the driver threatened her: "I'm gonna pop you Muslim". Hearing this and seeing how aggressive the man was becoming, Rachael's husband got out of the car and ran over to her. At this point, the driver got out of his car and started to punch her husband. With him lying on the ground, the perpetrator got back in his car and drove at her, running her over. Rachael was unable to get out of the way due to being pregnant. Noting the way in which her being Muslim appeared to be the primary cause for the man's anger and aggression, Rachael noted how: "It doesn't matter how white you are […] He gave me a really dirty look and said: 'Fucking paki bastards'."

As highlighted by the above examples, a relationship can be observed between the 11 September 2001 terrorist attacks and discrimination against Muslims (Islamic Human Rights Commission 2002). According to Copsey, et al. (2013), online anti-Muslim hate crime has recently become increasingly common, but research on the topic is still rare, despite 80% of adults using the internet every day. When specifically considering online incidents, 75% of the cases recorded by the Tell MAMA initiative were internet-based, with Twitter being the main source of abuse. Additionally, it was shown that victims of online abuse were also frequently victims of offline abuse. Due to the terrorist attacks committed by Islamic extremists, some victims of Islamophobia feel that other people may not take their victimisation seriously and indeed think that they deserve the abuse (BBC News 2013a). As a result of general distrust, many Muslim women also do not report their victimisation to governmental agencies (Allen, et al., 2013). Consequently, the Tell MAMA project is a useful solution for victims who wish to report their victimisation, but need an intermediary to do so (Allen, et al., 2013).

Huma Qureshi, a writer who discusses being Muslim, female and Asian in *The Observer*, was abused online and recalls the experience in an interview with *The Guardian* (2012a):

I didn't know what to expect and copped out pretty early on after some of the comments started saying horrible stuff directed towards my family, whom I'd mentioned in passing in a particular piece. Most of those comments were removed, but at the time they unsettled me enough to ask the comment editor not to run my next piece. Now that I'm older and wiser, I'm more prepared for what might be in store when I throw myself into the lion's den and write something about Islam. I know I'm going to get it from both sides. There are some Muslim readers who automatically assume I must be some liberal heathen, who have accused me of "Islam bashing", blasphemy and changing Islam to "suit my whims" – when I've done no such thing. I try to be indifferent, but occasionally these sort of comments make me angry, because for all their talk of piety, who are they to judge me on my faith? I'll engage with them on Cif, but mostly it's like talking to a brick wall. Then I get it from non-Muslims who use any Cif piece about Islam as a chance to point out what an abusive/violent/ oppressive/uncivilised religion I belong to, and how much they hate everything about it and everyone who is a part of it. Again, I try not to get involved, but those comments showing such hatred make me sad, because I don't see myself like that. It seems that, although people often ask to hear the "moderate Muslim voice", when they do they still don't listen. I choose what I write about very carefully, so I've been spared what some Muslim writers receive. (I mostly get harmless "Can't believe you get paid to write this shit" comments.) But the worst, serious abuse I've got was a lengthy email, sent anonymously after I wrote about Muslim marriage contracts, and listing everything they didn't like about me, saying my marriage was "fucked", that I was an "epic failure", and that I "didn't deserve happiness". I misguidedly read it while on honeymoon and it left me shaking. It was vile. Part of me is worried that this post might be an invitation to another email from whoever it was. But with hindsight I take it as a backhanded compliment that I provoked such irritation in this reader – that's the way I now try to deal with the comments that hit way below the belt.

By discussing issues in relation to her religion in the public sphere, Huma Qureshi became the target of online abuse. This account of online hatred illustrates how victimisation might be perpetrated by both Muslims and non-Muslims. In a report measuring anti-Muslim hate crime and the involvement of far-right organisations, Copsey, et al. (2013) state that far-right movements are making increasing use of online spaces. They found that the English Defence League is the far-right organisation that is most involved in disseminating online anti-Muslim hate. In particular, Facebook is used to communicate with its supporters. Copsey, et al. (2013, pp. 25–6) collated messages that were posted online by English Defence League members. Some examples of these messages include:

- 'Just pour pig's blood in every reservoir in Britain, the whole land will be tainted, goodbye muzzrats!'
- 'Have you seen the price of meat? And Muslim babies are so plentiful! Sharia allows sodomising babies!'
- 'Sadly, Britain is full of these filthy Muslim immigrants. Someone should "teach him a lesson" and cut his head off'.
- 'There is no such thing as a moderate Muslim. They are all nutjobs because they are animals'.
- 'Hope your mosque has fire insurance Muslim immigrant cunt. Fried halal'.
- 'You raped British women and children. Now you can pay'.

As can be observed by the above examples of messages, the messages range from abusive comments to hate speech, through to threats of serious violence against Muslims. Copsey, et al. (2013) show that the majority of perpetrators of online Islamophobia also threaten their victims with offline abuse. Additionally, repeat offenders tend to become increasingly aggressive over time and threats become more and more intimidating (for example, threats of killing an individual's children). There is an urgent need for research to assess the frequency in which online hate cases were a precursor for offline abuse (Copsey, et al., 2013).

A final example of a person who has experienced victimisation as a result of Islamophobia is that of Mehdi Hasan. Hasan was a contributing writer to the *New Statesman* between 2009 and 2012, and was a victim of Islamophobia on a nearly daily basis. He then joined the Huffington Post UK, but the abuse continued, as he was referred to as the 'HuffPo's house jihadi' (*The Guardian* 2012b). In his interview with *The Guardian* (2012b), Hasan states:

Have you ever been called an Islamist? How about a jihadist or a terrorist? Extremist, maybe? Welcome to my world. It's pretty depressing. Every morning, I take a deep breath and then go online to discover what new insult or smear has been thrown in my direction. Whether it's tweets, blogposts or comment threads, the abuse is as relentless as it is vicious. The mere mention of the words "Islam" or "Muslim" generates astonishing levels of hysteria and hate on the web. As one of only two Muslim columnists in the mainstream media – the other being *The Independent's* Yasmin Alibhai-Brown – I have the dubious distinction of being on the receiving end of much of it. In August 2011, for instance, I wrote a light-hearted column in *The Guardian* on Ramadan, examining how Muslim athletes cope with fasting while competing. The article provoked an astonishing 957 comments, the vast majority of which were malicious, belligerent or both. As one perplexed commenter observed: "There is much we might criticise Islam for … but to see the amount of hatred being spewed on this thread on an article about something as innocuous as fasting really makes one wonder".

This personal report on Hasan's experience of being a victim of Islamophobia and constant abuse illustrates the dread of discovering daily aggression directed at him, which also affects his family.

Government Policy that addresses Online Islamophobia

According to Awan (2014), there is an urgent need to examine in depth the rise of online anti-Muslim hate. He recommends the adoption of a new national and international online cyberhate strategy, where guidelines are provided to the police in terms of how to deal with these incidents. In order to ensure official recognition of Islamophobia, accurate figures and statistics are essential, and anti-Muslim attacks should be recorded independently from other incidents recorded as 'religious hate crimes'. Additionally, in general, 'underreporting remains a challenge in analysing crime data, especially for hate crimes' (Feldman and Littler 2014, p. 3). The Tell MAMA initiative's data shows that nearly five of every six victims of all anti-Muslim incidents (that is, online and offline) did not go to the police. Only 3% of victims of an offline attack went to both Tell MAMA and the police.

Feldman and Littler (2014) suggest a number of reasons that might explain the low rate of reporting abuse. These reasons include victims being afraid of further victimisation, victims not reporting repeat victimisation, and victims thinking the police may not or cannot do anything. However, it is worth noting that some victims tend to report abuse to their mosque as opposed to the police (Allen, et al., 2013). The low level of reporting online abuse might also be due to the victims not being aware that an online offence has been committed. Additionally, it is well known that the police have limited resources and that tracking online offences can be problematic in terms of online anonymity, the right to free speech, and from a jurisdictional stance (for example, internet service providers) (Awan 2014). Therefore, according to Awan (2014) the police need to consider using a range of policing models to address the issue. These models should include both those that are intelligence-led and community-led.

The Tell MAMA project has also recommended that there should be national guidance for all police forces with regard to how to deal with Islamophobia-related crimes. Additionally, they suggest introducing a system that accurately monitors Islamophobia-related crimes, as the faith of religious hate crime is not routinely recorded (*Daily Mail* Online 2013b). The Tell MAMA project has identified three primary issues in terms of reporting anti-Muslim hate crime. These are: (1) lack of understanding with regard to the language of

Islamophobia used during an incident; (2) not enough training in relation to asking relevant questions that can identify anti-Muslim cases; and (3) no uniformity in the recording process of these crimes (*Daily Mail* Online 2013b). Indeed, a clear and robust definition of online Islamophobia needs to be adopted, so that when it occurs it can be accurately recognised and effectively addressed (Awan 2014).

According to Allen, et al. (2013), the British government has recently introduced a range of policies that encourage better integration and cohesion within the community. However, the impact of questioning the identity of Muslims and the feeling of not belonging to the community should not be underestimated. Policy-makers need to consider the detrimental impact that anti-Muslim hate has on society as a whole, and put in place measures that can assist in addressing it (Allen, et al., 2013).

In the UK, the Communications Act (2003) regulates the improper use of public electronic communications and governs the Internet, e-mail, mobile telephone calls and text messaging. Section 127 of the Communications Act (2003) identifies that sending messages that can be considered 'grossly offensive or of an indecent, obscene or menacing character' is a punishable offence. If a message is sent on purpose to annoy, inconvenience or cause anxiety to the victim, or if the message contains information the sender knows is false, it is recognised as an offence and is punishable. This is regardless of whether or not the messages are persistent (Communications Act 2003). Additionally, the Defamation Act (2013) aims to ensure that there is a fair balance between the right of freedom of expression and the protection of reputation (see Chapter 7).

In 2013, the UK's Crown Prosecution Service published guidance on prosecuting cases involving communications sent via social media (see http:// www.cps.gov.uk/legal/a_to_c/communications_sent_via_social_media/). These guidelines cover communications that constitute a credible threat of violence, damage to property and instances where a specific individual or several individuals are targeted (for example, harassment or stalking). It also includes communications that lead to the breach of a court order (for example, sexual offences) and communications that may be considered grossly offensive, indecent, obscene, false, and that are intended to cause the victim to feel distressed (Crown Prosecution Service 2013).

An example of where these Acts and guidance prove useful is that of the Reece Elliott case. In July 2013, Reece Elliott, a 24-year-old British man, threatened to murder 200 individuals in the USA. He made these threats on Facebook via posts he wrote on a memorial page using a fabricated name. The memorial page was for two girls who had died in car accidents. As a result of Elliott's threats, 3,000 students were kept away from school for their safety. Elliott pleaded guilty, admitted to sending grossly offensive messages, and was sentenced for over two years in prison (BBC News 2013b). Many of the experiences of victims of Islamophobia, particularly those quoted in the previous sub-section of this chapter, could be addressed under the above legal Acts and guidance. Additionally, international guidance on how to deal with online Islamophobia across countries needs to be agreed, as often the perpetrators, much like Reece Elliott, target victims in a different country from themselves.

Conclusion

This chapter has highlighted the impact of online victimisation and, more specifically, online Islamophobia. The detrimental effect of the abuse experienced by victims has been described, and it is evident that much more needs to be done in terms of addressing the issue. Additionally, there is a clear lack of research regarding the topic, and more robust and empirical studies are required to assist with informing policy and how best to address the issue of online Islamophobia. Further, more research is needed with regard to appropriate victim support and putting in place measures that can assist those who suffer abuse.

Further Reading

Birmingham Mail. 2013. Death threats made to Salma Yaqoob after Question Time appearance, [Online] Available at: http://www.birminghammail.co.uk/news/local-news/death-threats-made-muslimpolitician-4219595 Accessed 1 September 2014.

Douglas, K. M., McGarty, C., Bliuc, A.M. and Lala, G. 2005. Understanding cyberhate: Social competition and social creativity in online white supremacist groups. *Social Science Computer Review,* 23 (1): 68–76.

Waddington, P.A.J. 2010. An examination of hate crime. *Police Review,* 23 April, Vol.118, No. 6077, 14–15.

References

Abu-Ras, W.M. and Suarez, Z.E., 2009. Muslim men and women's perception of discrimination, hate crimes, and PTSD symptoms post 9/11. *Traumatology,* 15(3): 48–63.

Allen, C., 2001. *Islamophobia in the Media since September 11th.* [Online]. Available at:http://www.fairuk.org/docs/Islamophobia-in-the-Media-since-911-ChristopherAllen.pdf [accessed: 26 January 2015].

Allen, C., Isakjee, A. and Young, O., 2013. *'Maybe we are Hated': The Expression and Impact of Anti-Muslim Hate on British Women*. [Online]. Available at: http://tellmamauk.org/wp-content/uploads/2013/11/maybewearehated.pdf [accessed: 26 January 2015].

Awan, I., 2014. Islamophobia and Twitter: A typology of online hate against Muslims on social media. *Policy and Internet*, 6 (2): 1944–2866.

Barkdull, C., Khaja, K., Queiro-Tajali, I., Swart, A., Cunningham, D. and Dennis, S., 2011. Experiences of Muslims in four Western countries post-911. *Affilia*, 26(2): 39–153.

BBC News, 2011a. 'Troll attack' on Georgia Varley Facebook tribute page. [Online]. Available at: http://www.bbc.co.uk/news/uk-england-merseyside-15463026 [accessed 26 January 2015].

BBC News, 2011b. Facebook page mocks dead Stoke-on-Trent girl. [Online]. Available at: http://www.bbc.co.uk/news/uk-england-stoke-staffordshire-14162669 [accessed: 26 January 2015].

BBC News, 2013a. 632 anti-Muslim hate incidents recorded by Tell Mama. [Online]. Available at: http://www.bbc.co.uk/news/uk-21712826 [accessed: 26 January 2015].

BBC News, 2013b. US Facebook death threats troll: Reece Elliott jailed. [Online]. Available at: http://www.bbc.co.uk/news/uk-england-tyne-22839359 [accessed: 26 January 2015].

BBC News, 2014. Trolling: who does it and why? [Online]. Available at: http://www.bbc.co.uk/news/magazine-14898564 [accessed: 26 January 2015].

Christopherson, K., 2007. The positive and negative implications of anonymity in internet social interactions: 'on the internet, nobody knows you're a dog'. *Computers in Human Behavior*, 23(6): 3038–56.

Communications Act 2003. London: HMSO.

Copsey, N., Dack, J., Littler, M. and Feldman, M., 2013. *Anti-Muslim Hate Crime and the Far Right*. [Online]. Available at: https://www.tees.ac.uk/docs/DocRepo/Research/Copsey_report3.pdf [accessed: 26 January 2015].

Crown Prosecution Service, 2013. *Guidelines on Prosecuting Cases involving Communications sent via Social Media*. [Online] Available at: http://www.cps.gov.uk/legal/a_to_c/communications_sent_via_social_media/ [accessed: 26 January 2015].

Daily Mail Online, 2013a. More than a quarter of young adults in Britain 'do not trust Muslims' because of terror attacks. [Online]. Available at: http://www.dailymail.co.uk/news/article-2432880/More-quarter-young-adults-Britain-trust-Muslims.html#ixzz3DfDRAAHi [accessed: 26 January 2015].

Daily Mail Online, 2013b. Anti-Muslim hate crimes soar in 2013 … and the month soldier Lee Rigby was murdered saw 104 incidents in just four weeks. [Online]. Available at:http://www.dailymail.co.uk/news/article-2529948/Surge-anti-

Muslim-hate-crimes-2013-Month-soldier-Lee-Rigby-killed-saw-104-incidents-just-four-weeks.html#ixzz3EKp5Dhe7 [accessed: 26 January 2015].

Defamation Act 2013. London: HMSO.

Feldman, M. and Littler, M., 2014. *Tell MAMA Reporting 2013/14 Anti-Muslim Overview, Analysis and 'Cumulative Extremism'*. [Online]. Available at: http://tellmamauk.org/wp-content/uploads/2014/07/finalreport.pdf [accessed 26 January 2015].

The Guardian, 2012a. Online racist abuse: We've all suffered it too. [Online]. Available at: http://www.theguardian.com/commentisfree/2012/jul/11/online-racist-abuse-writers-face [accessed: 26 January 2015].

The Guardian, 2012b. We mustn't allow Muslims in public life to be silenced. [Online]. Available at: http://www.theguardian.com/commentisfree/2012/jul/08/muslims-public-life-abuse [accessed: 26 January 2015].

The Guardian, 2013. Islamophobic hate crime: Is it getting worse? [Online]. Available at: http://www.theguardian.com/uk/2013/jun/05/islamophobic-hate-crime-getting-worse [accessed: 26 January 2015].

The Guardian, 2014. British Muslims fear backlash after David Haines murder. [Online]. Available at: http://www.theguardian.com/world/2014/sep/14/britain-muslims-backlash-fear-david-haines-murder [accessed: 26 January 2015].

Hardaker, C., 2010. Trolling in asynchronous computer-mediated communication: From user discussions to academic definitions. *Journal of Politeness Research*, 6: 215–42.

Herring, S., Job-Sluder, K., Scheckler, R. and Barab, S., 2002. Searching for safety online: Managing 'trolling' in a feminist forum. *The Information Society*, 18: 371–84.

Islamic Human Rights Commission, 2002. *The Hidden Victims of September 11: The Backlash against Muslims in the UK*. [Online]. Available at: http://www.ihrc.org.uk/publications/reports/7545-the-hidden-victims-of-september-11-the-backlash-against-muslims-in-the-uk [accessed: 26 January 2015].

Oxford, 2015. *Oxford Dictionary*. Oxford: Oxford University Press. [Online]. Available at: http://www.oxforddictionaries.com/definition/english/troll#troll-2 [accessed: 26 January 2015].

Philips, W., 2012. *What an Academic who wrote her Dissertation on Trolls thinks of Violentacrez*. [Online]. Available at: http://www.theatlantic.com/technology/archive/2012/10/what-an-academic-who-wrote-her-dissertation-on-trolls-thinks-of-violentacrez/263631/ [accessed: 26 January 2015].

Richardson, R., 2004. *Islamophobia: Issues, Challenges and Action*. Stoke-on-Trent: Commission on British Muslims and Islamophobia.

Semati, M., 2010. Islamophobia, culture, and race in the age of empire. *Cultural Studies*, 24(2): 256–75.

Spears, R. and Lea, M., 1994. Panacea or panopticon? The hidden power in computer-mediated communication. *Communication Research*, 21(4): 427–59.

Zimbardo, P.G., 1969. The human choice: Individuation, reason, and order versus deindividuation, impulse, and chaos, in W.J. Arnold and D. Levine, *Nebraska symposium on motivation*. Lincoln: University of Nebraska Press.

Chapter 10
Islamophobia, Hate Crime and the Internet

Imran Awan

Anti-Muslim hate crimes in the United Kingdom have increased since the Woolwich attacks in 2013, with a rise in attacks that have manifested themselves both offline and online (Feldman et al. 2013). Overall, the number of hate crimes reported in London, for example, rose by more than 20%, to a total of 11,400. In fact, faith related offences have also risen by 23%, to 1,048 (Gander 2014). A breakdown of the statistics shows these tend to be mainly from male perpetrators and are marginally more likely to be directed at women. Whilst online anti-Muslim hate crimes are on the increase, there are clearly three distinct areas where online hate crime emerges from. This is where: a) Muslims are stereotyped, demonised and dehumanised, b) where there are specific threats made against Muslims, and c) where experiences of online anti-Muslim hostility lead to communities feeling a sense of fear, insecurity and vulnerability.

This also has wider implications for society and can exacerbate the polarisation, thus creating a 'them versus us' narrative (Awan 2012). Online Islamophobia is therefore constructed by the notion of how some people view Muslim communities and how the real world converges with the online world which can have direct consequences for society and impact upon community cohesion as a whole (Allen 2010). Stuart Hall has noted that: 'some things are just off-limits' (Adams 2007) and as the dust settles after the Woolwich attack, it does appear that we are seeing a backlash against Muslim communities, which takes place offline and online after specific dramatic and mundane events.

These trigger events tend to emerge after events such as banning the face veil, the issue of halal food or the fact that Mohammed is the most popular baby's name in the UK. These trigger events also act as an echo chamber whereby anti-Muslim hostility is reinforced through 'tweets' or 'likes' that are perpetuated by 'cyber mobs' and can have a real life impact for those that are targeted (Tell MAMA 2013). The non-profit organisation, Faith Matters have also conducted research, post another flashpoint event, namely the Rotherham abuse scandal, analysing Facebook conversations from Britain First posts on Tuesday 26 August 2014 using the Facebook Graph API. The comments they analysed were from posts on the 26 August and compiled into a large corpus.

They found some common reappearing words to depict Muslims in a negative fashion which included; Scum (207); Asian (97); Deport (48); Paki (58); Gangs (27) and Paedo/Pedo (25). Indeed, a number of the comments and posts revealed that people had direct links to organisations such as Britain First, the English Brotherhood and the English Defence League. Indeed, the Faith Matters Report (2014:11) states that:

> This environment (around the Rotherham incident) activates and rationalises language that positions Muslims as irretrievably not-British, making them into an enemy. Derogatory language comes in place to paint all Muslims as criminals and action words turn this denigration into concrete demands for political action.

Internet hate crime can also cause significant distress for the people targeted and the communities affected by it. These cyber hate attacks can increase community tensions and act in some cases as a motivator for those offenders wishing to commit such online hate crimes. In the online world, the internet therefore reinforces the notion of how people feel in the real world and within cyberspace. As noted in Chapter 9, victims can also feel a sense of despair and anxiety, which can manifest itself with tragic cases of suicide and death (Williams and Tregidga 2013: 12).

For example in 2010, 18-year-old Tyler Clementi threw himself off the George Washington Bridge in the US. His last words which were posted on Facebook were: 'Jumping off the gw bridge sorry.' Clementi had been tormented by abusers online who were threatening to reveal details about his sexuality. Clementi's suicide is another example of how social media can have profound consequences when used for 'jokes', 'banter', 'pranks' and the subsequent abuse that follows from it (Pilkington 2010). Sadly, this is not an isolated case of online cyber bullying and suicide as we will see below.

In 2012, Ciara Pugsley committed suicide in the woods near her home in Ireland after incessant bullying on her online Ask.fm page. Users had described her as a 'slut' and 'ugly' and a month after Ciara's death, another Irish teenager, Erin Gallagher, took her own life after being bullied online (Broderick 2013). In December 2012, Jessica Laney, a 16-year-old from Florida, hanged herself after being bullied online about her weight. After her death a Change.org petition was launched asking for this particular online site Ask.fm to be taken down. Furthermore, Joshua Unsworth's body was discovered in April 2013 in the garden of his family's farmhouse in Lancashire. He allegedly was bullied for months leading up to his suicide, with anonymous online hate attacks targeting and harassing him. These cases highlight the power of social media and the dangers attached to it, when young people in particular are targeted (Broderick 2013).

Whilst the literature around online Islamophobia and abuse is limited, Tell MAMA refer to an actual case study of online abuse that was reported to them of a victim who was targeted with online anti-Muslim abuse for over two years. The case is important because it highlights the devastating impact of online abuse as the above cases have also identified. In this specific case reported to Tell MAMA, the victim feels uneasy about reporting the case to the police because she found the whole process 'daunting' and 'it's not treated in the same manner as other crimes'. When asked about what impact online abuse has had upon her, she states the following:

> I would say that unless you have been personally affected by an online troll threatening your life or your family/friends, no one will ever understand how this can affect you emotionally. You end up locking down to protect tweets and constantly managing your account to see whether it has been cloned again and your followers abused ... you feel suspicious, nervous and anxious as to who is behind that account. You can feel very isolated ... It's embarrassing. (Tell MAMA 2015)

This clearly can have a significant impact as shown above with respect to a person's private and family life as indicated above. This case highlights how as a society we can often neglect the importance of cyber bullying and cyber harassment because it is deemed as happening only in the online world and is not actual offline violence. Whilst anti-Muslim hate crime tends to involve people being directly targeted because of their clothing or the way they look, there clearly is a new rise in online Islamophobia which have often been amplified after events such as Woolwich, Isis and the recent Paris attacks. After the recent Paris attacks, the hashtag #KillAllMuslims was one of the UK terms trending on social media site Twitter (Barsocchini 2015). Figure 10.1 below is a selection of the tweets captured after Paris.

Facebook, Islamophobia and Hate: A Case Study

As noted above, anti-Muslim hate crime has been intensified following events such as the Woolwich attack, with a particular rise of the far-right (Whine 2003). The far-right as noted in Chapter 4, encompass a wide range of groups who have infiltrated cyberspace and used it as a means to target Muslim communities (Perry and Olsson 2009). A number of these groups have used ideological and political claims to target Muslims based on themes such as immigration, halal food and the veil (Williams 2010). A number of these groups have also used these events as a means to exacerbate an internal conflict. Neumann (2009) argues that the internet in such circumstances can be used by extremist groups to spread online hate and violence.

Figure 10.1 Social media hate collected after Paris attack

The internet therefore provides opportunities for online extremism and radicalism of the far-right. Coliandris (2012: 84) argues that:

> On the one hand, and as noted, increased connectivity has enabled social progress through greater opportunities to combine diverse resources, skills and ideas, while on the other, these same societies (their systems and by extension, their citizens) have become more and more vulnerable through their increasing dependence on such technologies.

The internet has been used in such circumstances by far-right groups and those such as the English Defence League and now Britain First, who have used the internet to create a public presence and been successful in using social media sites such as Facebook and Twitter, as a platform to disseminate further online hate and intolerance. Feldman et al. (2013) study found that most of the online hate was committed by people with a link to the far-right, specifically citing the English Defence League and the British National Party (BNP). As noted in chapter one, it is an offence to stir up and incite hatred through illegal hate content on the grounds of: race, religion and sexual orientation. Indeed, there are also other offences such as using the content of a website which can also be illegal when it threatens or harasses a person or a group of people. If this is posted because of hostility based on race, religion, sexual orientation, disability or transgender then it can be viewed as a hate crime.

Within this climate, and building upon the work in Chapter 3 of the Online Hate Prevention Institute, Awan's study also assesses and proposes five types of offender characteristics who have been engaged with online anti-Muslim hate crime on Facebook as a means to target Muslim communities with online hate, either through specific pages or comments and posts. These five types of offenders highlighted are the; *Opportunistic*, the *Deceptive, Fantasists, Producers* and *Distributors*. This typology is intended as a starting point for a framework around Islamophobia on Facebook (see Table 10.1). The majority of people involved in these acts were Males (80%) and Females (20%) (see Table 10.2). Whilst, a number of the individuals were primarily based in the UK (43%), there were also a number of online users who were identified as being from the United States (37%) and Australia (20%) (see Table 10.3). In particular, for the latter, there were a huge number of pages such as the 'Ban Islam in Australia' and 'Ban Islam in America' pages that had a large increase in anti-Muslim hate speech.

In 2013, the Online Hate Centre, published a report entitled: 'Islamophobia on the Internet', which analysed 50 Facebook pages and found 349 instances of online hate speech. They had identified 191 different examples of hate speech, with the most common themes appearing in seven distinct categories. They included Muslims being seen as:

Table 10.1 Offender Behaviour Typology

Type	Characteristics	Example Cases	No. of Cases
The Opportunist	Someone using Facebook to create a posts and comments of hate directed against Muslim communities after a particular incident. In particular, these individuals are using Facebook to post offline threats and promote violence following incidents such as Rotherham, ISIS and Trojan Horse.	Britain First Page English Defence League English Brotherhood	43
The Deceptive	Someone creating fear through the use of posts which are specifically related to false events in order to intensify the Islamophobic hate comments online. For example, a number of people were attempting to capitalise on false stories with links to incidents such as Peppa Pig and halal meat.	English Brotherhood English Defence League	32
Fantasists	Someone using Facebook webpages to fantasise over Muslim deaths and consequences with respect to Muslim events. In particular, these individuals have blurred the lines between reality and fiction and are making direct threats against Muslim communities.	Britain First Page English Brotherhood	36
Producers	People who are using and promoting racist images and videos which are used as a means to create a climate of fear, anti-Muslim hate and hostility. These individuals are closely linked to the distributors.	Britain First Page English Defence League	47
Distributors	People who are using social media and Facebook in order to distribute messages of online hate through posts, likes and comments on Facebook.	Britain First Page English Defence League	42

Table 10.2 Gender of perpetrator

Male	80%
Female	20%

Table 10.3 Country of residence

United Kingdom	43%
United States	37%
Australia	20%

1. a security threat;
2. a cultural threat;
3. as an economic threat;
4. dehumanising or demonising Muslims;
5. threats of violence, genocide and direct hate targeting Muslims;
6. hate targeting refugees/asylum seekers; and
7. other forms of hate. In this study, five distinct categories were established after analysing 100 different Facebook pages and comments.

As noted previously, they included:

8. Muslims viewed as terrorists;
9. Muslims viewed as rapists;
10. Muslim women viewed as a security threat because of their clothing;
11. a war between Muslims; and
12. that Muslims should be deported (see Table 10.4 for a full breakdown).

Table 10.4   The five walls of Islamophobic hate

Facebook Walls of Hate	Types of engagement	No. of cases
Muslims are Terrorists	Use of visual and written communications depicting Muslims as aggressive terrorists. The key being that there is no distinction made between Muslims and non-violent Muslims, as all are depicted as terrorists.	58
Muslims as Rapists	Use of material following incidents such as the Rotherham abuse scandal to depict Muslims as sexual groomers and serial rapists.	45
Muslim women are a security threat	The use of visual and written material to depict Muslims as a security threat. In particular, Muslim women wearing the veil are used as an example of a security threat.	76
A war between Muslims	Extremely dangerous and emotive piece, whereby Muslims are viewed in the lens of security and war. This is particularly relevant for the far-right who are using English history and patriotism as a means to stoke up anti-Islamic hate with the use of a war analogy.	53
Muslims should be deported	The use of immigration and particular campaigns such as banning halal food as a means to create online hate and fear. This also involves the use of casual racism which blurs the line between anti-Muslim comments and those which specifically target Muslims because of their race, gender, religion and beliefs. This is used to imply that Muslim's are taking over the country and should be deported before shariah law is adopted.	62

Offender Online Anti-Muslim Hate Engagement with Facebook

A number of examples of the above walls of Islamophobic hate, are used here via the Britain First, English Brotherhood and English Defence League Facebook webpages which aimed to create an atmosphere of fear and anti-Muslim hate. For example, following an incident involving someone committing an offence for drink and driving, the English Defence League Sikh Division on the 4 October 2013 posted a message entitled: 'HOW MUSLIM SCUM CELEBRATE EID' (see Figure 10.2).

Figure 10.2 English Defence League Sikh Division

This specific page had 93 likes, 50 shares and 39 comments. Some of those comments included:

> They all need the lethal injection dirty vile bastards.

> its not just paki muslims, all muslims are scum ... bengali muslims, Iraqi muslims, afghani muslims, indian muslims, english muslims etc.

In a previous post, the same webpage directs readers to a message regarding halal food. Interestingly, the association here is made with Islamic Jihad and the comments that accompany this also help create lazy assumptions that directly conflate and blur the lines between Muslims, halal food and acts of terrorism. This is done through the use of an image of halal food. This particular image had 186 likes and 163 shares (see Figure 10.3). Interestingly, whilst some of these images and comments should have been removed for inciting hate, Facebook

Figure 10.3 English Defence League posts on halal food

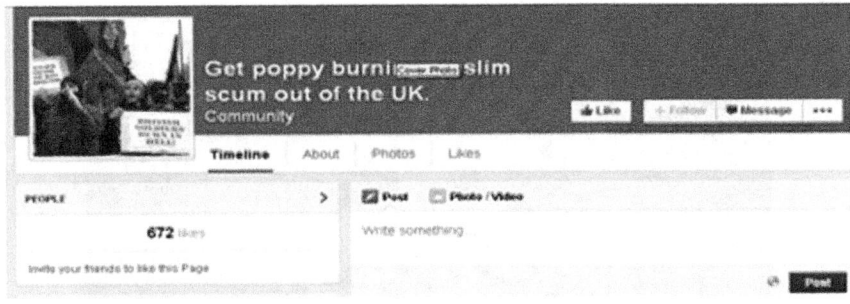

Figure 10.4 Get poppy burning Muslim scum out of the UK

has been criticised for their lack of action in such cases. For example, the Online Hate Prevention Institute (2013) which examined Islamophobia via Facebook, actually reported a number of pages for online hate, however despite this, Facebook administrators took little or no action.

Moreover, the 'Get poppy burning Muslim scum out of the UK' page was created as a direct result of the now banned group Islam4UK actions in burning poppies in relation to Britain soldiers' involvement in the wars in Iraq and Afghanistan. In May 2013, it began sending posts out following the Woolwich attacks in order to gather support and create further anti-Muslim rhetoric. The page has 672 likes but seems to be operating on the basis of reactionary events such as Woolwich and others. Clearly, this page and others similar to this, act as virtual repositories of news feeds that marginalise and demonise Muslims communities.

Similarly, the 'ban Islam in Australia' page has been much more successful at gathering widespread support for the anti-Muslim hate elements they have been posting (see Figure 10.4). Currently, they have 3,413 likes, and on the main webpage they describe Islam as being evil and that they are 'getting rid of this murderous cult'. It is also one of the most active and hostile pages using religious vilification against Muslims as a means towards promoting online hate speech and prejudice. This page is particularly significant, because as noted above, it has a wide range of followers. The images used are clearly intended to stir up racial and religious discord by inflaming tensions with the online hate rhetoric that it espouses. In a number of posts, the page uses images and videos to portray Muslims as violent extremists who are a threat to society because they are 'Muslim'. The attribution of extremism and terrorism are also used as a means to create racial and religious tensions with particular reference made also to mosques being build and the influx of immigrants as a means to create fear.

Allen (2014) has also found similar strong links of Facebook users and growing public opposition about mosques. In Allen's study, he investigated a

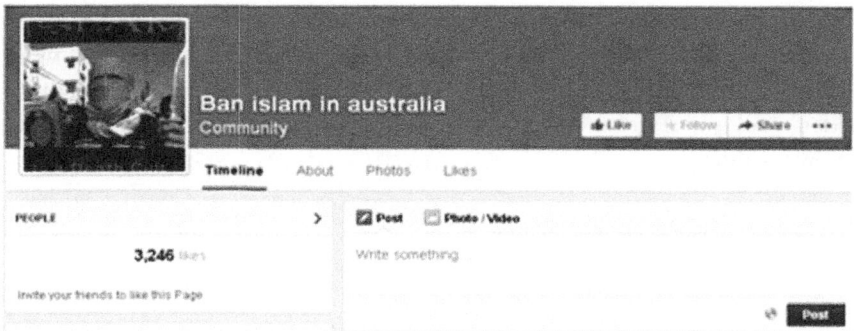

Figure 10.5 Ban Islam in Australia webpage

pilot study which sought to investigate opposition to a proposed Dudley 'super mosque'. By focusing on the Facebook group 'Stop Dudley Super Mosque' and 'Islamic Village', Allen found that members were engaged actively in online discourse which was opposed to the mosque. Some of the themes that emerged from this included issues regarding social identity, otherness and the Islamification of Britain. Allen (2014) also found that there was a rise of political disconnect which had been used as a vacuum to promote anti-Muslim tone and hate speech. Figure 10.6 is an image used via the 'Ban Islam in Australia page' which received considerable comments and posts regarding Muslims which are discussed below.

Figure 10.6 Image used via 'Ban Islam in Australia' webpage

This image had 159 likes, but it is the accompanying text that continue to show religious hate messages that are of concern. The images and words also were used and 'liked' by a number of individuals who form part of the wider typology of Islamophobia discussed above. Some of those comments below include:

Oh sorry Islam is like ebola virus

they are the worst of all human race full stop

Islam is cancer

Fuckn scum fuck every single one of you Muslim dogs

Another problem that emerged within the discourse of Islamophobia was the issue of Muslims being a threat to national security. This type of threat was intensified following high profile incidents such as Trojan Horse and ISIS actions to try and show that Muslims were attempting to adopt shariah law across Britain. This was particularly true for groups such as the English Brotherhood and Britain First who attempted to show that Britain adopting halal meat was just the 'tip of the iceberg'. This type of anti-Muslim hate, was used under the banner of English patriotism (see Figure 10.7) and was being used to demonise and dehumanise Muslim communities. This type of hate clearly was being used with respect to religious persecution of a group and the posts, comments and images all had a provocative and racial barrier attached towards them.

A number of these pages, have called for 'wiping out Muslims' and considering Muslim as intolerant, evil and inherently backward. Some of the examples they have used include depicting and showing Muslims as murderers, rapists, torturers and sexual predators.[1] Despite, this Facebook does have a legal liability to ensure that it removes such online hate, but critics argue that these pages may just reappear in a different format. Another valid concern is the issue of free speech which is enshrined under the US constitution and the First Amendment. This leads to a number of problems about how material is used online and also how far hate material can be censored without infringing and respecting a person's right to free speech.

Within this context, Muslim women were also deemed to be part of the 'Islamic problem'. This was true, when discussing the face veil and the comments used to describe Muslim women as a national security threat. The

---

1 See https://www.facebook.com/BanIslamInCanada?fref=ts; https://www.facebook.com/banislamfrommyanmar?fref=ts; https://www.facebook.com/pages/Ban-Islam/46037 6464099422?sk=photos_stream.

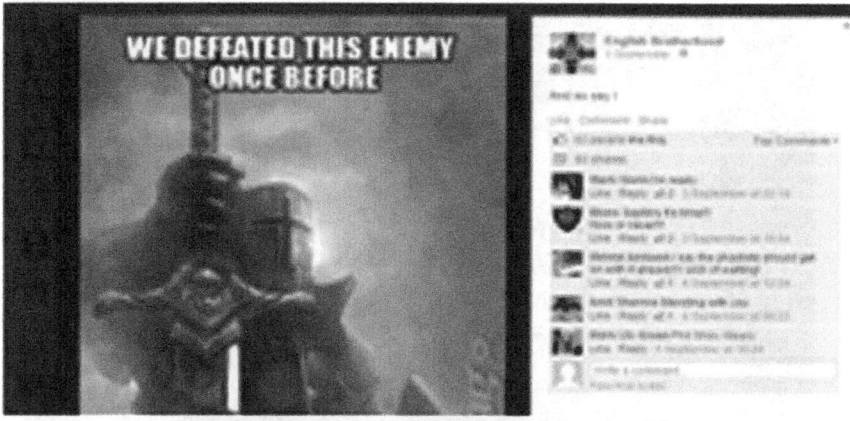

Figure 10.7 British Patriotism via the English Brotherhood

Figure 10.8 Muslim women are a security threat

hate images and posts in particular contained a number of loaded generalisations with respect to Muslim women and Muslim communities. Below is a selection of images accompanied by text and posts that showed an intensification of anti-Muslim tone. Clearly, some of the material posed on these pages were inciting hate against people on the basis of their religion, specifically Islam (see Figure 10.8). As a result, whilst it may look as though only Muslim women are considered a threat, it in fact shows that it stereotypes and legitimises all Muslims in the same fashion, and therefore considers them as not a race and a group that can be expelled, deported or killed[2] by using hostile imagery and depicting them in an innately negative fashion.

The above pages, posts, images and comments on Facebook reveal that Islamophobia whilst considered to be a threat on the streets, is also well and truly been infiltrated by the far-right and white supremacists, who have used it to inflame religious and racial tensions. Whilst the group has had little electoral success, it has via social media gained considerable momentum, with over half a million likes on Facebook within its first year of inception. Using British patriotism as a means to whip support for the group, it has been successful at also promoting a strong anti-Muslim tone. For example, after posting an image about eating British breakfast, a comment posted by one of the users included: 'For every sausage eaten or rasher of bacon we should chop of a Muslims head'. The worry is that such comments could lead to actual offline violence and clearly groups such as this, are using Facebook to promote racial tensions and disharmony (Allen 2010). Indeed, the language being used clearly attempts to agitate and bring in new members and as this study has highlighted revealed some of those emerging problems and concerns. Below the chapter will examine some key recommendations around how to tackle online anti-Muslim hate crime and looks to the future for measures at preventing online anti-Muslim hate crime.

The Future: Recommendations and Measures for Tackling Online Islamophobia

One of the aims of this book has been to examine the rise of online Islamophobia on social media and the Internet. Below the chapter offers some

---

2 See https://www.facebook.com/groups/131642910223888/; https://www.facebook.com/pages/All-Muslims-Are-Not-Terrorist-But-Most-Terrorists-Are-Muslim/1176715049 32480?fref=ts; https://www.facebook.com/groups/159328874220049/; https://www.face book.com/IslamPiss; https://www.facebook.com/pages/Piss-Islam-Pisslam/4690197464 96271; https://www.facebook.com/IslamFraud; https://www.facebook.com/pages/I-Hate-Islam/307956872572344; https://www.facebook.com/ifhix; https://www.facebook.com/search/results/?init=quick&q=hate%20islam&tas=0.7220548475161195.

practical examples for the future of online anti-Muslim hate crime and how government, social media companies and the police tackle online Islamophobia.

Exploration of Issues around Victim Support

There is a need to provide cyber hate related advice for those victims who are suffering online anti-Muslim abuse. This type of cyber counselling project could help empower the victim of abuse and offer them internal and external support. Perhaps a project called 'cyber counselling' for victims of online anti-Muslim hate may be a way forward for victims who have suffered online abuse via social networking sites.

Further Qualitative Research

There must be a continued effort to monitor online anti-Muslim hate and this should include resources for further research development. This would suggest a wider survey analysis, questionnaire design, focus groups and interviews with victims of online anti-Muslim abuse which allows us to understand the impact of this crime from the victim themselves could be the way forward. We know that the substantive quantitative data shows that online anti-Muslim abuse does exist. The next step is to now work with victims and ascertain what level of harm they have experienced and the impact on them.

Monitoring Online Hate

It is important to keep monitoring where the online hate is appearing and the inter-connected links as this can help inform not only policy but also help us get a better understanding of the relationships forming online. This would require in detail an examination of the various websites, blogs and social networking sites by monitoring the various URLs of those sites regarded as having links to anti-Muslim hate.

Long-Term Educational Programmes

The evidence does suggest that what young people see online will have an impact upon their understanding of key issues. An initiative which uses a programme that works with the perpetrators who have formed racial prejudice online could also have benefits. Having an educational toolkit and a specific programme might help us examine the culture that permeates this type of hate and ensure that we look at the root causes of such problems within our society. Being innovative and flexible and getting young people involved is crucial. This could be done with gaming and getting youngsters to look at cyber hate in a more nuanced approach that can reach people at the earliest stages and can help us promote and publicise the dangers of online Islamophobia.

Local and Global Conference on Online Anti-Muslim Abuse/ Free Speech

A series of discussions, focus groups and round the table meetings with a range of stakeholders, academics, online users and community groups could help facilitate a wider discussion of online anti-Muslim abuse. Bringing together a range of experts such as lawyers, academics, teachers, young adults and victims of online hate crime for a local and global conference could have many benefits. Firstly, it would be an ideal way to share and disseminate best practice. Furthermore, because of the many jurisdictional issues with online hate and ISPs this would be an ideal way to form joint collaborative links with other countries. Moreover, this would also lead to more joint work with ISPs.

Website Designed by Victims of Online Anti-Muslim Abuse

This would be a great way of empowering those victims of online anti-Muslim abuse. It could also encourage others to report incidents to them not as a policing agency but as a collaborative hub for people who have suffered this form of abuse. It also could have a lead from the people affected and provide a platform which helps tackle the online anti-Muslim bigotry that exists. The victims of this form of cyber bullying will have the most important stories to share and therefore could provide real expertise in this area.

A Clearer and Stronger Strategy that Examines Online Islamophobia

Despite the excellent work of groups such as Tell MAMA in measuring online Muslim abuse, this area remains one that gets little attention. This is because there are issues around free speech and how best to deal with jurisdictional problems. However a commitment made by Government to examine and look at online anti-Muslim abuse with a real working definition would be much needed at this important time post Woolwich.

Examining Online Threats with Offline Violence

Online anti-Muslim hate crime does appear to have a significant impact upon communities and therefore research which can help examine the link between online abuse with actual offline physical violence would be poignant and critical for government.

Consultation with Young People, Offenders and Victims

It is important that we begin a process of consultation with victims of online anti-Muslim abuse and indeed reformed offenders who could work together on publishing a detailed report that highlights the issues they think are important when examining online Islamophobia.

Methods at Improving Reporting Online Anti-Muslim abuse

Clearly, the internet offers an easy and accessible way of reporting online abuse. However the problematic relationship with the police and Muslim community in some areas means much more could be done with improving Muslim relations with the police and therefore this could have an impact on the overall reporting of online abuse. An improved rate of prosecutions which might culminate as a result could also help identify the issues around online anti-Muslim abuse.

Conclusion

Cyber hate crime remains a complex problem and with the emerging rise of online anti-Muslim hate, prejudice, discrimination and threats there is an urgent need to look at this area in more depth. This chapter provides a snapshot of the problem of online anti-Muslim abuse and suggests that positive ways of dealing with such problems will require a multifaceted partnership approach. As a result a new international and national strategy should be adopted that highlights online anti-Muslim abuse and ways in which the police can deal with such incidents. Perhaps a further strengthening of cyber hate regulation and protocols could be used to tackle online threats made against people of all backgrounds including anti-Muslim abuse and at the same time ensuring free speech is protected. This chapter makes the case that cyber hate and online anti-Muslim abuse must be considered as a key priority for government. Accordingly, the UK government, ISs and the police service must examine all online threats and the links with actual offline violence as this could help agencies have a better understanding of what they are dealing with.

The reporting of online anti-Muslim abuse must also be taken seriously and improved relations with the police and Muslim community may help to achieve that. A more robust and clearer definition of what is online Islamophobia could help provide a more nuanced approach to this problem. Ultimately a hate crime committed against someone will have a detrimental impact upon the victims and much more needs to be done to also recognise the rights of victims. Too often the issue of online anti-Muslim hate is used as a stick to beat the victim with as opposed to helping them. The right to offend, for example is not the same as the obligation to offend or target individuals because of their specific religious beliefs or race. The worry is that these online groups and virtual communities will use this support to foster an offline extremist counter-narrative. Clearly, from the evidence established within this case, Islamophobia on the internet is rife and is being used by groups and individuals to inflame religious and racial hate. This is prohibited by English law and can be in most cases construed as an offence in England and Wales. Prejudice and discrimination come in many forms, from offline physical violence, verbal abuse and hate, but also to online hate which can equally have a damaging impact upon community cohesion and society.

This chapter has shed light on helping us have a better understanding of Islamophobia on the internet. It should be noted that freedom of speech is a fundamental right that everyone should enjoy conflated those principles of free speech with religious and racial hatred of communities, simply because of the way they dress and what they practice. Clearly, Muslim communities are not the sole group that are targeted via social media platforms. However, this chapter has attempted to identify and collect messages of online hate and found a considerable amount of hate speech directed against Muslim communities online.

Further Reading

Back, M.D., Stopfer, J.M., Vazire, S., Gaddis, S., Schmukle, S.C., Egloff, B. and Gosling, S.D. 2010. Facebook profiles reflect actual personality, not self-idealization. *Psychological Science*, 21: 372–4.

Douglas, K., McGarty, C., Bliuc, A.M. and Lala, G. 2005. Understanding Cyberhate: Social Competition and Social Creativity in Online White Supremacist Groups. *Social Science Computer Review*, 23 (1): 68–76.

Gurak, L.J. and Logie, J. 2003. Internet protests, from text to Web. In M. McCaughey and M.D. Ayers (eds), *Cyberactivism: Online activism in theory and practice* (pp. 25–46). London, England: Routledge.

Hewson, C., Yule, P., Laurent, D. and Vogel, C. 2003. *Internet Research Methods: A practical guide for the behavioural and social sciences*. London, England: Sage.

Taras, R. 2012. *Xenophobia and Islamophobia in Europe*. Edinburgh: Edinburgh University Press.

References

Adams, T. 2007. Cultural Hallmark, *The Guardian*, [Online]. Available at: http://www.theguardian.com/society/2007/sep/23/communities.politics philosophyandsociety [accessed: 15 January 2014].

Allen, C. 2010. *Islamophobia*, Ashgate, London.

Allen, C. 2014. Findings from a Pilot Study on Opposing Dudley Mosque Using Facebook Groups as Both Site and Method for Research, *Sage Open*. [Online]. Available at: http://sgo.sagepub.com/content/4/1/2158244014522074. fulltext.pdfþhtml [accessed: 20 September 2014].

Awan, I. 2012. The Impact of Policing British Muslims: A Qualitative Exploration, *Journal of Policing, Intelligence and Counter-terrorism*, 7(1): 22–35.

Barsocchini, R. 2015. *Reactions to France Terror Attacks include Citizens' Calls 'to Kill All Muslims'*, Global Research, [Online]. Available at: http://www. globalresearch.ca/reactions-to-france-attacks-include-citizens-calls-to-kill-all-muslims/5423702 [accessed: 15 January 2015].

Broderick, R. 2013. 9 Teenage Suicides In The Last Year Were Linked To Cyber-Bullying On Social Network Ask.fm, [Online]. Available at: http:// www.buzzfeed.com/ryanhatesthis/a-ninth-teenager-since-last-september-has-committed-suicide#.rw17YdOPQ [accessed: 15 January 2014].

Coliandris, G. 2012. Hate in a Cyber Age. In I. Awan and B. Blakemore, *Policing Cyber Hate, Cyber Threats and Cyber Terrorism* (pp. 75–94). Farnham: Ashgate.

Faith Matters, 2014. Rotherham, hate and the far-right online, [Online]. Available at: http://tellmamauk.org/wp-content/uploads/2014/09/Rotherham.pdf [accessed: 10 January 2014].

Feldman, M., Littler, M., Dack, J. and Copsey, N. 2013. Anti-Muslim Hate Crime and the Far Right, Teeside University, [Online]. Available at: http:// tellmamauk.org/wpcontent/uploads/2013/07/antimuslim2.pdf [accessed: 4 September 2013].

Gander, K. 2014. Rise in racist, religious and homophobic hate crimes in London, *The Independent*, [Online]. Available at: http://www.independent. co.uk/news/uk/crime/rise-in-racist-religious-and-homophobic-hate-crimes-in-london-9899009.html [accessed: 15 January 2015].

Neumann, P.R. 2009. *Old and New Terrorism*. Cambridge: Polity Press.

Online Hate Prevention Centre. 2013. *Islamophobia on the Internet: The Growth of Online Hate Targeting Muslims*. [Online]. Available at: http://ohpi.org.au/ islamophobia-on-the-internet-the-growth-of-online-hate-targetingmuslims/ [accessed: 10 January 2015].

Perry, B. and Olsson, P. 2009. Cyberhate: The Globalisation of Hate. *Information & Communications Technology Law*. [Online]. 18(2): 185–99. [Online]. Available at: http://www.informaworld.com/smpp/content~content=a912569634~ db=all~jumptype=rss [accessed: 10 January 2015].

Pilkington, E. 2010. Tyler Clementi, student outed as gay on internet, jumps to his death, The Guardian, [Online]. Available at: http://www.theguardian. com/world/2010/sep/30/tyler-clementi-gay-student-suicide [accessed: 10 January 2015].

Tell MAMA (Measuring Anti-Muslim Attacks), 2013. Anti-Muslim Hate Crime, [Online]. Available at: http://tellmamauk.org/ [accessed: 2 September 2014].

Tell MAMA, 2015. A Victim's Personal Perspective on the Impacts of Online Hate. [Online]. Available at: http://tellmamauk.org/a-victims-personal-perspective-on-the-impacts-of-online-hate/ [accessed: 11 January 2015].

Whine, M. 2003. Far right extremists on the Internet, in *CyberCrime: Law Enforcement, Security and Surveillance in the Information Age*, edited by D. Thomas and B.D. Loader. London: Routledge, 234–50.

Williams, M and Tregidga, J. 2013. All Wales Hate Crime Research Project, [Online]. Available at: http://www.refweb.org.uk/files/Wales%20Hate%20Crime%20Report.pdf [accessed: 9 January 2015].

Index